INTRODUCTION TO OPERATIONS RESEARCH

This is Volume 47 in
MATHEMATICS IN SCIENCE AND ENGINEERING
A series of monographs and textbooks
Edited by RICHARD BELLMAN, *University of Southern California*

A partial list of the books in this series appears at the end of this volume. A complete listing is available from the Publisher upon request.

INTRODUCTION TO OPERATIONS RESEARCH

A. Kaufmann

Institut Polytechnique de Grenoble
Grenoble, France

R. Faure

Paris Transport Authority
Paris, France

Translated by Henry C. Sneyd

1968

ACADEMIC PRESS NEW YORK · LONDON

ACADEMIC PRESS, INC.
111 Fifth Avenue, New York, New York 10003

United Kingdom Edition published by
ACADEMIC PRESS, INC. (LONDON) LTD.
Berkeley Square House, London W1X 6BA

LIBRARY OF CONGRESS CATALOG CARD NUMBER: 67-23162

Third Printing, 1972

PRINTED IN THE UNITED STATES OF AMERICA

FOREWORD

Operations research may be defined as the art of applying precise reasoning to problems which, for a variety of reasons, cannot be formulated in the usual precise terms of science. We meet questions of this perplexing nature in the consideration of economic, engineering, industrial, and medical processes and, generally, in the human direction of human affairs.

As in any art form, there are basically two types of principles: those that can be explicitly taught, and readily learned, and those which are just as real, but imponderable and incapable of explicit statement. In some mysterious fashion, which we do not now understand, and most likely will never comprehend, concepts of the second kind can be absorbed by means of suitable case histories, a sort of intellectual osmosis. The basic task is that of choosing the appropriate examples.

This is what Kaufmann and Faure have done so brilliantly in this book. They have constructed eighteen charming and witty vignettes which lucidly illustrate many of the fundamental ideas and methods of operations research. This work is based upon years of application of mathematical theories to real life situations.

It is therefore a pleasure to welcome this book into the series that I edit. There may be no royal road to knowledge, but there are some with more attractive scenery along the way, and some that can be traversed with gay and learned companions. How I wish that I had had the benefit of a book such as this when I first started out!

RICHARD BELLMAN

June, 1968

PREFACE TO THE FRENCH EDITION

Introduction to Operations Research is primarily intended for decision-makers in the fields of industrial economics and management. It was conceived and written with the aim of interesting such men in the recent developments in applied mathematics which can assist them in their work.

It is a fact that these men do not have sufficient time in which to read and digest scholarly scientific works. It is, however, very desirable that they keep abreast of new methods since they, in the end, are the men who are in a position to apply them. Like many others, we believed that a work of instruction in these new methods was sorely needed.

We proposed these criteria: Could our book be read in a train, subway, airplane, or even at home; would the reader feel inclined to put the book aside and complete some of the very simple calculations in it for himself; would it persuade the reader to progress to more serious works on the same subject? Some people, we have no doubt, will read it behind closed doors, so as to satisfy their curiosity without damaging their reputations.

With the help of 18 short anecdotes, which are actually studies of simplified problems, we have explained the principal methods and analytical procedure for setting up equations or constructing models for solving the problems. In most of the chapters, a resume of the theoretical aspect of each problem has been given. These sections, which are rather more difficult, are set off by ornamental borders. A bibliography according to chapter is included at the end of the volume.

To be a successful popularizer, an author needs to have understood the most advanced research in the subject, and also to have experienced the daily anxieties of those confronted with the harsh realities of life. If our qualifications fall short of this, we must reply that we completed this book not only to be useful, but because writing it afforded us enjoyment.

It may be asked why we have chosen to jest about serious matters, why these anecdotes have been used and treated in a facetious style. Our answer must be that we should take our work seriously, but not ourselves. Even if the aim of our book has not been achieved, its subject matter is so important that we hope, as we said earlier, that those who read it will not stop here.

A. Kaufmann
R. Faure

CONTENTS

INTRODUCTION TO OPERATIONS RESEARCH

CHAPTER 1

STORY OF A NEWSVENDOR

(A Problem of Stock)

In countries other than the United States there are cases, sometimes factual though more often legendary, of millionaires who have begun their careers as newsvendors. Alas, the recipe for becoming a millionaire has not been vouchsafed to us, and until such time as someone is kind enough to let us into the secret, we propose to sell newspapers without too great a loss or, if that is possible, with sufficient profit to provide a modest livelihood. Will fortune smile on us if we study the methods of *operations research*? Anyhow, out of modesty, we shall tell the story of our friend, Theophrastus, from whom we always buy our newspapers.

Theophrastus buys a stock of newspapers which he resells at 1 F (Franc) a copy; the wholesale price of a paper is 0.50 F, and he is allowed 0.20 F the following day for each unsold copy. Such a sales system may appear abnormal or even harsh, but the wholesaler is subject to the demands of the printer, who is subject to the demands of his suppliers, who themselves . . ., but that is another story as harsh as this one.

Theophrastus can never predict the lucky days, and not infrequently he does not break even. It is said that hunger is a bad counsellor, but it may also lead to wisdom *and* statistical analysis. It will be our business to show that the conjunction *and* is not to be confused with the exclusive *or*.

On the morrow of a particularly unprofitable day (the reasons for which we need not discuss), our friend takes an important first step toward improving his knowledge of his trade: he determines to make an analysis of his sales. From his daily records he finds that he has never sold more than 50 newspapers on one day, and rarely more than 40; on the other hand, sales of over 30 have been somewhat less infrequent, and sales of 20 or more have been frequent. It is clear to him that his sales are increased by important political events or even by the photograph of an appetizing creature on the front page; as to the latter attraction, he can well recall occasions when he refused to dispose of his last copy.

A businessman becomes an accountant (indeed, some jealous persons hold the converse to be true), and our hero accordingly prepares a table of possible profits, calculating his purchases and sales in units of ten. At the intersection of a line, corresponding to a particular quantity purchased, and of a column, representing a given demand, the profit in Francs can be found (Table 1.1).

TABLE 1.1

Purchase \ Demand	0	10	20	30	40	50
0	0	0	0	0	0	0
10	— 3	5	5	5	5	5
20	— 6	2	10	10	10	10
30	— 9	— 1	7	15	15	15
40	— 12	— 4	4	12	20	20
50	— 15	— 7	1	9	17	25

A study of this table leaves our friend much perplexed. If he buys 50 newspapers, he may make a profit of 25 F, but there is a risk of losing 15 F; by buying only 20, his profit may be 10 F, but he may equally lose 6 F. Indeed, the only assurance of avoiding a loss is not to buy any papers! But to be a newsvendor, one must have newspapers.

Success in business is nearly always allied to an observant nature. In his perplexity, our friend determines to make a more thorough study of the situation, and it is as a result of this decision that the statistical demon finds an entry into a mind that is, admittedly, ill prepared for receiving it. This is how our friend sums up his reflections.

"What I have to consider is not my daily profit, but how much I can earn over a monthly or two monthly or even longer period. Surely it must be possible to calculate my profit over a lengthy period if I always order (except on those exceptional days which I should be able to predict) a fixed number of newspapers every day. All that is needed is to discover this number and to anticipate the purchasing habits of my customers.

"Very well, for a certain period, instead of leaving my kiosk when all my newspapers have been disposed of, I shall stay there until 7:00 p.m. every evening as if I still had copies for sale. Rather than note the sales, I shall in future record the demand, satisfied or otherwise, and in the latter event, I will make a polite excuse for being unable to serve a customer. Finally, to obtain a rough estimate, I shall study what happens over a normal 100-day period."

Let us agree that our newsvendor has shown some of the qualities required for a statistician or millionaire. His findings are shown in Table 1.2.[1]

TABLE 1.2

Demand in groups of ten	0	10	20	30	40	50
Number of days when this demand occurs	3	17	37	29	12	2

"Assuming," he continues, "that the future has the same pattern as the past, it would be useful to learn what would happen if I buy the same number (0, 10, 20, etc.) of newspapers every day. Using my table of frequencies, it should be possible to calculate the total profit for 100 days in each case, and hence, simply by dividing by 100, the average daily profit. To find the latter directly I need merely use 0.03, 0.17, 0.37, etc. instead of the corresponding numbers 3, 17, 37, etc., in the table."

The details and results of his calculations are given in Table 1.3. The reader may be surprised at a newsvendor rediscovering the basic principles of statistics and probabilities. But why not? The majority of newsvendors share the common fund of intelligence and ability to a much greater degree than is generally supposed.

[1] To be precise, he has recorded the daily demand; next, he has formed class 0 by combining the days when the demand was between 0 and 4, and class 10 by combining those when it was between 5 and 14, etc. In this way he has obtained Table 1.2.

TABLE 1.3

If I buy	My average profit will be
0	$= 0$
10	$(-3)(0.03) + (5)(0.17) + (5)(0.37) + (5)(0.29) + (5)(0.12) + (5)(0.02) = 4.76$
20	$(-6)(0.03) + (2)(0.17) + (10)(0.37) + (10)(0.29) + (10)(0.12) + (10)(0.02) = 8.16$
30	$(-9)(0.03) + (-1)(0.17) + (7)(0.37) + (15)(0.29) + (15)(0.12) + (15)(0.02) = 8.60$
40	$(-12)(0.03) + (-4)(0.17) + (4)(0.37) + (12)(0.29) + (20)(0.12) + (20)(0.02) = 6.72$
50	$(-15)(0.03) + (-7)(0.17) + (1)(0.37) + (9)(0.29) + (17)(0.12) + (25)(0.02) = 3.88$

"Accordingly," he concludes, "I shall purchase 30 papers a day, which will give me an average profit of 8.60 F."

It is by such reasoning as this that we rediscover *the expected gain*, *the optimization of an economic function*, and *the economic horizon*.

However, this is not the end of our story, for one of Theophrastus's regular customers was a young mathematics student who was fond of discussions. Rather than converse about the usual inexhaustible topics of the weather, the future, or the good old times, he preferred to talk about more technical subjects; and thus there developed another case of collaboration between science and industry to the value of which it added a further modest example.

Our young mathematician was anxious to provide his friend with a handy formula as a guide in his business, and one evening found them seated together in a small café. Making use of the detailed records which Theophrastus had kept in a small notebook, the student was able to draw up a more elaborate statistical table (Table 1.4) than Table 1.2, in which the purchases and sales had been grouped in classes of ten. Based on the frequencies of the sales, the cumulative frequency could also be easily calculated. For example, the frequency of a demand less than or equal to 11 is found from the table to be

$$0 + 0 + 1 + 1 + 1 + 2 + 1 + 1 + 1 + 2 + 2 + 1 = 13\,.$$

The graph of Fig. 1.1, showing the values of the cumulative frequency as a function of the demand, was then drawn by the student.

TABLE 1.4[a]

D	F	CF	D	F	CF	D	F	CF	D	F	CF
0	0	0	13	1	17	26	4	64	39	1	94
1	0	0	14	3	20	27	3	67	40	2	96
2	1	1	15	3	23	28	3	70	41	0	96
3	1	2	16	3	26	29	4	74	42	1	97
4	1	3	17	4	30	30	2	76	43	1	98
5	2	5	18	3	33	31	3	79	44	0	98
6	1	6	19	4	37	32	3	82	45	0	98
7	1	7	20	3	40	33	2	84	46	1	99
8	1	8	21	4	44	34	2	86	47	0	99
9	2	10	22	5	49	35	2	88	48	0	99
10	2	12	23	4	53	36	1	89	49	1	100
11	1	13	24	4	57	37	2	91	50	0	100
12	3	16	25	3	60	38	2	93	> 50	0	100

[a] D, demand; F, frequency; CF, cumulative frequency.

The newsvendor was naturally dubious as to how such a representation could be used to advantage. The concept of probability, in the sense attached to it here, has been studied by mathematicians for some 300 years, yet it exists intuitively for everyone in an undefined form under the name of *chance*.

Let us now listen to the conversation on this subject that took place between our two friends.

"If the future repeats itself with the same frequencies as those of the past," said the mathematician, "you will have 12 *chances* in 100 of selling a maximum of 10 newspapers, 13 chances of selling a maximum of 11, . . ., and 44 chances of selling a maximum of 21. This association of chance, to a limit of 100, with a given demand, will be called the *probability* of this demand, and we shall take $P(x)$ to represent the probability

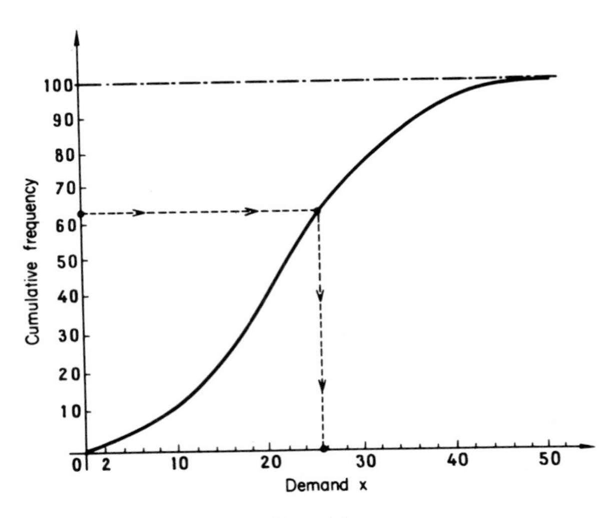

FIG. 1.1

of a demand equal to a maximum of x. A very simple method of reasoning, which is often referred to as *marginal calculation*, will quickly reveal the number of newspapers to order so as to obtain a maximal profit, *if* (and I repeat this proviso), *the same frequencies occur in the future as in the past.*

"Let us suppose that your daily order is $s - 1$ and then enquire what would happen if you decided to order an extra paper. You would gain 0.50 F with the probability $1 - P(s - 1)$, which is that of a demand greater than $(s - 1)$, and you would lose 0.30 F with the probability $P(s - 1)$, which is that of a demand equal to a maximum of $(s - 1)$. Hence, your additional profit would amount to

$$(0.5)[1 - P(s - 1)] - (0.3)\, P(s - 1)$$

or

$$0.5 - (0.8)\, P(s - 1)\,.$$

It is therefore advantageous to buy an extra paper, as long as

$$0.5 - 0.8\, P(s - 1) > 0\,,$$

that is,

$$P(s - 1) < \frac{0.50}{0.80} = 0.625\,.$$

You must stop for a value of s such that

$$P(s-1) \leqslant 0.625;$$

that is to say that s must be such that

$$P(s-1) < 0.625 < P(s)\,.$$

"Let us examine the curve I have just drawn; you observe that if $s = 26$, we have

$$P[(s-1) = 25] = 0.60 \qquad \text{and} \qquad P[s = 26] = 0.64\,.$$

The optimal order is therefore $s = 26$."

To find the average profit corresponding to this number, we must evaluate all the possible hypotheses with their respective probabilities. In this way we obtain Table 1.5, where $\bar{G}(26)$ represents the average daily profit.

TABLE 1.5

Hypothesis		Probable profit	
Purchase	Demand		
26	0	$(0) \cdot [-(0.30) \cdot (26)]$	$= 0$
26	1	$(0) \cdot [-(0.30) \cdot (25) + (0.50) \cdot 1]$	$= 0$
26	2	$(0.01) \cdot [-(0.30) \cdot (24) + (0.50) \cdot 2]$	$= -0.062$
26	3	$(0.01) \cdot [-(0.30) \cdot (23) + (0.50) \cdot 3]$	$= -0.054$
26	4	$(0.01) \cdot [-(0.30) \cdot (22) + (0.50) \cdot 4]$	$= -0.046$
26	5	$(0.02) \cdot [-(0.30) \cdot (21) + (0.50) \cdot 5]$	$= -0.076$
⋮	⋮		⋮
26	25	$(0.03)[-(0.30)(1) + (0.50) \cdot 25]$	$= 0.366$
26	26	$(0.04)[-(0.30)(0) + (0.50) \cdot 26]$	$= 0.520$
26	27	$(0.03)[(0.50) \cdot 26]$	$= 0.390$
26	28	$(0.03)[(0.50) \cdot 26]$	$= 0.390$
⋮	⋮		⋮
26	48	$(0) \cdot [(0.50) \cdot 26]$	$= 0$
26	49	$(0.01) \cdot [(0.50) \cdot 26]$	$= 0.130$
26	50	$(0) \cdot [(0.50) \cdot 26]$	$= 0$
		Total: $\bar{G}(26)$	$= 8.424$

But it is also possible to calculate the average profit for a stock s by using a recurring formula which enables us to find $\bar{G}(s)$ by a *step-by-step* method of calculation. The formula we shall use is

$$\bar{G}(s) = \bar{G}(s-1) + 0.50 - 0.80P(s-1)\,.$$

$\bar{G}(0)$ is obviously zero, and we find that

$$\begin{aligned}
\bar{G}(1) &= 0.50 - (0.80)(0) = 0.50 \\
\bar{G}(2) &= 0.50 + 0.50 - (0.80)(0) = 1 \\
\bar{G}(3) &= 1 + 0.50 - (0.80)(0.01) = 1.492 \\
\bar{G}(4) &= 1.492 + 0.50 - (0.80)(0.02) = 1.976 \\
\bar{G}(5) &= 1.976 + 0.50 - (0.80)(0.03) = 2.452 \\
&\vdots \qquad\qquad\qquad\qquad\qquad \vdots
\end{aligned}$$

and so on, until we obtain

$$\bar{G}(26) = 8.424\,,$$

then

$$\bar{G}(27) = 8.412\,, \qquad \bar{G}(28) = 8.376\,, \qquad \text{etc.}$$

"Your best plan," concluded the young mathematician, "is always to order 26 copies, and you will then obtain on average the maximal profit, namely 8.43 F a day. At the same time, you should exclude any exceptional days—the launching of a satellite that is to orbit Mars or Venus (if the public is still interested in such projects), the escape of a master criminal, or a large reduction in income tax. For such days I can give you no useful advice, and you will agree that commerce still retains an element of adventure. But as outstanding events are, by their very nature, of rare occurrence, you can safely base your business on normal days which are far more frequent. Now, if you want to expand your business, or in modern terminology *promote your sales*, mathematics might still be of use to you, and we will discuss this possibility another evening."

Problems of Stock

1. Nature of the Problem

In most problems concerning stock, of which the preceding example is only one, different *random* variables make their appearance: first, the customer demand, and second, the delays experienced by the supplier in restocking. Moreover, since unsold articles cannot be returned, efforts have to be made to sell them off. Finally, as our newsvendor perceived by a kind of vague intuition, a problem of this sort cannot strictly be a subject of mathematical treatment until we have established a *penalty for shortage* or, more objectively stated, the sum of money corresponding to a lost sale.[2]

It would be very difficult to take all these factors into account simultaneously, and we shall begin by restricting the problem to a case in which we are able to define a demand of r articles by its probability $p(r)$ and also the cost of stocking c_s and of shortage or penury c_p, for a given article.

Let us assume that between the bounds of period T, during which our stock evolves, the variation in it may be treated as linear. Hence, we are confronted by one of two situations: either the stock s was sufficient to supply the demand r, and the end of the period finds us with a surplus $s - r$, or s was insufficient, and we have experienced a shortage, $r - s$; both situations are shown diagrammatically in Fig. 1.2.

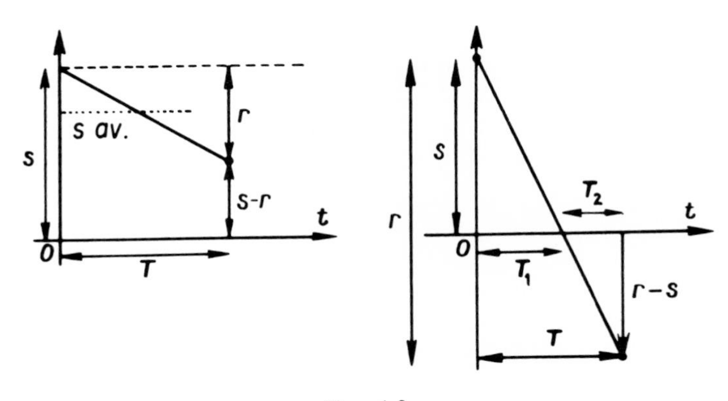

Fig. 1.2

[2] Let us recognize that very often part of such an evaluation is of a psychological nature.

In the first case the average stock is clearly

$$\frac{s + s - r}{2} = s - \frac{r}{2}$$

and, in the second, $\frac{1}{2}s$, during a period of time equal to T_1/T, that is, s/r or

$$\tfrac{1}{2}s \cdot \frac{T_1}{T} = \tfrac{1}{2}s \cdot \frac{s}{r} = \frac{1}{2}\frac{s^2}{r}.$$

In the second case the shortage lasts

$$\frac{T_2}{T} = \frac{r - s}{r}$$

and its average level is $(r - s)/2$, from which we obtain an average shortage

$$\frac{r - s}{2} \cdot \frac{r - s}{r} = \frac{(r - s)^2}{2r}.$$

Provided the demand r follows the law of probability $p(r)$, as long as r is less than or equal to s, our cost of restocking will be

$$c_s \cdot (s - r/2)\, p(r)$$

for each value of r.

If the demand r is greater than s, our cost of restocking will be

$$c_s \cdot \frac{1}{2}\frac{s^2}{r} \cdot p(r),$$

to which we must add a cost of shortage,

$$c_p \cdot \frac{(r - s)^2}{2r} \cdot p(r),$$

for each value of r.

Let us assume that the demand r is not limited, and the sum of the costs can be expressed as

$$\begin{aligned} \Gamma(s) = c_s \cdot \sum_{r=0}^{s} \left(s - \frac{r}{2}\right) \cdot p(r) \\ + c_s \cdot \sum_{r=s+1}^{\infty} \frac{1}{2}\frac{s^2}{r} \cdot p(r) \\ + c_p \cdot \sum_{r=s+1}^{\infty} \frac{1}{2}\frac{(r - s)^2}{r} \cdot p(r). \end{aligned}$$

If there is a value s_0 of the stock such that

$$\Gamma(s_0 - 1) > \Gamma(s_0) \quad \text{and} \quad \Gamma(s_0 + 1) > \Gamma(s_0),$$

then s_0 clearly will be the optimal value to which restocking should be carried.

It can be shown that if $L(s)$ is taken for the function

$$L(s) = p(r \leqslant s) + (s + \tfrac{1}{2}) \sum_{r=s+1}^{\infty} \frac{p(r)}{r},$$

and ρ for the ratio

$$\rho = \frac{c_p}{c_s + c_p},$$

the cost becomes minimal when

$$L(s_0 - 1) < \rho < L(s_0).$$

An example will help to elucidate this statement.

Example. A manufacturer, producing each year a small number of machines to order, has noticed that the demand of his customers for a certain part, essential for the operation of the machines, follows the law of probability given in Table 1.6.

TABLE 1.6

Demand r (number of parts per machine manufactured)	0	1	2	3	4	5	6	7	8	9	>9
Probability $p(r)$	0.01	0.05	0.08	0.12	0.16	0.16	0.18	0.14	0.08	0.02	0

The cost of stocking amounts to 100 F for each part, and the penalty for shortage is estimated at 1000 F. The manufacturer wishes to evaluate the optimal stock per machine of this separate part, so as to include its production in that of the year's series.

N.B. Annual modifications are made in the machines, and the part in question has particular specifications for a given series.

The optimal stock is found by drawing up Table 1.7, in which the third column contains the values of $p(r)$ and the seventh column the

TABLE 1.7

s	r	$p(r)$	$\frac{p(r)}{r}$	$\sum_{r=s+1}^{\infty} \frac{p(r)}{r}$	$(s + \frac{1}{2}) \sum_{r=s+1}^{\infty} \frac{p(r)}{r}$	$p(r \leqslant s)$	$L(s)$
0	0	0.01	—	0.2642	0.1321	0.01	0.1421
1	1	0.05	0.05	0.2142	0.3213	0.06	0.3813
2	2	0.08	0.04	0.1742	0.4355	0.14	0.5755
3	3	0.12	0.04	0.1342	0.4697	0.26	0.7297
4	4	0.16	0.04	0.0942	0.4239	0.42	0.8439
5	5	0.16	0.032	0.0622	0.3421	0.58	0.9221
6	6	0.18	0.03	0.0322	0.2093	0.76	0.9693
7	7	0.14	0.02	0.0122	0.0915	0.90	0.9915
8	8	0.08	0.01	0.0022	0.0187	0.98	0.9987
9	9	0.02	0.002	0	0	1	1
>9	>9	0	0	0	0	1	1

cumulative probability that the demand r will be smaller than a given value of s or equal to it: $p(r \leqslant s)$. The supplementary calculations for the fifth and sixth columns are required in order that the eighth column may contain the values of the expression

$$L(s) = p(r \leqslant s) + (s + \tfrac{1}{2}) \sum_{r=s+1}^{\infty} \frac{p(r)}{r} .$$

We see that $s_0 = 5$; indeed,

$$\rho = \frac{c_p}{c_s + c_p} = 0.909$$

and

$$L(s_0 - 1) = L(4) = 0/8439 < 0.909 < L(s_0) = L(5) = 0.9221 .$$

In addition, a rough calculation of

$$\Gamma(s) = c_s \cdot \sum_{r=0}^{s} \left(s - \frac{r}{2}\right) \cdot p(r)$$

$$+ c_s \cdot \sum_{r=s+1}^{\infty} \frac{1}{2} \frac{s^2}{r} \cdot p(r)$$

$$+ c_p \cdot \sum_{r=s+1}^{\infty} \frac{1}{2} \frac{(r - s)^2}{r} \cdot p(r) ,$$

gives us

$$\Gamma(4) = 456.90, \qquad \Gamma(5) = 385.20, \qquad \Gamma(6) = 399.50 .$$

2. Introduction of a Random Delay in Deliveries

Another aspect of the problem concerns delays in the delivery of orders, and we shall now consider the selection of a policy which takes these into account.

Policy P_1 Whenever a particular stock falls to a critical or danger level, an amount of stock is ordered equal to the sales of the preceding week, the delay in delivery varying from three to eight days in accordance with the law

$$p(3) = 0.05 , \qquad p(4) = 0.25 , \qquad p(5) = 0.40 ,$$

$$p(6) = 0.20 , \qquad p(7) = 0.08 , \qquad p(8) = 0.02 .$$

Policy P_2 A fixed quantity of stock is ordered at the end of each week, and it is always received a week later, so that it can be put on sale the following Monday morning.

Policy P_3 The order for stock is placed at the end of the week, and the stock is received a week later, but the quantity ordered is equal to N (which has to be determined) less the existing amount of stock.

In all these cases, with a five-day work week, the demand follows a law of Poisson's with an average of 4; in other words, it possesses the following probabilities:

$$p(0) = 0.018 , \quad p(1) = 0.073 , \quad p(2) = 0.146 , \quad p(3) = 0.195 ,$$

$$p(4) = 0.195 , \quad p(5) = 0.156 , \quad p(6) = 0.104 , \quad p(7) = 0.060 ,$$

$$p(8) = 0.030 , \quad p(9) = 0.014 , \quad p(10) = 0.006 , \quad p(11) = 0.002 ,$$

$$p(12) = 0.001 .$$

The choice among the three policies should be such that the loss of sales never exceeds 2.5 %, a lost sale being regarded as one which cannot be made on the day of the demand. Hence, the problem consists of calculating the danger level of stock for P_1, the fixed quantity to be ordered for P_2, and the constant N, on which the variable order depends, for P_3.

The method of choice for a problem of this kind is to study it by simulation. This method is fully explained in Chapter 12, and in the present problem we shall merely make use of tables of random numbers to obtain artificial samples of the daily demand. These will be valid for each of the policies, and for the delay in restocking required for P_1.

DELAY IN RESTOCKING. Let us open our table of random numbers at any place and extract a series of numbers with equiprobability. We shall divide them into groups with two digits, and to each group we shall relate a delay conforming to the law which we have observed; see Table 1.8.

TABLE 1.8

Law of probability	$p(3) = 0.05$	$p(4) = 0.25$	$p(5) = 0.40$	$p(6) = 0.20$	$p(7) = 0.08$	$p(8) = 0.02$
Number included between→	00	05	30	70	90	98
and between→	04	29	69	89	97	99
Random delay	3	4	5	6	7	8

In this way we obtain an artificial sample of the delays in restocking, which we shall use to gauge policy P_1.

Series taken from Table 1.8:

17, 40, 50, 89, 66, 65, 36, 98, 96, 80, 17, 56, 97, 84, 91, 22, 16, 12, 46, 19, 05, 22, 04, ...

Artificial samples of the delays:

4, 5, 5, 6, 5, 5, 5, 8, 7, 6, 4, 5, 7, 6, 7, 4, 4, 4, 5, 4, 4, 4, 3, ...

DAILY DEMAND. Let us again open our tables of numbers at random, but at a different page from the previous one, so as to avoid any connection between the first series and the one we shall now choose.

A correspondence by groups of three digits will be established in the following manner (Table 1.9).

TABLE 1.9

Chance number included between→	000	018	091	237	432	627	783	887	947	977	991	997	999
and between→	017	090	236	431	626	782	886	946	976	990	996	998	—
Random demand	0	1	2	3	4	5	6	7	8	9	10	11	12

Here is the sequence found from Table 1.9:

430; 998; 837; 380; 091; 350; 583; 575; 547; 555; 996; 027; 174;
470; 442; 923; 128; 866; 674; 451; 580; 435; 171; 403; 258; 898;
708; 930; 109; 859; 023; 656; 856; 648; 700; 995; 736; 769; 307;
109; 027; 143; 952; 292; 479; 902; 313; 174; 362; 027; 370; 581;
406; 181; 663; 154; 178; 447; 370; 254; 481; 368; 080; 784; 674;
052; 583; 037; 232; 555; 103; 816; 976; 129; 983; 306; 779; 476;
191; 290; 160; 179; 237; 804; 994; 330; 139; 079; 322; 926; 701
934; 195; 841; 335; 635; 803; 902; 849; 756; ...,

from which we can at once deduce the following values for the demand:

3 - 11 - 6 - 3 - 2 - 3 - 4 - 4 - 4 - 4 - 10 - 1 - 2 - 4 - 4 - 7 - 2 - 6 - 5 - 4 - 4 - 4 - 2 -
3 - 3 - 7 - 5 - 7 - 2 - 6 - 1 - 5 - 6 - 5 - 5 - 10 - 5 - 5 - 3 - 2 - 1 - 2 - 8 - 3 - 4 - 7 -
3 - 2 - 3 - 1 - 3 - 4 - 3 - 2 - 5 - 2 - 2 - 4 - 3 - 3 - 4 - 3 - 1 - 6 - 5 - 1 - 4 - 1 - 2 -
4 - 2 - 6 - 8 - 2 - 9 - 3 - 5 - 4 - 2 - 3 - 2 - 2 - 3 - 6 - 10 - 3 - 2 - 1 - 3 - 7 - 5 - 7 -
2 - 6 - 3 - 5 - 6 - 7 - 6 - 5 - ...

Let us first test policy P_1 with a danger level of 35 for the stock. Table 1.10 reveals that the rate of shortage is very low (1/410), so that it is permissible to diminish the amount of stock by successively testing for 34, 33, etc. From Table 1.11 we find that a danger level of 30 gives a shortage rate of 10/410, which is still slightly below the permitted limit of 2.5%.

As soon as the average sales reach $4 \times 5 = 20$ a week, we shall test a constant restocking of 20 units at the end of each week, in accordance with policy P_2. As we find from Table 1.12, the rate of shortage is nil, but this does not authorize us to lower the amount ordered below 20, lest at the end of a certain number of periods we should find ourselves unable to meet the demand. We might, however, consider bringing the stock down to 20 at the end of a particular week by ordering a smaller quantity, such as 19, before resuming the normal weekly order of 20 units.

TABLE 1.10[a]

POLICY P_1 : DANGER LEVEL OF STOCK IS 35

Day	Demand	Stock	Cost of restocking	Delay	Shortage	Day	Demand	Stock	Cost of restocking	Delay	Shortage
Initial stock		40									
1	3	37				51	3	24			
2	11	26	(20)	4		52	4	20			
3	6	20				53	3	35	16	4	
4	3	17				54	2	33			
5	2	15	25	5		55	5	28			
6	3	32				56	2	26			
7	4	28				57	2	40			
8	4	24				58	4	36			
9	4	20				59	3	33	17	5	
10	4	41				60	3	30			
11	10	31	19	5		61	4	26			
12	1	30				62	3	23			
13	2	28				63	1	22			
14	4	24				64	6	33	14	7	
15	4	20				65	5	28			
16	7	32	21	6		66	1	27			
17	2	30				67	4	23			
18	6	24				68	1	22			
19	5	19				69	2	20	19	6	
20	4	15				70	4	16			
21	4	11	24	5		71	2	28			
22	4	28				72	6	22			
23	2	26				73	8	14	12	7	
24	3	23				74	2	12			
25	3	20				75	9	22	27	4	
26	7	37				76	3	19			
27	5	32	16	5		77	5	14			
28	7	25				78	4	10			
29	2	23				79	2	35			
30	6	17	27	5		80	3	44			
31	1	16				81	2	42			
32	5	27				82	2	40			
33	6	21				83	3	37			
34	5	16				84	6	31	17	4	
35	5	38				85	10	21			
36	10	28	22	8		86	3	18			
37	5	23				87	2	16	23	4	
38	5	18				88	1	32			
39	3	15				89	3	29			
40	2	13	25	7		90	7	22			
41	1	12				91	5	40			
42	2	10				92	7	33	16	5	
43	8	2				93	2	31			
44	3	22			1	94	6	25			
45	4	18				95	3	22			
46	7	11				96	5	17	23	4	
47	3	33	18	6		97	6	27			
48	2	31				98	7	20			
49	3	28				99	6	14			
50	1	27				100	5	32	29	4	
							410				1

[a] When the stock, including an expected delivery, falls below 36, the order is given for stocking up.

TABLE 1.11

POLICY P_1 : DANGER LEVEL OF STOCK IS 30

Day	Demand	Stock	Cost of restocking	Delay	Shortage	Day	Demand	Stock	Cost of restocking	Delay	Shortage
Initial stock		40									
1	3	37				51	3	27			
2	11	26	(20)	4		52	4	23			
3	6	20				53	3	20			
4	3	17				54	2	18			
5	2	15				55	5	13	17	4	
6	3	32				56	2	27			
7	4	28	25	5		57	2	25			
8	4	24				58	4	21			
9	4	20				59	3	35			
10	4	16				60	3	32			
11	10	6				61	4	28	14	5	
12	1	30	19	5		62	3	25			
13	2	28				63	1	24			
14	4	24				64	6	18			
15	4	20				65	5	13	19	7	
16	7	13				66	1	26			
17	2	30	21	6		67	4	22			
18	6	24				68	1	21			
19	5	19				69	2	19			
20	4	15				70	4	15			
21	4	11				71	2	13			
22	4	7	24	5		72	6	26	12	6	
23	2	26				73	8	18	12	7	
24	3	23				74	2	16			
25	3	20				75	9	7			
26	7	13				76	3	4	27	4	
27	5	32				77	5	0			1
28	7	25	16	5		78	4	12			4
29	2	23				79	2	10			
30	6	17				80	3	46			
31	1	16				81	2	44			
32	5	11	27	5		82	2	42			
33	6	21				83	3	39			
34	5	16				84	6	33			
35	5	11				85	10	23	23	4	
36	10	1	22	8		86	3	20			
37	5	27			4	87	2	18			
38	5	22				88	1	17			
39	3	19				89	3	37			
40	2	17				90	8	30	16	4	
41	1	16				91	5	25			
42	2	14				92	7	18			
43	8	6	25	7		93	2	16			
44	3	25				94	6	26	16	5	
45	4	21				95	3	23			
46	7	14				96	5	18			
47	3	11				97	6	12	23	4	
48	2	9				98	7	5			
49	3	6				99	6	16			1
50	1	30	16	6		100	5	11			
							410				10

TABLE 1.12

POLICY P_2: FIXED QUANTITY ORDERED AT END OF EACH WEEK IS 20

Day	Demand	Stock	Cost of restocking	Delay	Shortage	Day	Demand	Stock	Cost of restocking	Delay	Shortage
Initial stock		40	(20)								
1	3	37				51	3	24			
2	11	26				52	4	20			
3	6	20				53	3	17			
4	3	17				54	2	15			
5	2	35	20			55	5	30	20		
6	3	32				56	2	28			
7	4	28				57	2	26			
8	4	24				58	4	22			
9	4	20				59	3	19			
10	4	36	20			60	3	36	20		
11	10	26				61	4	32			
12	1	25				62	3	29			
13	2	23				63	1	28			
14	4	19				64	6	22			
15	4	35	20			65	5	37	20		
16	7	28				66	1	36			
17	2	26				67	4	32			
18	6	20				68	1	31			
19	5	15				69	2	29			
20	4	31	20			70	4	45	20		
21	4	27				71	2	43			
22	4	23				72	6	37			
23	2	21				73	8	29			
24	3	18				74	2	27			
25	3	35	20	End of following week		75	9	38	20	End of following week	
26	7	28				76	3	35			
27	5	23				77	5	30			
28	7	16				78	4	26			
29	2	14				79	2	24			
30	6	28	20			80	3	41	20		
31	1	27				81	2	39			
32	5	22				82	2	37			
33	6	16				83	3	34			
34	5	11				84	6	28			
35	5	26	20			85	10	38	20		
36	10	16				86	3	35			
37	5	11				87	2	33			
38	5	6				88	1	32			
39	3	3				89	3	29			
40	2	21	20			90	7	42	20		
41	1	20				91	5	37			
42	2	18				92	7	30			
43	8	10				93	2	28			
44	3	7				94	6	22			
45	4	23	20			95	3	39	20		
46	7	16				96	5	34			
47	3	13				97	6	28			
48	2	11				98	7	21			
49	3	8				99	6	15			
50	1	27	20			100	5	30	20		
							410				0

TABLE 1.13

POLICY P_2: FINAL STOCK FOR 7TH WEEK IS BROUGHT UP TO 20 BY ORDERING ONLY 19 UNITS AT END OF WEEKS 1 TO 6, AFTER WHICH WEEKLY ORDER OF 20 IS RESUMED

Day	Demand	Stock	Cost of restocking	Delay	Shortage	Day	Demand	Stock	Cost of restocking	Delay	Shortage
Initial stock		40	(20)								
1	3	37		End of following week		51	3	23		End of following week	
2	11	26				52	4	19			
3	6	20				53	3	16			
4	3	17				54	2	14			
5	2	35	19			55	5	29	20		
6	3	32				56	2	27			
7	4	28				57	2	25			
8	4	24				58	4	21			
9	4	20				59	3	18			
10	4	35	19			60	3	35	20		
11	10	25				61	4	31			
12	1	24				62	3	28			
13	2	22				63	1	27			
14	4	18				64	6	21			
15	4	33	19			65	5	36	20		
16	7	26				66	1	35			
17	2	24				67	4	31			
18	6	18				68	1	30			
19	5	13				69	2	28			
20	4	28	19			70	4	44	20		
21	4	24				71	2	42			
22	4	20				72	6	36			
23	2	18				73	8	28			
24	3	15				74	2	26			
25	3	31	19			75	9	37	20		
26	7	24				76	3	34			
27	5	19				77	5	29			
28	7	12				78	4	25			
29	2	10				79	2	23			
30	6	23	19			80	3	40	20		
31	1	22				81	2	38			
32	5	17				82	2	36			
33	6	11				83	3	33			
34	5	6				84	6	27			
35	5	20	20			85	10	37	20		
36	10	10				86	3	34			
37	5	5				87	2	32			
38	5	0				88	1	31			
39	3	0			3	89	3	28			
40	2	20	20		2	90	7	41	20		
41	1	19				91	5	36			
42	2	17				92	7	29			
43	8	9				93	2	27			
44	3	6				94	6	21			
45	4	22	20			95	3	38	20		
46	7	15				96	5	33			
47	3	12				97	6	27			
48	2	10				98	7	20			
49	3	7				99	6	14			
50	1	26	20			100	5	29	20		
							410				5

TABLE 1.14

Policy P_3: Fixed Quantity Ordered Is N Less Stock at End of Each Week ($N = 46$)

Day	Demand	Stock	Cost of restocking	Delay	Shortage	Day	Demand	Stock	Cost of restocking	Delay	Shortage
Initial stock		40	(20)								
1	3	37				51	3	27			
2	11	26				52	4	23			
3	6	20				53	3	20			
4	3	17				54	2	18			
5	2	35	11			55	5	29	17		
6	3	32				56	2	27			
7	4	28				57	2	25			
8	4	24				58	4	21			
9	4	20				59	3	18			
10	4	27	19			60	3	32	14		
11	10	17				61	4	28			
12	1	16				62	3	25			
13	2	14				63	1	24			
14	4	10				64	6	18			
15	4	25	21			65	5	27	19		
16	7	18				66	1	26			
17	2	16				67	4	22			
18	6	10				68	1	21			
19	5	5				69	2	19			
20	4	22	24			70	4	34	12		
21	4	18				71	2	32			
22	4	14				72	6	26			
23	2	12				73	8	18			
24	3	9				74	2	16			
25	3	30	16	End of following week		75	9	19	27	End of following week	
26	7	23				76	3	16			
27	5	18				77	5	11			
28	7	11				78	4	7			
29	2	9				79	2	5			
30	6	19	27			80	3	29	17		
31	1	18				81	2	27			
32	5	13				82	2	25			
33	6	7				83	3	22			
34	5	2				84	6	16			
35	5	27	19		3	85	10	23	23		
36	10	17				86	3	20			
37	5	12				87	2	18			
38	5	7				88	1	17			
39	3	4				89	3	14			
40	2	21	25			90	7	30	16		
41	1	20				91	5	25			
42	2	18				92	7	18			
43	8	10				93	2	16			
44	3	7				94	6	10			
45	4	28	18			95	3	23	23		
46	7	21				96	5	18			
47	3	18				97	6	12			
48	2	16				98	7	5			
49	3	13				99	6	0			1
50	1	30	16			100	5	23	23		5
							410				9

It will be found from Table 1.13 that seven weeks would be required to reach a final stock of exactly 20, and for the overall management of the stock the shortage rate would then amount to 5/410.

Turning to policy P_3, any value of N between 40 and 45 produces too high a rate of shortage, but for $N = 46$ the rate drops to 9/410 (Table 1.14).

Let us now compare the restocking costs for the various policies over the 20 weeks we are studying, including those days that the business is closed. With a danger level of 30 policy P_1 gives an average daily stock of 17.08. With a fixed order of 20 at the end of each week P_2 gives one of 25.75 (24.45 if the order is modified for the first seven weeks), and P_3 gives a daily average of 19.13.

To sum up, P_1 appears to be the best policy, *but there are serious reservations as to this conclusion*, since we have limited the study by simulation to a period of 20 weeks, which is completely insufficient to allow us to make a sound decision.[3] Indeed, the use of an electronic computer, which has made it possible to take 1000 samples of the demand over a period of 200 weeks, shows that policy P_3 is actually preferable.

[3] A close study of the tables would enable us to eliminate certain *transitory* phenomena, which we did not wish to discuss here.

CHAPTER 2

HOW SHOULD INVESTMENTS BE DISTRIBUTED?

(A Combinatorial Problem of Allocation. Dynamic Program)

Even a Frenchman would have to admit that the red wines produced in Mexico by the firm of *Nueva Carta* are excellent for their taste, color, and bouquet.[1] Wine is not, it is true, the popular drink of the Mexicans who prefer *pulque*, made from the fermented sap of a species of aloe, or a very strong and aromatic drink called *tequila*, which is produced from another species of this plant. In the cities, however, beer and Coca Cola are the most popular beverages, but with the growth of the average income the consumption of quality wines is steadily increasing; therefore, the Nueva Carta company has decided to invest ten million pesos in promoting its products.

An ambitious campaign is to be launched in the four major cities: Mexico City in the center of the country, Monterrey in the northeast, Guadalajara in the north, and Vera Cruz in the south. A careful study of the market has been undertaken in the four regions I, II, III, and IV, corresponding to these cities, and curves of the expected average profit have been drawn as a function of the overall expenditures on warehouses, shops, salesmen, publicity, etc.; see Fig. 2.1 and Table 2.1. Reliable data for such graphs are as difficult to obtain in Mexico as elsewhere, and we assume that the company has employed the most competent specialists in market research they could obtain. To simplify our calculations, we shall assume that the funds to be invested are allocated in units of one million pesos each. How then, given the curves of Fig. 2.1, are these ten millions of pesos to be distributed among the four regions so as to provide a maximal total profit?

[1] Naturally, the name of the firm is imaginary, but any visitor to Mexico can verify that the excellence of certain of the wines is not.

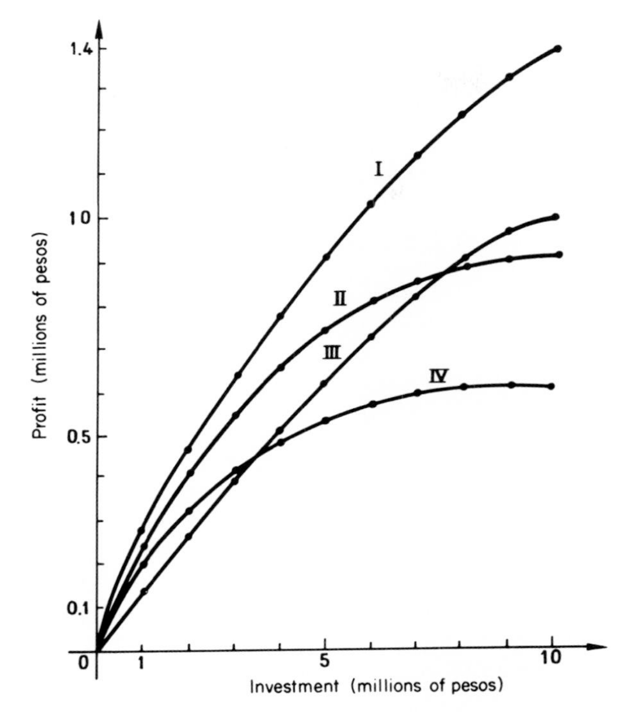

FIG. 2.1

TABLE 2.1

Investment (in millions)	Profit			
	Region I	Region II	Region III	Region IV
0	0	0	0	0
1	0.28	0.25	0.15	0.20
2	0.45	0.41	0.25	0.33
3	0.65	0.55	0.40	0.42
4	0.78	0.65	0.50	0.48
5	0.90	0.75	0.62	0.53
6	1.02	0.80	0.73	0.56
7	1.13	0.85	0.82	0.58
8	1.23	0.88	0.90	0.60
9	1.32	0.90	0.96	0.60
10	1.38	0.90	1.00	0.60

A problem of this kind is combinatorial; in effect, we are required to allocate ten units to four positions, so that we might calculate the profits corresponding to each of the combinations:

$$
\begin{array}{llll}
(10, 0, 0, 0)\,, & (9, 1, 0, 0)\,, & (9, 0, 1, 0)\,, & (9, 0, 0, 1)\,, \ldots\,, \\
(8, 1, 1, 0)\,, & (8, 1, 0, 1)\,, & (8, 0, 1, 1)\,, & (8, 2, 0, 0)\,, \\
(8, 0, 2, 0)\,, & (8, 0, 0, 2)\,, & (7, 1, 1, 1)\,, & (7, 2, 1, 0)\,, \\
(7, 2, 0, 1)\,, & (7, 1, 2, 0)\,, & & \\
& \vdots & \vdots & \vdots
\end{array}
$$

$$
\begin{array}{lll}
(4, 4, 2, 0)\,, \ldots\,, & (4, 4, 1, 1)\,, \ldots\,, & (4, 3, 3, 0)\,, \ldots\,, \\
(4, 3, 2, 1)\,, \ldots\,, & (4, 2, 2, 2)\,, \ldots\,, &
\end{array}
$$

which would necessitate 286 separate calculations!

This would not be unduly burdensome, but the company also wishes to know all the optimal solutions for total investments of only one to nine millions, and this would require several days work. It is therefore advantageous to introduce the method of *dynamic programming* for this combinatorial problem, and we shall now explain how it is to be employed.

Let us call $f_1(\psi)$, $f_2(\psi)$, $f_3(\psi)$, and $f_4(\psi)$ the functions corresponding to regions I, II, III, and IV, respectively. We next call:

$F_{1,2}(A)$ the optimal allocation when A millions are invested in regions I and II combined;

$F_{1,2,3}(A)$ the optimal allocation when A millions are invested in regions I, II, and III combined;

$F_{1,2,3,4}(A)$ the optimal allocation when A millions are invested in regions I, II, III, and IV combined.

Hence, to evaluate $F_{1,2}(2)$, we must calculate

$$
\begin{aligned}
f_1(0) + f_2(2) &= 0.00 + 0.41 = 0.41\,, \\
f_1(1) + f_2(1) &= 0.28 + 0.25 = 0.53\,, \\
f_1(2) + f_2(0) &= 0.45 + 0.00 = 0.45\,.
\end{aligned}
$$

We thus find

$$F_{1,2}(2) = 0.53\,.$$

In the same manner we now calculate the values of

$$F_{1,2}(0),\quad F_{1,2}(1),\quad F_{1,2}(2), \ldots, F_{1,2}(9),\quad F_{1,2}(10)\,,$$

which gives us Table 2.2.

TABLE 2.2

$F_{1,2}(A) = \mathrm{MAX}[f_1(x) + f_2(A - x)]$

Investment A	$f_1(x)$	$f_2(x)$	$F_{1,2}(A)$	Optimal policy for investing in regions I and II
0	0	0	0	(0, 0)
1	0.28	0.25	0.28	(1, 0)
2	0.45	0.41	0.53	(1, 1)
3	0.65	0.55	0.70	(2, 1)
4	0.78	0.65	0.90	(3, 1)
5	0.90	0.75	1.06	(3, 2)
6	1.02	0.80	1.20	(3, 3)
7	1.13	0.85	1.33	(4, 3)
8	1.23	0.88	1.45	(5, 3)
9	1.23	0.90	1.57	(6, 3)
10	1.38	0.90	1.68	(7, 3)

Table 2.2 shows us the optimal policies for a given investment. For example, if four millions are invested in regions I and II combined, three millions should be allocated to I and one million to II, which is the meaning of the notation (3, 1) in the fifth column, the corresponding profit amounting to 0.90. For a combined investment of ten millions, the policy to choose would be (7, 3), for which the profit is optimal and is equal to 1.68.

Next we shall calculate $F_{1,2,3}(A)$ in order to discover the optimal distribution when A millions are invested in I, II, and III regions. Table 2.3 gives the results. It shows, for example, that if we have seven millions to distribute among the three regions, the optimal policy is (3, 3, 1), which will yield a profit of 1.35 million.

We conclude our calculations by evaluating $F_{1,2,3,4}(A)$ for regions I, II, III, and IV, and summarize the results in Table 2.4. An economic adviser can now present his recommendations to the company in the form of Table 2.5.

TABLE 2.3

$F_{1,2,3}(A) = \text{MAX}[F_{1,2}(x) + f_3(A - x)]$

A	$F_{1,2}(x)$	$f_3(x)$	$F_{1,2,3}(A)$	Optimal policy for investing: In I and II	Optimal policy for investing: In I, II, and III
0	0	0	0	(0, 0)	(0, 0, 0)
1	0.28	0.15	0.28	(1, 0)	(1, 0, 0)
2	0.53	0.25	0.53	(1, 1)	(1, 1, 0)
3	0.70	0.40	0.70	(2, 1)	(2, 1, 0)
4	0.90	0.50	0.90	(3, 1)	(3, 1, 0)
5	1.06	0.62	1.06	(3, 2)	(3, 2, 0)
6	1.20	0.73	1.21	(3, 3)	(3, 2, 1)
7	1.33	0.82	1.35	(4, 3)	(3, 3, 1)
8	1.45	0.90	1.48	(5, 3)	(4, 3, 1)
9	1.57	0.96	1.60	(6, 3)	(5, 3, 1) or (3, 3, 3)
10	1.68	1.00	1.73	(7, 3)	(4, 3, 3)

TABLE 2.4

$F_{1,2,3,4}(A) = \text{MAX}[F_{1,2,3}(x) + f_4(A - x)]$

A	$F_{1,2,3}(x)$	$f_4(x)$	$F_{1,2,3,4}(A)$	Optimal policy for investing: In I, II, and III	Optimal policy for investing: In I, II, III, and IV
0	0	0	0	(0, 0, 0)	(0, 0, 0, 0)
1	0.28	0.20	0.28	(1, 0, 0)	(1, 0, 0, 0)
2	0.53	0.33	0.53	(1, 1, 0)	(1, 1, 0, 0)
3	0.70	0.42	0.73	(2, 1, 0)	(1, 1, 0, 1)
4	0.90	0.48	0.90	(3, 1, 0)	(3, 1, 0, 0) or (2, 1, 0, 1)
5	1.06	0.53	1.10	(3, 2, 0)	(3, 1, 0, 1)
6	1.21	0.56	1.26	(3, 2, 1)	(3, 2, 0, 1)
7	1.35	0.58	1.41	(3, 3, 1)	(3, 2, 1, 1)
8	1.48	0.60	1.55	(4, 3, 1)	(3, 3, 1, 1)
9	1.60	0.60	1.68	(5, 3, 1) or (3, 3, 3)	(4, 3, 1, 1) or (3, 3, 1, 2)
10	1.73	0.60	1.81	(4, 3, 3)	(4, 3, 1, 2)

The reader may be interested in verifying that these results are still valid for any other order of calculation such as

$$F_{3,1}(A), \qquad F_{3,1,2}(A), \qquad F_{3,1,2,4}(A) .$$

When the wine is drawn, it must be sold, and the company is now in a position to know the optimal profits to be obtained whatever sum it

TABLE 2.5

If your capital is (millions of pesos)	Invest in (millions of pesos) I	II	III	IV	Optimal profit will be (millions of pesos)
1	1	0	0	0	0.28
2	1	1	0	0	0.53
3	1	1	0	1	0.73
4	3	1	0	0	0.90
	or				
	2	1	0	1	
5	3	1	0	1	1.10
6	3	2	0	1	1.26
7	3	2	1	1	1.41
8	3	3	1	1	1.55
9	4	3	1	1	1.68
	or				
	3	3	1	2	
10	4	3	1	2	1.81

decides to invest. Here we must again stress that these results depend entirely on the validity of the first table.

A useful graph is given in Fig. 2.2, which shows how the marginal optimal profit decreases as a function of A, and it can be stated

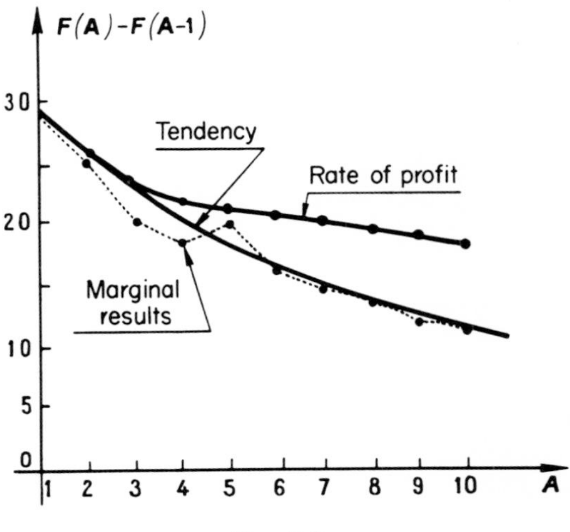

FIG. 2.2

that in general the extra profit obtained by investing one million pesos more, that is, by investing A instead of $A-1$ millions, decreases as a function of the investment A.

This decrease is clearly connected with the general tendency towards saturation, evidenced by the curves in Fig. 2.1, and it is confirmed by the manner in which the rate of profit evolves.

In spite of the amplitude of our calculations, many points still remain obscure. To what economic horizon—one year or several years—do the millions to be invested apply ? Ought we not to differentiate between the initial investments and the operating expenses ? Let us remind the critical reader that all we promised was to provide him with some ideas which might be of service in his own problems. Remember, in *vino veritas*!

Combinatorial Problems—Use of Dynamic Programming

The example we have just studied was mainly intended to emphasize the combinatorial character of problems of investment. In such conditions the only real difficulty consists in the large number of solutions to be considered.

In the foregoing problem, for all the possible investments up to ten million, there are 1001 solutions. We suggest that the reader study the graph in Fig. 2.3. By calculation, preferably with the aid of an office

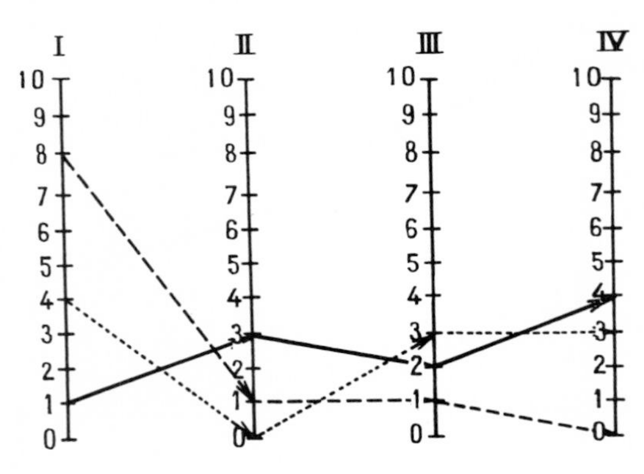

FIG. 2.3

machine, all these solutions can eventually be obtained; but in such problems as production scheduling and transport programs, in which dozens or even hundreds of variables are involved, the number of possible solutions becomes astronomical. Hence the need to discover a shorter method, or what mathematicians term an *algorithm*.[2]

As before we note that if $A = 10$, the maximal profit is 1.81 million pesos, whereas the minimal profit, which is simple to calculate, is 0.60 million, a difference of 1.21 million pesos, or 0.484 million Francs between the best and the worst solutions. It might be possible to choose intuitively a solution approaching the optimal one, but this is by no means certain. Moreover, it is very arbitrary to limit our estimates to whole numbers in millions of pesos (1 peso = 0.4 Franc); the choice of a smaller unit would eliminate any possibility of using the method of enumeration.

The algorithm we have selected is taken from the works of Richard Bellman and is called *dynamic programming*.

Given N functions with nonnegative values[3]:

$$f_1(x) \quad \text{where} \quad x \in d_1 ; \qquad f_2(x) \quad \text{where} \quad x \in d_2 ; \quad \cdots$$
$$f_n(x) \quad \text{where} \quad x \in d_n ,$$

let us determine the maximum (or minimum) of the function

$$F(x_1, x_2, ..., x_n) = f_1(x_1) + f_2(x_2) + \cdots + f_n(x_n) ,$$

the variables x_1, x_2, ..., x_n being subject to a system of constraints for which we assume the maximum (or minimum) of F exists.

In the problem that we studied above this system of constraints reduces to the equation

$$x_1 + x_2 + \cdots + x_n = A . \tag{1}$$

Then, to obtain

$$\mathscr{F}(A) = \underset{\substack{x_1, x_2, \ldots, x_n \\ x_1+x_2+\ldots+x_n=A}}{\text{MAX}} [f_1(x_1) + f_2(x_2) + \cdots + f_n(x_n)] ,$$

[2] This word is a corruption of the name of the 9th century Arab mathematician Al Khwârizmi.

[3] $x \in d$ means that x belongs to the domain, or set, d. We assume here that this domain includes zero.

we work by stages, or sequences. Let

$$\begin{aligned} F_{1,2}(A) &= \underset{x \in d_1}{\text{MAX}}\,[f_1(x) + f_2(A - x)]\,, \\ F_{1,2,3}(A) &= \underset{x \in d_2}{\text{MAX}}\,[F_{1,2}(x) + f_3(A - x)]\,, \\ &\vdots \\ F_{1,2,\ldots,(n-1)}(A) &= \underset{x \in d_{n-2}}{\text{MAX}}\,[F_{1,2,\ldots,(n-2)}(x) + f_{n-1}(A - x)]\,, \\ \mathscr{F}(A) &= \underset{x \in d_{n-1}}{\text{MAX}}\,[F_{1,2,\ldots,(n-1)}(x) + f_n(A - x)]. \end{aligned} \tag{2}$$

Hence, we calculate the maximum of f_1 and f_2 for all the values of x_1 and x_2 to be considered and such that

$$A = x_1 + x_2\,.$$

We thus obtain a function $F_{1,2}$ of A. We next find the maximum of $F_{1,2}$ and f_3 for the different values of x_1, x_2, and x_3 to be considered such that

$$A = x_1 + x_2 + x_3\,,$$

thereby obtaining a function $F_{1,2,3}(A)$, and so on.

In this problem the nature of the constraints—the solitary one given in Eq. (1)—allows us to proceed to the sequential optimization in an arbitrary order. This property, as we might suspect, is not at all general, and the nature of the constraints frequently obliges us to proceed in one or more special orders of operation and forbids us to use others. We say that the sequential problem is *strictly ordered* if only one *order*, taken in *either direction*, is possible. If only one order in one direction is possible, the problem is said to be *strictly ordered and strictly oriented*, a condition of particular importance when we are studying states (situations) that are defined by random variables. It is also possible to envisage a sequential optimization with two or more variables, but the advantages of dynamic programming are quickly lost as a result of the complications which these cause.

The formulas of Eq. (2) can be generalized for the case where a set of variables, or a state vector, is considered at each stage of the optimization. It is this modification which enables us to find the optimum of an economic system into which, each time it is considered, a number of relations between production and consumption enter, a decision being made on the basis of the state vector or another vector on which it depends. In this way, stage by stage, either proceeding toward the future or, if the nature of the problem requires it, toward the past, we can calculate the optimum corresponding to the given economic horizon.

The properties of dynamic programming are based on a general "principle," which Bellman has called the *principle of optimality*, and which he has defined as follows:

"A policy is optimal if, at a given period, whatever the previous decisions have been, the decisions still to be taken constitute an optimal policy, regard being paid to those which have already been taken."

CHAPTER 3

THE PUPPET MANUFACTURER

(Markov Chain. Problem of Sequential Decisions)

On the occasions when his patience is severely tested by a prolonged stoplight at one of the main intersections in Mexico City, a motorist is certain to be approached by some youthful and agile salesman. These young vendors, who thread their way so adroitly between the cars with typical Mexican disregard for danger, will offer him a variety of attractive purchases: automobile accessories, lottery tickets, mangoes when they are in season, and also marionettes. It is with the marionettes that we are concerned.

In Mexico puppets are called *titeres*, and as the name suggests, they should certainly provide parents with some respite from the demands of their children. It is the humorous aspect with which these puppets invest characters taken from Mexican folklore that is their most striking feature; and this folklore is admittedly one of the most abundant and entertaining in the world. How, then, could a visitor fail to admire their vivid coloring and humorous expressions and avoid becoming acquainted with that agile and gifted salesman of puppets, Lupe?

When the authors first purchased a puppet, Lupe told himself we must be *gringos*—not *Americans*, since the Mexicans are also Americans—but men from the north, with well-lined wallets. When we bought another, he decided we were "characters." With the third purchase we became collectors, and after the fourth very rich gringos, eccentric enough to be driving around in a small European car. It was only when Lupe discovered his mistake that we all became friends, and then over Coca Colas (now almost the national beverage), he divulged the address of his uncle Manuel, artist and manufacturer, and the father of a modest family of fourteen. We are convinced that if the airlines were more generous with their baggage allowance most visitors to Mexico City would return with a suitcase filled with the remarkable puppets produced by this charming man.

The manufacture and sale of marionettes is a serious enough subject to arouse the interest of anyone concerned with business management, but it was not until Señor Manuel confided his difficulties to us that we discovered he had his own ideas about production.

Señor Manuel's puppets are sold to some 20 young men such as Lupe, and each week he manufactures a single type. If it is successful, he continues the production of it the following week; if it is a failure, he changes to a new model.

Since he is not rich and is unable to accumulate capital, his economic horizon is limited to a period of a week, and his policy is based on the results of the previous week. Moreover, if he produces only one type at a time, this is largely because his salesmen, such as Lupe, do not have the opportunity while the stoplights are red to offer a variety of puppets. Accordingly, he concentrates on a single model, relying on future visitors to his factory to buy those which are unsold.

Every Monday morning Manuel decides what he will produce, according to the rule given above. If L_1 represents a particular Monday, and the production of the preceding week S_0 is reckoned a success, his possible future production can be shown by a simple diagram (Fig. 3.1).

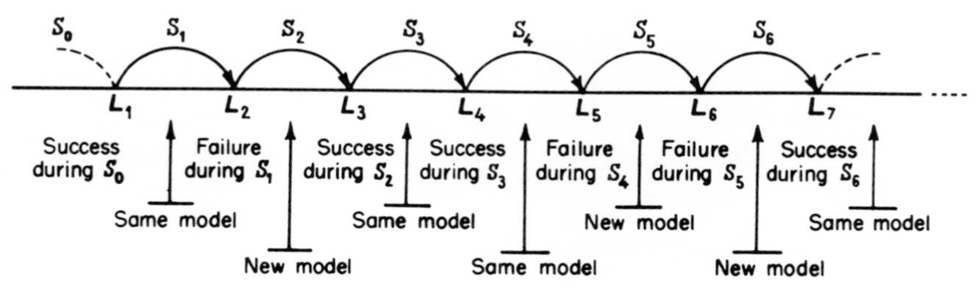

FIG. 3.1

Such is the way in which the random character of demand leads to new and original products, thereby proving that art and commerce are not as entirely distinct as some people would contend.

Mexicans may be easygoing, but they are shrewd observers, and Manuel had noticed that, if the model sold one week was successful, there was a fifty-fifty chance of its being successful the following week. Conversely, if a model was a failure, seven times out of ten the new model introduced the next week would prove a success.

To be sure, such statistics may seem very arbitrary, and it may well be asked why purchasers of marionettes should conform to any of the business and economic laws that we have discovered. Nonetheless, if we use the concept of probability, the random[1] future represented by the following week can be shown as a diagram (Table 3.1) in which

TABLE 3.1

		Week S_{i+1} Success	Week S_{i+1} Failure
Week S_i	Success	0.5	0.5
	Failure	0.7	0.3

0.5, 0.5, 0.7, 0.3 represent probabilities. This table gives the *probabilities of a change of state* between the two states of Manuel's business, success and failure. Figure 3.2 shows all the possible changes of state in a different way, by means of a *graph*.

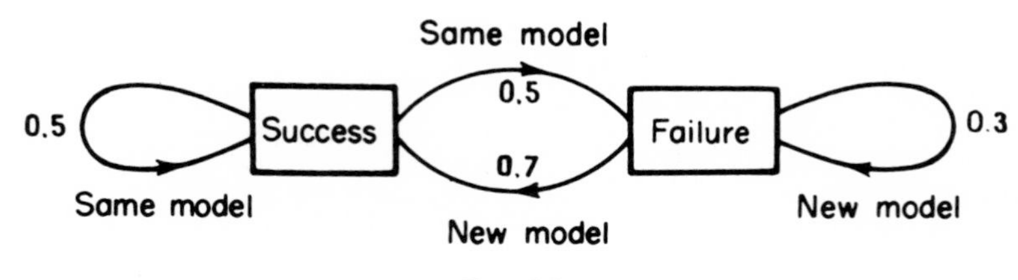

FIG. 3.2

What Manuel did not know (and would have disdained anyhow), is that mathematicians have made a study of the properties of random sequences of this kind. A sequential process that corresponds to the random nature of the sales and to the production decisions for these puppets, belongs to a very important class of random sequential processes: Markov decision chains. Let us therefore temporarily remove our thoughts from Mexico and fix them on the work of the great contemporary Russian mathematician after whom they are named. In considering his theory we shall try to simplify matters as much as possible.

[1] In conformity with the authors' preference, the French *aléatoire* has been translated as *random* rather than as *uncertain* or *incertain*.—Translator's note.

According to Table 3.1 and Fig. 3.2, if E_1 represents a success, and E_2 represents a failure, the probabilities p of a change of state, or a transition, from any week S_i to the following week S_{i+1} may be expressed conveniently as

$$\begin{array}{cccc} E_1 \to E_1 & E_1 \to E_2 & E_2 \to E_1 & E_2 \to E_2 \\ p_{11} = 0.5 & p_{12} = 0.5 & p_{21} = 0.7 & p_{22} = 0.3 \end{array}$$

These transition probabilities can also be conveniently shown *en bloc* in the form of a table known as a *matrix*. If $\mathscr{P}$ is this matrix, then

$$\mathscr{P} = \begin{bmatrix} 0.5 & 0.5 \\ 0.7 & 0.3 \end{bmatrix}.$$

As we have seen, if the week S_0 has been successful for Manuel, his probability of success (and equally, of failure) the next week is 0.5. If $P_1(1)$ and $P_2(1)$ represent the probabilities at the end of week 1, we have

$$\begin{aligned} P_1(1) &= 0.5, \quad \text{probability of success,} \\ P_2(1) &= 0.5, \quad \text{probability of failure.} \end{aligned}$$

With this information, what would the probabilities of success or of failure be at the end of the second week?

Taking $P_1(2)$ and $P_2(2)$ for these probabilities, we have

$$\begin{aligned} \text{probability of success:} \quad P_1(2) &= P_1(1) \cdot (0.5) + P_2(1) \cdot (0.7) \\ &= (0.5) \cdot (0.5) + (0.5) \cdot (0.7) = 0.60\,, \end{aligned}$$

with

$$p_{11}(E_1 \to E_1) = 0.5 \quad \text{and} \quad p_{21}(E_2 \to E_1) = 0.7,$$

$$\begin{aligned} \text{probability of failure:} \quad P_2(2) &= P_1(1) \cdot (0.5) + P_2(1) \cdot (0.3) \\ &= (0.5) \cdot (0.5) + (0.5) \cdot (0.3), \end{aligned}$$

with

$$p_{12}(E_1 \to E_2) = 0.5 \quad \text{and} \quad p_{22}(E_2 \to E_2) = 0.3\,.$$

By similar reasoning, the probabilities of success or failure at the end of the third week will be

$$\begin{aligned} P_1(3) &= P_1(2) \cdot (0.5) + P_2(2) \cdot (0.7) \\ &= (0.60) \cdot (0.50) + (0.40) \cdot (0.70) = 0.58, \\ P_2(3) &= P_1(2) \cdot (0.5) + P_2(2) \cdot (0.3) \\ &= (0.60) \cdot (0.50) + (0.40) \cdot (0.30) = 0.42. \end{aligned}$$

Continuing our calculations, we find

$$P_1(4) = 0.584, \qquad P_1(5) = 0.5832, \qquad P_1(6) = 0.58336, \ldots$$
$$P_2(4) = 0.416, \qquad P_2(5) = 0.4168, \qquad P_2(6) = 0.41663, \ldots$$

and that for any value of n,

$$P_1(n) = 0.5833 \cdots = 7/12,$$
$$P_2(n) = 0.4166 \cdots = 5/12.$$

Let us now carry out the same calculations on the assumption that week S_0 was a failure, using primes to denote the corresponding probabilities for this case. We now find:

$$P_1'(1) = 0.7, \qquad P_2'(1) = 0.3.$$
$$P_1'(2) = 0.56, \qquad P_1'(3) = 0.588, \qquad P_1'(4) = 0.5824,$$
$$P_2'(2) = 0.44, \qquad P_2'(3) = 0.412, \qquad P_2'(4) = 0.4176,$$
$$P_1'(5) = 0.58352, \qquad P_1'(6) = 0.583296, \ldots$$
$$P_2'(5) = 0.41648, \qquad P_2'(6) = 0.416704, \ldots$$
$$P_1'(n) = 0.5833 \cdots = 7/12,$$
$$P_2'(n) = 0.4167 \cdots = 5/12.$$

Thus,

$$P_1'(n) = P_1(n) \qquad \text{and} \qquad P_2'(n) = P_2(n).$$

This shows that after a certain number of weeks the probabilities no longer depend on the initial situation. Whether the first week was a success or a failure, a state of equilibrium rapidly develops and the probabilities of success or failure remain constant.

Manuel himself had discovered this state of equilibrium and had found satisfaction in the discovery. All he needed to support himself and his extensive family was that over a fairly large number of weeks, the probability of success should be appreciably greater than the probability of failure.

It is extremely important to realize the possibility of a state of equilibrium existing in an economic system, whether we are considering a small-scale manufacturer of puppets or a nation. Just as the life of a man can be regarded as an alternation between adventure and equilibrium, the existence of a business can, happily, be looked upon in the same way.

Several glasses of pulque had loosened Manuel's tongue, and he now recalled a whole series of figures in connection with his small business.

As a general rule, when a successful week has been followed by another successful one, his return amounts to 500 pesos; a success followed by a failure gives a return of 150 pesos for the week; a failure followed by a success gives a return of 200 pesos; finally, a failure followed by a failure means a loss of 400 pesos. Accordingly, if we take r_{11}, r_{12}, r_{21}, and r_{22} for the returns corresponding to the situations just described, we have

$$\begin{array}{cccc} E_1 \to E_1 & E_1 \to E_2 & E_2 \to E_1 & E_2 \to E_2 \\ r_{11} = 500 & r_{12} = 150 & r_{21} = 200 & r_{22} = -400 \end{array}$$

In calculating the totals for Manuel's income as the weeks pass, we shall introduce notation designed to render our explanations more precise and intelligible. Accordingly, time $n - 1$ will represent the beginning of week n, time 0 the beginning of week 1; time 1 will represent the end of week 1 and the commencement of week 2, time 2 will mean the end of week 2 and the commencement of week 3 and so on.

We shall take $\bar{R}_1(0, N)$ as the average total income from time 0 to time N or, in other words, as the expected value of the total income, in the case where time 0 has been preceded by a success. In the same way $\bar{R}_2(0, N)$ will represent the corresponding income when time 0 has been preceded by a failure. Obviously, the future will depend on the initial conditions which connect it with the past.

For the first week, from time 0 to time 1, we have

$$\bar{R}_1(0, 1) = p_{11}r_{11} + p_{12}r_{12} = (0.5)(500) + (0.5)(150) = 325,$$

$$\bar{R}_2(0, 1) = p_{21}r_{21} + p_{22}r_{22} = (0.7)(200) + (0.3)(-400) = 20.$$

For two weeks, from time 0 to time 2, we shall have

$$\bar{R}_1(0, 2) = p_{11}\bar{R}_1(0, 1) + p_{12}\bar{R}_2(0, 1) + p_{11}r_{11} + p_{12}r_{12},$$

$$\bar{R}_2(0, 2) = p_{21}\bar{R}_2(0, 1) + p_{22}\bar{R}_2(0, 1) + p_{21}r_{21} + p_{22}r_{22}.$$

Since these formulas are rather more complicated, some explanation of them is required. Let us, therefore, suppose that at time 0 we are in state E_1; see Fig. 3.3. From time 0 to time 1 the expected value of gain is

$$p_{11}r_{11} + p_{12}r_{12}.$$

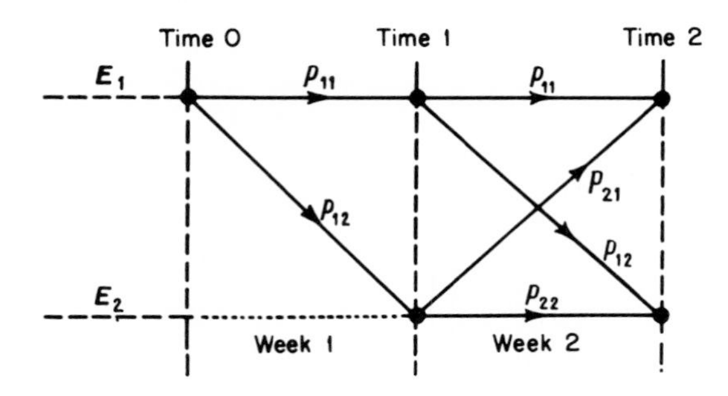

FIG. 3.3

Next, at time 1 we may find ourselves in either E_1 or E_2. If we are in E_1, the expected value of gain is

$$p_{11}(p_{11}r_{11} + p_{12}r_{12}) = p_{11}\bar{R}_1(0, 1),$$

and if we are in E_2, this profit is

$$p_{12}(p_{21}r_{21} + p_{22}r_{22}) = p_{12}\bar{R}_2(0, 1),$$

and it corresponds to the interval between time 1 and time 2. With the proviso that we do not prescribe our state as E_1 or E_2 at time 2, the expected income from time 1 to time 2 is

$$p_{11}\bar{R}_1(0, 1) + p_{12}\bar{R}_2(0, 1).$$

The same reasoning will be followed to explain $\bar{R}(0, 2)$. Substituting numerical values, we now have

$$\bar{R}_1(0, 2) = (0.5)(325) + (0.5)(20) + 325 = 497.5,$$
$$\bar{R}_2(0, 2) = (0.7)(325) + (0.3)(20) + 20 = 253.5.$$

The same form of reasoning will give us

$$\begin{aligned}\bar{R}_1(0, 3) &= p_{11}\bar{R}_1(0, 2) + p_{12}\bar{R}_2(0, 2) + p_{11}r_{11} + p_{12}r_{12}\\ &= (0.5)(497.5) + (0.5)(253.5) + 325 = 700.5.\\ \bar{R}_2(0, 3) &= p_{21}\bar{R}_1(0, 2) + p_{22}\bar{R}_2(0, 2) + p_{21}r_{21} + p_{22}r_{22}\\ &= (0.7)(497.5) + (0.3)(253.5) + 20 = 444.3.\end{aligned}$$

and, similarly,

$$\bar{R}_1(0, 4) = 897.4, \qquad \bar{R}_1(0, 5) = 1095.52, \qquad \bar{R}_1(0, 6) = 1293.396,$$
$$\bar{R}_2(0, 4) = 643.64, \qquad \bar{R}_2(0, 5) = 841.272, \qquad \bar{R}_2(0, 6) = 1039.2456.$$

It can be proved that

$$\bar{R}_1(0, N) - \bar{R}_2(0, N)$$

approaches the following value as N grows larger:

$$\lim_{N\to\infty} [\bar{R}_1(0, N) - \bar{R}_2(0, N)] = 254.167.$$

When N represents a large number of weeks, we shall find[2]

$$\bar{R}_1(0, N) = 197.916N + 105.902,$$
$$\bar{R}_2(0, N) = 197.916N - 148.264.$$

Then we have Manuel's average weekly return:

$$\bar{r}_1(N) = \frac{\bar{R}_1(0, N)}{N} = 197.916 + \frac{105.902}{N},$$

$$\bar{r}_2(N) = \frac{\bar{R}_2(0, N)}{N} = 197.916 - \frac{148.264}{N}.$$

When $N \to \infty$,

$$\bar{r}_1(N) = \bar{r}_2(N) = \bar{r} = 197.916.$$

Manuel will obtain an average income of 197.916 pesos a week on which to support his family.

Like all shrewd merchants, Manuel was always looking for ways of increasing his profit and had experimented with a number of plans, of which we shall consider only two. The first of these plans was to have his youthful salesmen distribute small cardboard cutouts of his puppets to motorists in the hope that this would induce them to purchase a real puppet when they were stopped at one of these same red lights the next day. The second plan was simply to reduce the price of his puppets by some ten percent. Obviously, such decisions as these are bound to affect the weekly profit, and on the basis of Manuel's records a tabulation was prepared in which, for the sake of simplification, we have reduced to four the many alternatives which Manuel might have chosen. These four alternatives will be represented as

P_1 : the decision not to distribute cutouts after a success,

P_2 : the decision to distribute cutouts after a success,

[2] For the method of calculation the reader should consult the works of Howard and of Kaufmann and Cruon given in the Bibliography.

Q_1 : the decision not to alter the price after a failure,

Q_2 : the decision to reduce the price by 10% after a failure.

The figures which we shall now use were obtained from Manuel's records, and we shall employ the same notation as before, adding a superscript to represent the type of decision.

$$P_1: \; p_{11}^{(1)} = 0.5, \quad p_{12}^{(1)} = 0.5, \quad r_{11}^{(1)} = 500, \quad r_{12}^{(1)} = 150,$$

$$P_2: \; p_{11}^{(2)} = 0.6, \quad p_{12}^{(2)} = 0.4, \quad r_{11}^{(2)} = 400, \quad r_{12}^{(2)} = 200,$$

$$Q_1: \; p_{21}^{(1)} = 0.7, \quad p_{22}^{(1)} = 0.3, \quad r_{21}^{(1)} = 200, \quad r_{22}^{(1)} = -400,$$

$$Q_2: \; p_{21}^{(2)} = 0.8, \quad p_{22}^{(2)} = 0.2, \quad r_{21}^{(2)} = 100, \quad r_{22}^{(2)} = -800.$$

In the case of P_2 and Q_2 we are, of course, dealing with net returns after allowing for the respective costs of the decisions.

Those of our readers who are acquainted with matrix notation will have observed that

$$\mathscr{P}^{(1)} = \begin{bmatrix} 0.5 & 0.5 \\ 0.7 & 0.3 \end{bmatrix}, \qquad \mathscr{R}^{(1)} = \begin{bmatrix} 500 & 150 \\ 200 & -400 \end{bmatrix} \begin{matrix} \leftarrow P_1 \\ \leftarrow Q_1 \end{matrix}$$

$$\mathscr{P}^{(2)} = \begin{bmatrix} 0.6 & 0.4 \\ 0.8 & 0.2 \end{bmatrix}, \qquad \mathscr{R}^{(2)} = \begin{bmatrix} 400 & 200 \\ 100 & -800 \end{bmatrix} \begin{matrix} \leftarrow P_2 \\ \leftarrow Q_2 \end{matrix}$$

Figure 3.4 represents several weeks' management under these conditions.

Since a decision has to be taken weekly for a set of N consecutive weeks, what policy or, in other words, what sequence of decisions must Manuel adopt to maximize the cumulative value of his takings for these N weeks?

To calculate this, we shall employ dynamic programming, commencing

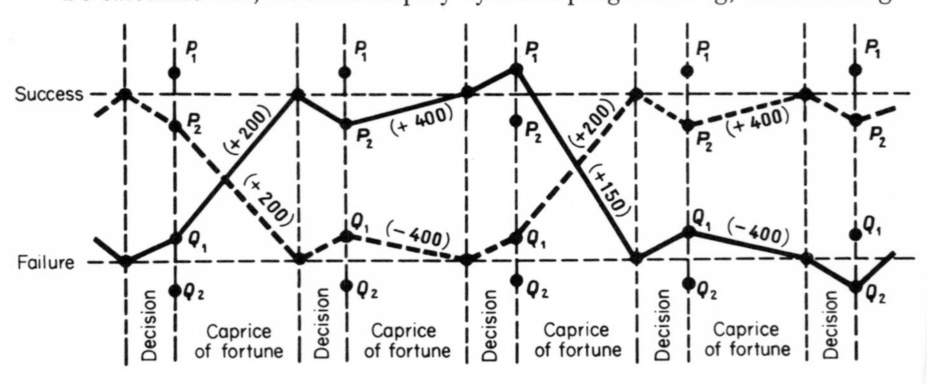

FIG. 3.4

our operations with the Nth (that is, the *last*) week and then passing to weeks $N-1$, $N-2$, until we finally reach the first week.

Let us use the notation:

$\bar{R}_1(N-1, N)$, the expected value of profit for a week from time $N-1$ to time N, when at time $N-1$ the previous week could be counted a success,

$\bar{R}_2(N-1, N)$, the same, when the previous week has been a failure,

$\bar{R}_1(N-2, N)$, the expected value of the total profit for two weeks from time $N-2$ to time N, when time $N-2$ has been preceded by a success,

$\bar{R}_2(N-2, N)$, the same definition, when time $N-2$ has been preceded by a failure.

In the same manner we can define

$$\bar{R}_1(N-3, N), \qquad \bar{R}_2(N-3, N), \ldots, \quad \text{etc.}$$

up to $N-20=0$, if the management period is one of 20 weeks.[3]

Optimal Management for One Week, Time $N-1$ to Time N

We have

$$\begin{aligned}\bar{R}_1(N-1, N) &= \text{MAX}[p_{11}^{(1)}r_{11}^{(1)} + p_{12}^{(1)}r_{12}^{(1)}, p_{11}^{(2)}r_{11}^{(2)} + p_{12}^{(2)}r_{12}^{(2)}]\\ &= \max[325, 320]\\ &= 325.\end{aligned}$$

If at time $N-1$ Manuel is in situation E_1, he should choose decision P_1 to ensure an optimal state from $N-1$ to N.[4]

$$\begin{aligned}\bar{R}_2(N-1, N) &= \text{MAX}[p_{21}^{(1)}r_{21}^{(1)} + p_{22}^{(1)}r_{22}^{(1)}, p_{21}^{(2)}r_{21}^{(2)} + p_{22}^{(2)}r_{22}^{(2)}]\\ &= \max[20, -80]\\ &= 20.\end{aligned}$$

If at time $N-1$ Manuel is in situation E_2, he should choose decision Q_1 to ensure an optimal state from $N-1$ to N.

[3] We are assuming here than Manuel will end his operations after N weeks and will close his business without any compensation, whatever the final situation may be. Otherwise, we could generalize the present method and consider what happens under the assumption that his business will be sold.

[4] We must admit that Manuel is scarcely qualified to carry out such calculations, but there has been so much study of operations research in Mexico that he would have no difficulty in finding a competent adviser.

Let us now try to discover the optimum for two weeks from time $N-2$ to time N.

Optimal Management for Two Weeks, Time $N-2$ to Time N

We shall now compare Figs. 3.3 and 3.5. The same reasoning will apply, but to calculate $\bar{R}_1(N-2, N)$, then $\bar{R}_2(N-2, N)$, and the other

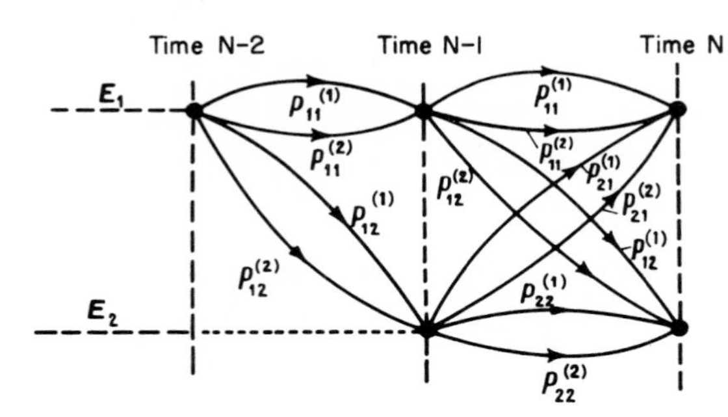

Fig. 3.5

expected values of the income for three, four, and more weeks, we must in each case seek these values by comparing the results of the different possible decisions. Thus, Manuel should choose as the value of $\bar{R}_1(N-2, N)$ the highest of the values:

$$p_{11}^{(1)}\bar{R}_1(N-1, N) + p_{12}^{(1)}\bar{R}_2(N-1, N) + p_{11}^{(1)}r_{11}^{(1)} + p_{12}^{(1)}r_{12}^{(1)}$$

$$p_{11}^{(2)}\bar{R}_1(N-1, N) + p_{12}^{(2)}\bar{R}_2(N-1, N) + p_{11}^{(2)}r_{11}^{(2)} + p_{12}^{(2)}r_{12}^{(2)},$$

which gives

$$(0.5)(325) + (0.5)(20) + 325 = 497.5,$$

$$(0.6)(325) + (0.4)(20) + 320 = 523.$$

He should, therefore, choose decision P_2 at time $N-2$ if the preceding week was a success, and the management from $N-2$ to N will then be optimal with a return of 523 pesos. That is to say,

$$\bar{R}_1(N-2, N) = 523.$$

If at time $N-2$ his situation is E_2 instead of E_1, a similar method of calculation leads him to compare

$$p_{21}^{(1)}\bar{R}_1(N-1, N) + p_{22}^{(1)}\bar{R}_2(N-1, N) + p_{21}^{(1)}r_{21}^{(1)} + p_{22}^{(1)}r_{22}^{(1)},$$

$$p_{21}^{(2)}\bar{R}_1(N-1, N) + p_{22}^{(2)}\bar{R}_2(N-1, N) + p_{21}^{(2)}r_{21}^{(2)} + p_{22}^{(2)}r_{22}^{(2)}.$$

This gives

$$(0.7)(325) + (0.3)(20) + 20 = 253.5,$$

$$(0.8)(325) + (0.2)(20) - 80 = 184.$$

He should, therefore, choose decision Q_1 at time $N - 2$ if the preceding week was a failure, and the management from $N - 2$ to N will then be optimal, with a return of 253.5 pesos. That is,

$$\bar{R}_2(N - 2, N) = 253.5.$$

Optimal Management for Three Weeks, Time $N - 3$ to Time N

The same process is repeated. To find $\bar{R}_1(N - 2, N)$ we must compare

$$p_{11}^{(1)}\bar{R}_1(N - 2, N) + p_{12}^{(1)}\bar{R}_2(N - 2, N) + p_{11}^{(1)}r_{11}^{(1)} + p_{12}^{(1)}r_{12}^{(1)},$$

$$p_{11}^{(2)}\bar{R}_1(N - 2, N) + p_{12}^{(2)}\bar{R}_2(N - 2, N) + p_{11}^{(2)}r_{11}^{(2)} + p_{12}^{(2)}r_{12}^{(2)}.$$

This gives

$$\bar{R}_1(N - 3, N) = \max[713.5, 735.2] = 735.2$$

with P_2 as the decision; in the same way,

$$\bar{R}_2(N - 3, N) = \max[462.15, 389.1] = 462.15,$$

and the choice must be Q_1.

Proceeding in a similar manner and assuming $N = 20$, we obtain a tabulation.

Optimal management for n weeks	Average total revenue	Optimal decision
$n = 4$	$\bar{R}_1(N - 4, N) = 945.98$	P_2
	$\bar{R}_2(N - 4, N) = 673.28$	Q_1
$n = 5$	$\bar{R}_1(N - 5, N) = 1156.90$	P_2
	$\bar{R}_2(N - 5, N) = 884.17$	Q_1
$\vdots$	$\vdots$	$\vdots$
$n = N = 20$	$\bar{R}_1(0, 20) = 4320.33$	P_2
	$\bar{R}_2(0, 20) = 4047.60$	Q_1

Finally, the optimal management for 20 weeks, from time 0 to time 20 (assuming Manuel ends his production after 20 weeks, regardless of the situation at time 18), will be:

For all times 0, 1, 2, 3, ..., 18

(a) if the previous week has been a success, choose P_2;
(b) if the previous week has been a failure, choose Q_1.

For time 19

(a) if the previous week has been a success, choose P_1;
(b) if the previous week has been a failure, choose Q_1.

By following this policy Manuel will earn 4320.33 pesos for 20 weeks if the first week was preceded by a successful one, and 4047.60 pesos if it was preceded by a week of failure.

If the calculations are extended beyond 20 weeks, Manuel's optimal policy will still be that just given, whatever period is considered.

By a procedure similar to the one used earlier we can discover Manuel's average weekly return by assuming

$$\bar{r}_1(N) = \frac{\bar{R}_1(0, N)}{N}, \qquad \bar{r}_2(N) = \frac{\bar{R}_2(0, N)}{N}.$$

It can be proved[5] that

$$\lim_{N\to\infty} \bar{r}_1(N) = \lim_{N\to\infty} \bar{r}_2(N) = \bar{r}^* = 210.91.$$

Limiting the period of management to 20 weeks, we find

$$\bar{r}_1(20) = \frac{4320.33}{20} = 216.02, \qquad \bar{r}_2(20) = \frac{4047.60}{20} = 202.38.$$

As N increases, the difference $\bar{r}_1(N) - \bar{r}_2(N)$ approaches zero, as we would readily discover if our calculations were pursued over a greater period than 20 weeks.

Finally, by following policy P_2, Q_1 every week except the last and P_1, Q_1 for the last week, Manuel's average weekly return will amount to 210.91 pesos instead of 197.91 pesos.[6]

[5] The method to be used will be found in Howard and in Kaufmann and Cruon (see the Bibliography for Chapter 2).

[6] This small increase of profit will enable him, for example, to take his family for lunch to the floating garden of Xochimilco, a pleasant reward for a more scientific management.

Thus, by associating the theory of Markov decision chains with dynamic programming (it should be observed that in passing from the management for one week to that for two weeks, then for three weeks, and so on, we have strictly applied Bellman's principle of optimality, as defined in Chapter 2), it is possible to treat numerous problems of management with random influences and discover the optimal policy or policies.

A Glance at the Theory of Markov Decision Chains

Given a system capable of assuming a certain number of states $E_0, E_1, \ldots, E_k, \ldots$, the changes of state taking place at predetermined times 0, 1, 2, ..., n, ... if $p_k(n)$ is the probability of state E_k at time n, we may represent the state of the system at time n by the state vector

$$p(n) = [p_0(n)\, p_1(n)\, p_2(n) \cdots p_k(n) \cdots],$$

where all the $p_k(n)$ terms are included between 0 and 1, and the sum of all the probabilities relative to the same time

$$\sum_k p_k(n)$$

is equal to 1.

If with every pair of states (E_i, E_j) it is possible to associate the *probability of transition* p_{ij} such that the system in state E_i at time n will be in state E_j at time $n + 1$, then

$$p_j(n + 1) = \sum_i p_i(n) \cdot p_{ij},$$

which amounts in practice to first multiplying each element of the state vector $p(n)$ by the corresponding probability of its transition to state E_j at time $n + 1$, and then finding the sum of these results. From this we discover the probability of state E_j at time $n + 1$.

Let us now give all the elements of the vector:

$$\begin{aligned} p(n + 1) &= [p_0(n + 1), p_1(n + 1), \ldots, p_j(n + 1), \ldots] \\ &= \left[\sum_i p_i(n) \cdot p_{i0}, \sum_i p_i(n) \cdot p_{i1}, \ldots, \sum_i p_i(n) \cdot p_{ij}, \ldots\right] \\ &= [p_0(n) \cdot p_{00} + p_1(n) \cdot p_{10} + \ldots, p_0(n) \cdot p_{01} + p_1(n) \cdot p_{11} + \cdots] \end{aligned}$$

We observe that this gives us the matricial product:

$$p(n+1) = [p_0(n)\, p_1(n) \cdots p_i(n) \cdots] \cdot \begin{bmatrix} p_{00} & p_{01} & p_{02} & \cdots & p_{0j} & \cdots \\ p_{10} & p_{11} & p_{12} & \cdots & & \cdots \\ & & & \vdots & & \vdots \\ p_{i0} & p_{i1} & p_{i2} & \cdots & p_{ij} & \cdots \\ & & & \vdots & & \vdots \end{bmatrix}$$

$$= p(n) \cdot [\mathscr{M}].$$

We note that the elements of each line of the matrix $[\mathscr{M}]$ formed by the p_{ij} terms have a sum equal to unity. In fact, such a line represents the sum of the probabilities of passing from a given state to all the other possible states (including itself). In these conditions the transition matrix belongs to the category of *stochastic matrices.*[7]

If the p_{ij} terms do not depend on times, the Markov process is stationary, and we can easily see that

$$p(n) = p(0) \cdot [\mathscr{M}]^n.$$

Example. Let us consider a workshop which specializes in the repair of two different types of automobile engine. The overhaul of engine M_1 requires two days; that of engine M_2 can be completed in one day. Each morning the probability of receiving an M_1 engine for repair is $\frac{1}{3}$, the probability of receiving an M_2 engine is $\frac{1}{2}$. Work which cannot be completed by the firm is sent to other workshops.

We assume that if the first day's repair has been completed on an M_1 type engine, any work received the following day will be refused, and that on any other day either type will be accepted if only one engine is received, but we hesitate between two possible policies when both types are received simultaneously. Stated as hypotheses the possible policies are:

(1) Give preference to M_1.
(2) Give preference to M_2.

To discover the best policy, we begin by writing the matrices of transition between the various possible states created by the two hypo-

[7] See M. D. Papin and A. Kaufmann, *Cours de calcul matriciel appliqué*, Albin Michel, 3rd ed., Annexe IV.

theses. In both cases the possible states are: no work (state 0), first day of work on M_1 (state 1), second day of work on M_1 (state 2), work on M_2 (state 3).

The probability that no M_1 engine will be received for repair is $1 - \frac{1}{3}$; the same probability for M_2 is $1 - \frac{1}{2}$.

For both hypotheses:

(a) The probability of not receiving any work in the course of a day is always $(1 - \frac{1}{3})(1 - \frac{1}{2})$, whatever state existed on the previous day, except when the commencement of work on an M_1 engine has eliminated the possibility of idleness.

(b) The probability of repairing an M_1 engine on the second day is uniformly nil except in those cases when overhaul has been begun on the previous day, when the probability is 1.

In the two transition matrices corresponding respectively to each hypothesis, the columns which represent cases a and b will be identical.

For the first hypothesis:

(c) We accord preference to the repair of an M_1 engine on those days when both types are received simultaneously. Thus, the probability of overhauling an M_1 engine (state 1) is always equal to $\frac{1}{3}$, except when the workshop was in state 1 on the previous day, the only case when it has to refuse other work (probability 0).

(d) The fact that priority is not given to the M_2 engine means that the probability of undertaking repair of one (state 3) is always the product of the probability of receiving an M_2 engine and the probability of not receiving an M_1 engine. This amounts to $\frac{1}{2}(1 - \frac{1}{3})$, with the obvious exception of the case when one day's work has been completed on an M_1 engine, in which case the probability is 0.

For the second hypothesis:

As the repair of an M_2 engine now receives priority, a similar form of reasoning enables us to find the column corresponding to state 1. All the elements in this column are equal to $(1 - \frac{1}{2})(\frac{1}{3})$, except the second one, which is 0. In the same way the elements of the column representing state 3 are all equal to $\frac{1}{2}$, with the exception of the second element, which is 0.

TRANSITION MATRIX. FIRST HYPOTHESIS

Present day

States		0 No work	1 $M_1(1)$	2 $M_1(2)$	3 M_2
Previous day	0 No work	$(1-\frac{1}{3})(1-\frac{1}{2})$	$\frac{1}{3}$	0	$\frac{1}{2}(1-\frac{1}{3})$
	1 $M_1(1)$	0	0	1	0
	2 $M_1(2)$	$(1-\frac{1}{3})(1-\frac{1}{2})$	$\frac{1}{3}$	0	$\frac{1}{2}(1-\frac{1}{3})$
	3 M_2	$(1-\frac{1}{3})(1-\frac{1}{2})$	$\frac{1}{3}$	0	$\frac{1}{2}(1-\frac{1}{3})$

$$
\begin{array}{c} \begin{matrix} 0 & 1 & 2 & 3 \end{matrix} \\ = \begin{bmatrix} \frac{1}{3} & \frac{1}{3} & 0 & \frac{1}{3} \\ 0 & 0 & 1 & 0 \\ \frac{1}{3} & \frac{1}{3} & 0 & \frac{1}{3} \\ \frac{1}{3} & \frac{1}{3} & 0 & \frac{1}{3} \end{bmatrix} \begin{matrix} 0 \\ 1 \\ 2 \\ 3 \end{matrix} \end{array}
$$

TRANSITION MATRIX. SECOND HYPOTHESIS

$$
\begin{bmatrix} (1-\frac{1}{3})(1-\frac{1}{2}) & (1-\frac{1}{2})\frac{1}{3} & 0 & \frac{1}{2} \\ 0 & 0 & 1 & 0 \\ (1-\frac{1}{3})(1-\frac{1}{2}) & (1-\frac{1}{2})\frac{1}{3} & 0 & \frac{1}{2} \\ (1-\frac{1}{3})(1-\frac{1}{2}) & (1-\frac{1}{2})\frac{1}{3} & 0 & \frac{1}{2} \end{bmatrix} = \begin{array}{c} \begin{matrix} 0 & 1 & 2 & 3 \end{matrix} \\ \begin{bmatrix} \frac{1}{3} & \frac{1}{6} & 0 & \frac{1}{2} \\ 0 & 0 & 1 & 0 \\ \frac{1}{3} & \frac{1}{6} & 0 & \frac{1}{2} \\ \frac{1}{3} & \frac{1}{6} & 0 & \frac{1}{2} \end{bmatrix} \begin{matrix} 0 \\ 1 \\ 2 \\ 3 \end{matrix} \end{array}
$$

For each hypothesis the transition matrix can be represented by a graph (Fig. 3.6). For the first hypothesis we have

$$
p(n) = p(0)\,[\mathscr{M}_1]^n,
$$

with

$$
\mathscr{M}_1 = \frac{1}{3} \begin{bmatrix} 1 & 1 & 0 & 1 \\ 0 & 0 & 3 & 0 \\ 1 & 1 & 0 & 1 \\ 1 & 1 & 0 & 1 \end{bmatrix},
$$

Next, if we raise matrix $\mathscr{M}_1$ to the power of n, we find that it takes the form

$$
[\mathscr{M}_1]^n = \frac{1}{4} \cdot \frac{1}{3^n} \cdot \begin{bmatrix} 3^n - 1 & 3^n - 1 & 3^n & 3^n - 1 \\ 3^n & 3^n & 3^n - 2 & 3^n \\ 3^n - 1 & 3^n - 1 & 3^n & 3^n - 1 \\ 3^n - 1 & 3^n - 1 & 3^n & 3^n - 1 \end{bmatrix},
$$

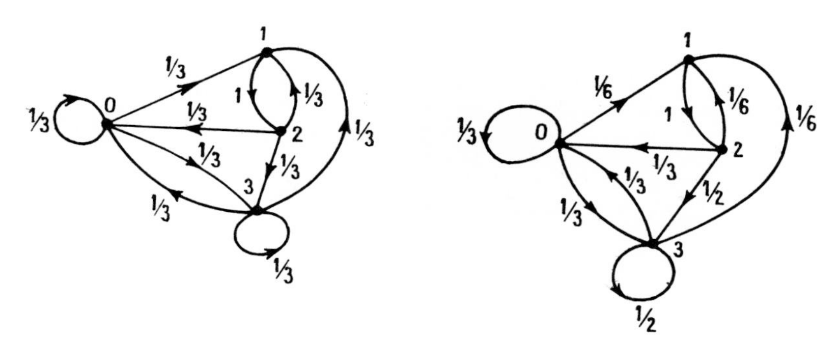

FIG. 3.6. Left: first hypothesis. Right: second hypothesis.

whence, if n increases indefinitely,

$$\lim_{n\to\infty} [\mathscr{M}_1]^n = \frac{1}{4}\begin{bmatrix} 1 & 1 & 1 & 1 \\ 1 & 1 & 1 & 1 \\ 1 & 1 & 1 & 1 \\ 1 & 1 & 1 & 1 \end{bmatrix}.$$

In these conditions, whatever the value of $p(0)$, we obtain

$$\lim_{n\to\infty} p(n) = [\tfrac{1}{4} \quad \tfrac{1}{4} \quad \tfrac{1}{4} \quad \tfrac{1}{4}].$$

Assuming that a similar property applies to the second hypothesis, and taking π_0, π_1, π_2, and π_3 for the probabilities of being in states 0, 1, 2, and 3 as $n \to \infty$, we have

$$\begin{bmatrix} \pi_0 & \pi_1 & \pi_2 & \pi_3 \\ \pi_0 & \pi_1 & \pi_2 & \pi_3 \\ \pi_0 & \pi_1 & \pi_2 & \pi_3 \\ \pi_0 & \pi_1 & \pi_2 & \pi_3 \end{bmatrix} = \lim_{n\to\infty} [\mathscr{M}_2]^n,$$

whence

$$\begin{bmatrix} \pi_0 & \pi_1 & \pi_2 & \pi_3 \\ \pi_0 & \pi_1 & \pi_2 & \pi_3 \\ \pi_0 & \pi_1 & \pi_2 & \pi_3 \\ \pi_0 & \pi_1 & \pi_2 & \pi_3 \end{bmatrix} [\mathscr{M}_2] = \{\lim_{n\to\infty} [\mathscr{M}_2]^n\} \cdot [\mathscr{M}_2] = \begin{bmatrix} \pi_0 & \pi_1 & \pi_2 & \pi_3 \\ \pi_0 & \pi_1 & \pi_2 & \pi_3 \\ \pi_0 & \pi_1 & \pi_2 & \pi_3 \\ \pi_0 & \pi_1 & \pi_2 & \pi_3 \end{bmatrix}$$

and

$$[\pi_0 \quad \pi_1 \quad \pi_2 \quad \pi_3][\mathscr{M}_2] = [\pi_0 \quad \pi_1 \quad \pi_2 \quad \pi_3],$$

with

$$\pi_0 + \pi_1 + \pi_2 + \pi_3 = 1.$$

Numerically,

$$[\pi_0 \quad \pi_1 \quad \pi_2 \quad \pi_3] \begin{bmatrix} \frac{1}{3} & \frac{1}{6} & 0 & \frac{1}{2} \\ 0 & 0 & 1 & 0 \\ \frac{1}{3} & \frac{1}{6} & 0 & \frac{1}{2} \\ \frac{1}{3} & \frac{1}{6} & 0 & \frac{1}{2} \end{bmatrix} = [\pi_0 \quad \pi_1 \quad \pi_2 \quad \pi_3].$$

From this we can deduce the system of equations

$$\frac{\pi_0}{3} + \frac{\pi_2}{3} + \frac{\pi_3}{3} = \pi_r ,$$

$$\frac{\pi_0}{6} + \frac{\pi_2}{6} + \frac{\pi_3}{6} = \pi_1 ,$$

$$\pi_1 = \pi_2 ,$$

$$\frac{\pi_0}{2} + \frac{\pi_2}{2} + \frac{\pi_3}{2} = \pi_3 ,$$

with

$$\pi_0 + \pi_1 + \pi_2 + \pi_3 = 1.$$

We find that

$$\pi_1 = \pi_2 = \pi_0/2, \qquad \pi_3 = 3\pi_0/2:$$

consequently,

$$\pi_0 + \pi_0 + 3\pi_0/2 = 1,$$

whence

$$\pi_0 = \tfrac{2}{7}, \qquad \pi_1 = \pi_2 = \tfrac{1}{7}, \qquad \pi_3 = \tfrac{3}{7}.$$

Thus,

$$\lim_{n\to\infty} p(n) = [\tfrac{2}{7} \quad \tfrac{1}{7} \quad \tfrac{1}{7} \quad \tfrac{3}{7}].$$

It is not difficult to see that the first hypothesis, which would keep the workshop employed for three-quarters of its time, is better than the second, which would only keep it employed for five-sevenths of its time: $\frac{3}{4} > \frac{5}{7}$. This completes our example.

The transition matrices having an nth power which approaches a limit, and having equal rows as $n \to \infty$, are called *fully ergodic*. In this case the Markov chain leads to a stable state which is independent of the initial conditions.

This is not always true of stochastic matrices, which can be placed in several categories. If they are *reducible* matrices, that is to say, matrices of the form

$$\begin{bmatrix} A & 0 \\ 0 & D \end{bmatrix},$$

where A and D are square submatrices, if we leave a state contained in A, we can never find ourselves in state D, and inversely. Let us consider, for example, matrix $[\mathscr{M}]$ and its associated graph, Fig. 3.7.

$$[\mathscr{M}] = \begin{bmatrix} 0.2 & 0.8 & 0 & 0 \\ 0.4 & 0.6 & 0 & 0 \\ 0 & 0 & 0.1 & 0.9 \\ 0 & 0 & 0.7 & 0.3 \end{bmatrix} \begin{matrix} 0 \\ 1 \\ 2 \\ 3 \end{matrix}$$
$$\begin{matrix} 0 & 1 & 2 & 3 \end{matrix}$$

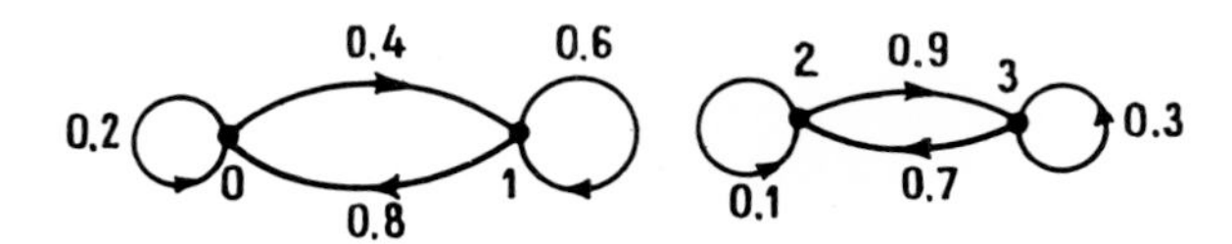

FIG. 3.7

We observe that the graph is composed of two disjoint subgraphs, and we have

$$\lim_{n\to\infty} [\mathscr{M}]^n = \begin{bmatrix} \frac{1}{3} & \frac{2}{3} & 0 & 0 \\ \frac{1}{3} & \frac{2}{3} & 0 & 0 \\ 0 & 0 & 0.4375 & 0.5625 \\ 0 & 0 & 0.4375 & 0.5625 \end{bmatrix}.$$

If the matrices are *periodic*, that is to say, of the form

$$\begin{bmatrix} 0 & B \\ C & 0 \end{bmatrix},$$

where the zero matrices are square matrices, the system will oscillate between states B and C. Our example is a matrix $[\mathscr{M}]$ and its associated graph, Fig. 3.8.

$$[\mathscr{M}] = \begin{bmatrix} 0 & \frac{1}{2} & \frac{1}{2} \\ 1 & 0 & 0 \\ 1 & 0 & 0 \end{bmatrix} \begin{matrix} 0 \\ 1 \\ 2 \end{matrix}$$
$$\begin{matrix} 0 & 1 & 2 \end{matrix}$$

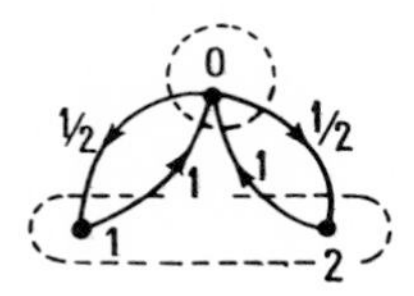

Fig. 3.8

The system passes from state 0 to state 1 or 2, to return to state 0, and so on. It can be easily seen that

$$[\mathscr{M}]^2 = \begin{bmatrix} 1 & 0 & 0 \\ 0 & \frac{1}{2} & \frac{1}{2} \\ 0 & \frac{1}{2} & \frac{1}{2} \end{bmatrix} \qquad \text{and} \qquad [\mathscr{M}]^3 = \begin{bmatrix} 0 & \frac{1}{2} & \frac{1}{2} \\ 1 & 0 & 0 \\ 1 & 0 & 0 \end{bmatrix};$$

hence,

$$[\mathscr{M}]^{2n} = [\mathscr{M}]^2 \qquad \text{and} \qquad [\mathscr{M}]^{2n+1} = [\mathscr{M}].$$

This shows that if we have started from state 0 we shall return to it after an even number of stages, whereas there is a probability equal to $\frac{1}{2}$ of finding ourselves in either state 1 or 2 after an uneven number of stages. Inversely, if we left from either state 1 or 2, there is a probability equal to $\frac{1}{2}$ of returning to one of these two states after an even number of stages. Again, after an uneven number of stages, if we have started from state 1 or state 2 we shall, in both cases, find ourselves in state 0.

Finally, stochastic matrices can also conform to either of the special forms

$$\begin{bmatrix} A & 0 \\ C & D \end{bmatrix} \qquad \text{or} \qquad \begin{bmatrix} A & B \\ 0 & D \end{bmatrix}$$

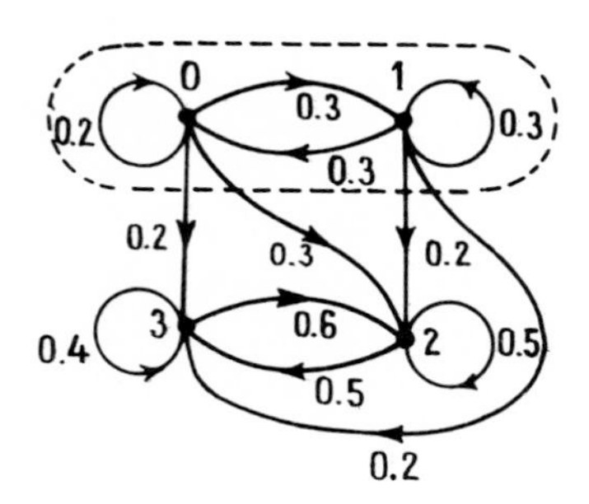

Fig. 3.9

in which A and D are square matrices. If, for example, we have the matrix $[\mathscr{M}]$ and its corresponding graph, Fig. 3.9,

$$[\mathscr{M}] = \begin{bmatrix} 0.2 & 0.3 & 0.3 & 0.2 \\ 0.3 & 0.3 & 0.2 & 0.2 \\ 0 & 0 & 0.5 & 0.5 \\ 0 & 0 & 0.6 & 0.4 \end{bmatrix} \begin{matrix} 0 \\ 1 \\ 2 \\ 3 \end{matrix}$$

$$\begin{matrix} 0 & \quad 1 & \quad 2 & \quad 3 \end{matrix}$$

it can easily be seen that, if we have started from state 0 or 1 to go toward state 2 or 3, we can never return to our starting point. States 0 and 1 are in this case *transitory states* of the system.

CHAPTER 4

PATIENCE IN THE FACE OF DELAYS

(Distribution of Tools in a Factory. The Theory of Waiting-Line Phenomena)

The *Lavenbloc* factory, which is situated on the outskirts of Paris, produces dishwashers. At the present time its products do not greatly interest French males, but the pernicious example of their American counterparts, who have a solid experience of dishwashing, is likely to alter this situation and produce a sharp increase in the value of the company's shares.

The firm has some thousand employees and produces six types of dishwasher, for a Frenchman would find it disagreeable to own the same model as his neighbor or to use a standard size of plate. As a result Lavenbloc produces only a modest number of each model and has to employ a large variety of tools for their assembly. It would be impractical for the workers to retain all the tools which they have to handle, and a number of these have to be drawn from the store, which is situated in the assembly building, for the different operations which they perform. The unfortunate result of this necessity is that waiting lines form at the window counters of the store, and there is an obvious need to reduce the time wasted in this way since it is time lost from actual production.

The number of storekeepers whose job it is to issue the tools will, of course, have a direct influence on this waiting time. On the one hand, if they are too numerous, there will, it is true, be no more waiting lines, but it would be illogical to pay storekeepers whose enforced leisure time is filled discussing such subjects as the racing form. On the other hand, if there are too few storekeepers the waiting lines will become long, frequent, and costly.

The economic problem is therefore to employ the number of storekeepers that will result in a minimal overall loss of time for them as well as for the factory workers, the hourly wage of the former being, say, 3 F and that of the latter 6 F.

Let us begin solving this problem by discovering the overall cost of the waiting time if there are 1, 2, 3, ..., n storekeepers employed. The diagram of a waiting-line phenomenon is shown in Fig. 4.1, where the

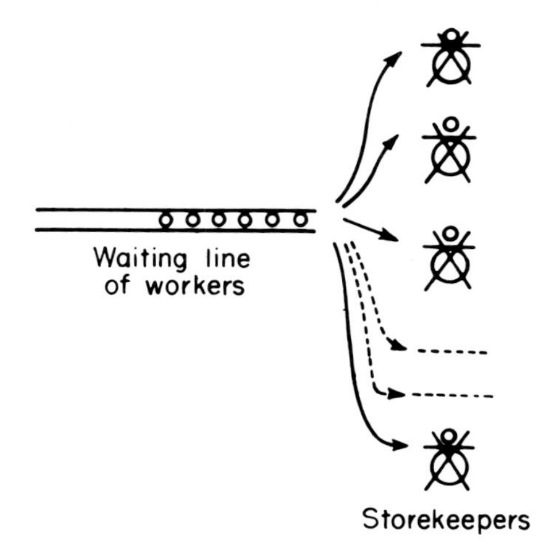

FIG. 4.1

turnstiles represent window counters, each of which can only serve one worker at a time. The first operation is to analyze the law governing the arrival of workers at the windows by means of a statistical count. From this count we shall eliminate both the first and last half-hours of the working day, as well as the half-hour preceding and following the lunch break. Apart from these special periods, we assume that the statistical law of arrivals at the windows remains constant or, in mathematical terms, that we are dealing with a stationary regime.

To obtain the required statistics, one hundred samplings are made over ten-minute periods of the number of workers appearing at the windows to draw tools. From these samplings corresponding frequencies are calculated, both results being shown in the first two columns of Table 4.1. Next, the average number of arrivals per ten-minute period is found from the two sets of figures; that is,

$$\bar{L} = (5)(0.01) + (6)(0) + (7)(0.01) + \cdots + (14)(0.10) + \cdots + (25)(0.01) = 15.61 \approx 16.$$

TABLE 4.1

Number of arrivals per period of 10 minutes	Frequencies observed (%)	Theoretical frequencies (Poisson's law)	Number of arrivals per period of 10 minutes	Frequencies observed (%)	Theoretical frequencies (Poisson's law)
5	1	0.1	16	12	9.9
6	0	0.2	17	8	9.3
7	1	0.6	18	9	8.3
8	2	1.2	19	7	6.9
9	1	2.1	20	5	5.5
10	3	3.4	21	4	4.2
11	5	4.9	22	3	3.1
12	6	6.6	23	1	2.1
13	9	8.1	24	1	1.4
14	10	9.3	25	1	0.9
15	11	9.9			

This gives an average of 16 workers arriving every ten minutes, or (to employ a cannibalistic concept) an average of 1.6 workers every minute. We shall now endeavor to reconcile this statistical average with a very popular and convenient theoretical law of probability. With this as our aim, let us assume that these hypotheses are satisfied: (1) the workers arrive independently of each other at the windows; (2) two or more workers never arrive simultaneously; and (3) the average rate of arrivals is constant.

Given these assumptions, it can be proved (as we shall do later) that the chance underlying the arrivals is governed by the following law, known as *Poisson's law*,

$$p_n(t) = \frac{e^{-\lambda t}(\lambda t)^n}{n!} \tag{1}$$

where e is the base of the Naperian logarithms and $n!$ represents

$$1 \cdot 2 \cdot 3 \cdot \cdots \cdot (n - 1) \cdot n,$$

that is to say, the product of the n positive integers from 1 to n inclusive. This formula gives the probability that n arrivals will appear during an interval of time equal to t; the value λ represents the average rate of arrival for the unit of time chosen, and in our example is equal to 1.6 arrivals per minute. The third column of Table 4.1 shows the values, obtained from an appropriate table, corresponding to $\lambda t = 16$.

Our reason for introducing Poisson's law is that it provides convenient formulas in those cases where it is permissible to use it. Indeed, when successive events take place at random intervals, and the three hypotheses given earlier are satisfied, at least to an approximate degree, we often discover that the conditions are governed by this law.

To verify whether the statistical law shown in the second column approximates sufficiently to the theoretical law represented by the third column, we calculate the squares of the differences between the observed and theoretical frequencies and then add them

$$\chi^2 = \frac{(1-0.1)^2}{0.1} + \frac{(0-0.2)^2}{0.2} + \frac{(1-0.6)^2}{0.6} + \frac{(2-1.2)^2}{1.2}$$
$$+ \frac{(1-2.1)^2}{2.1} + \cdots + \frac{(1-1.4)^2}{1.4} + \frac{(1-0.9)^2}{0.9} = 12,$$

the result being called χ_2 (*chi-square*).

Tables are available for χ^2 from which it is possible to determine whether the theoretical law is a sufficiently exact interpretation of the phenomena observed. In the present case, the probability that the law is acceptable is 0.88, which we shall consider sufficient, and we shall therefore associate the law based on statistics with the theoretical law having an average of $\lambda t = 16$, that is to say, a rate $\lambda = 1.6$. It will be noted that, for every arbitrary period t, and given λ, Poisson's law [Eq. (1)] will provide the values of the probabilities of n arrivals.

Thus, the probabilities of n arrivals during an interval of ten minutes are given by

$$p_n = \frac{e^{-16}(16)^n}{n!},$$

where n has the values 0, 1, 2, 3, ...

We must now consider the method of issuing the tools. When a worker appears, an unoccupied storekeeper (if there is one) obtains the required tools and issues them in return for a token, a service which may vary in duration from 15 seconds to 30, or 90, etc. If all the storekeepers are busy, waiting lines begin to form. Finally, since we have assumed that no preference is shown by the workers for particular storekeepers, there is an equal probability of a worker being issued tools by any of the storekeepers when several are available.

To obtain a law for the duration of service, an electric timing device was employed, with a red button which was pressed by the storekeeper as soon as a worker appeared, and a green button which was pressed by the latter when the tools had been issued. One thousand periods of service were measured by this device, and frequencies for periods of 0–15, 15–30, 30–45 seconds, and so on, were calculated; they are shown in the first two lines of Table 4.2, where the intervals appear as classes of 15, 30, 45, etc.

From the table of the noncumulative frequencies (Table 4.1) it was easy to establish the average time required for issuing tools, which was 1.1 minutes. Next, on line 3 of Table 4.2 the values were entered corresponding to a law of intervals, called the *exponential law*, for the periods

$$\Pr\{\Theta \geqslant \theta\} = 1000e^{-\mu\theta},$$

where the left-hand member represents "the probability that an interval Θ is greater than or equal to a given value θ," e is the base of the Naperian logarithms, and μ is the rate of service, in other words, the average number of services performed in the given unit of time. In our case $\mu = 1/1.1 \approx 0.9$, and θ is given in minutes.

We may ask why the law based on actual figures should be compared with the theoretical exponential.[1] The answer is that if Poisson's law is satisfied when the intervals of time separating events are arranged contiguously, then the statistics for the given periods can be shown to follow an exponential law. The three hypotheses given in connection with Poisson's law must be satisfied for the periods of service, but in this case the intervals of time are not always contiguous, since there are occasions when the storekeepers are idle.

It is now time to introduce a very important value, the *rate of traffic* or *intensity of traffic*, per storekeeper. If μ is the rate of service of one storekeeper, the rate for S storekeepers of equal efficiency will amount to μS. It is important, since we are dealing with averages, that the rate of arrivals should not exceed the overall rate of service, whence

$$\lambda < \mu S$$

or, alternatively,

$$\frac{\lambda}{\mu S} < 1.$$

The value $\lambda/\mu S$, which we shall call ψ, constitutes the intensity of traffic. The reader will readily see that the average length of the waiting

[1] A test for χ^2 applied here to the noncumulative laws yields $\chi^2 = 8.85$ (percentage of variance 19), a result which justifies us in treating the experimental law as exponential.

TABLE 4.2

Intervals of time, *s*	0	15	30	45	60	75	90	105	120	135	150	165	180	195	210	225	240	255	270	285	300
Cumulative frequencies observed (‰)	1000	813	652	512	408	330	261	210	163	125	95	79	62	51	44	35	26	21	17	13	10
Theoretical frequencies (exponential law)	1000	798	637	508	406	324	259	207	165	131	105	84	67	53	42	34	27	21	17	14	11

line and the average period of waiting of any unit in the line are a function of ψ, as can be proved. In the present problem, we have

$$\psi = \frac{1.6}{0.9S} = \frac{1.77}{S}.$$

To examine the economic aspect of our problem we shall use a number of classic formulas which were discovered some forty years ago by the Danish engineer Erlang in the course of his famous analytical study of delays in a telephone exchange.

We must first calculate the probability of a zero waiting time p_0, and we then find that

$$p_0 = \left[\frac{S^S \psi^S}{S!(1-\psi)} + 1 + \frac{S\psi}{1!} + \frac{S^2\psi^2}{2!} + \cdots + \frac{S^{S-1}\psi^{S-1}}{(S-1)!}\right]^{n-1},$$

and the average waiting time on the line

$$\bar{t}_f = \frac{1}{\mu} \frac{S^S \psi^S}{S!(1-\psi)} \cdot p_0.$$

These formulas may seem very complicated; many more of equal difficulty are encountered in operations research. We need not, however, extend too much sympathy to the specialists in this field, since they can usually make use of a nomogram, such as the one shown in Fig. 4.2, which gives us $\bar{t}_f$ as a function of ψ, μ, and S.

For the convenience of the reader, we shall therefore abandon the calculation of p_0 and shall make use of the nomogram. Taking different values of S, we first calculate the corresponding values of $\psi = 1.77/S$. For each abscissa of S considered, we find the intersection of the ordinate from this point with the curve which has the required value for ψ, interpolating whenever necessary. For example, if $S = 2$ and $\psi = 1.77/2 \approx 0.88$, we interpolate between the curves marked 0.85 and 0.90 and find an ordinate value of 3.6. This ordinate represents $\mu\bar{t}_f$, and here $\mu = 0.9$; hence, we obtain $\bar{t}_f = 4$ (minutes) for $S = 2$. The reader can check the following results obtained for different values of S:

$$S = 2, \quad \psi = 0.88, \quad \mu\bar{t}_f = 3.6, \quad \text{whence} \quad \bar{t}_f = \frac{3.6}{0.9} = 4,$$

$$S = 3, \quad \psi = 0.59, \quad \mu\bar{t}_f = 0.28, \quad \text{whence} \quad \bar{t}_f = \frac{0.28}{0.9} = 0.31,$$

$$S = 4, \quad \psi = 0.44, \quad \mu\bar{t}_f = 0.054, \quad \text{whence} \quad \bar{t}_f = \frac{0.054}{0.9} = 0.06.$$

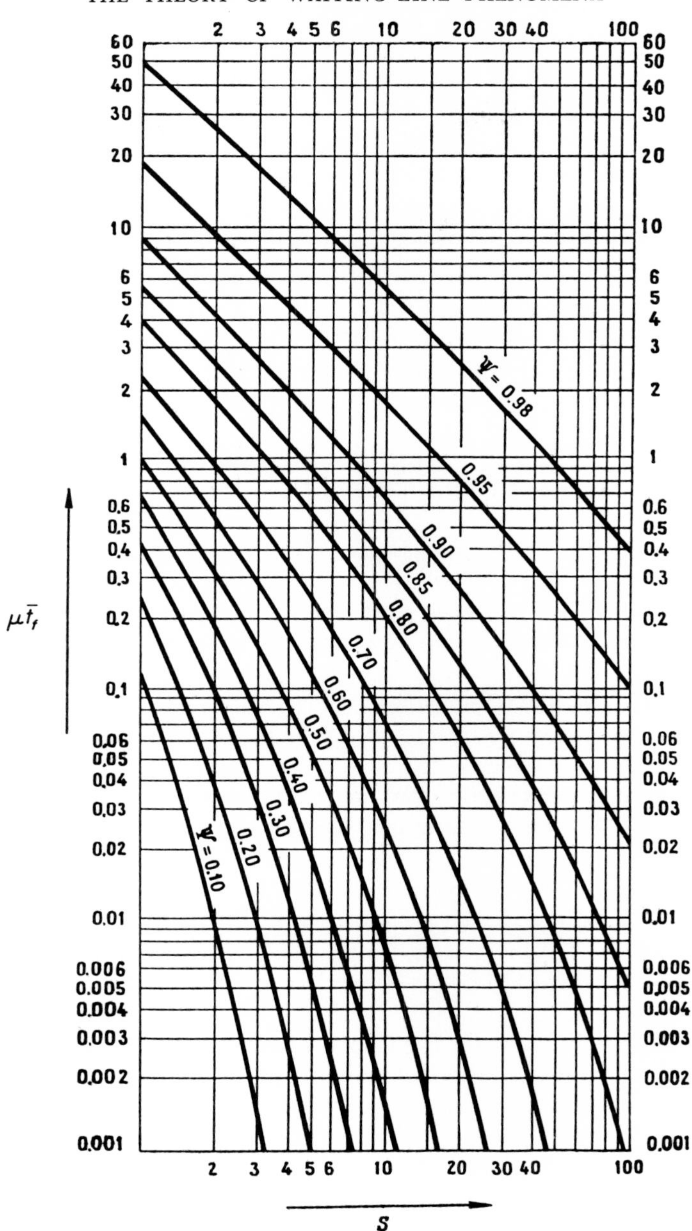
2
3
4
5
6
10
20
30
40
100
60
50
40
30
20
10
6
5
4
3
2
1
0.6
0.5
0.4
0.3
0.2
0.1
0.06
0.05
0.04
0.03
0.02
0.01
0.006
0.005
0.004
0.003
0.002
0.001
Ψ = 0.98
0.95
0.90
0.85
0.80
0.70
0.60
0.50
0.40
0.30
0.20
Ψ = 0.10
μt̄f
s

Fig. 4.2

We have not calculated the value of $\bar{t}_f$ for $S = 1$, since in this case $\psi > 1$, and the average waiting time would be infinite; in other words, once a waiting line formed it would continue to increase. Armed with the knowledge of the average waiting time of any workman in the line, we are now in a position to study the economic aspects of the problem.

In the course of an eight-hour day, at a rate of 1.6 a minute, 768 workers visit the windows.

$$\lambda \times 60 \times 8 = 1.6 \times 60 \times 8 = 768.$$

With an average service time of $1/\mu$, the daily overall service time for this number of workers is

$$768 \times \frac{1}{\mu} = \frac{768}{0.9} = 853 \text{ min.}$$
$$= 14 \text{ h, } 13 \text{ min.} = 14.21 \text{ h.}$$

Next, the daily period during which the storekeepers are idle is easily found to be

for two storekeepers $(S = 2)$: $2 \times 8 - 14.21 = 16 - 14.21 = 1.79$ h,

for three storekeepers $(S = 3)$: $3 \times 8 - 14.21 = 24 - 14.21 = 9.79$ h,

for four storekeepers $(S = 4)$: $4 \times 8 - 14.21 = 32 - 14.21 = 17.79$ h.

Let us now discover the time lost by the workers through waiting at the windows. For the three hypotheses given earlier this is

$$S = 2: \quad 768 \times 4 = 3072 \text{ min.} = 51.2 \text{ h,}$$
$$S = 3: \quad 768 \times 0.31 = 238 \text{ min.} = 3.96 \text{ h,}$$
$$S = 4: \quad 768 \times 0.06 = 46 \text{ min.} = 0.76 \text{ h.}$$

Given the hourly pay as 3 F and 6 F for the storekeepers and workers, respectively, the total daily cost of the time lost by both categories of employees can be calculated for the three different cases

$$S = 2: \quad C_2 = 1.79 \times 3 + 51.2 \times 6 = 312.57 \text{ F,}$$
$$S = 3: \quad C_3 = 9.79 \times 3 + 3.96 \times 6 = 53.13 \text{ F,}$$
$$S = 4: \quad C_4 = 17.79 \times 3 + 0.76 \times 6 = 57.93 \text{ F.}$$

If we calculate C_5 for $S = 5$, we obtain a result of 75.37 F, and we conclude that the function of cost is minimal for $S = 3$.

To convince the factory manager that the optimal solution was to employ three storekeepers, the operations research specialist had to explain in detail why it was advantageous for an average of at least one storekeeper to be idle, a situation which at first glance appeared illogical. Once the manager had been convinced, he decided to employ *four* storekeepers, basing his decision on the following reasoning. "From your calculations," he said, "a fourth storekeeper would cost me only an extra 4.80 F a day. From our records, absenteeism in the factory averages 8 %, so that if I employed only three storekeepers and one of them was absent, the added expense would be

$$312.57 - 53.13 = 259.44 \text{ F},$$

that is,

$$259.44 \times 0.08 = 20.75 \text{ F}$$

as a daily average. In the end, four storekeepers will cost less than three. Further, by engaging four I shall virtually eliminate the possibility of being left with only one storekeeper, a situation which your figures have shown would greatly increase the length of the lines, and would interfere with the efficiency of the whole factory."

Some Ideas on the Theory of Waiting-Line Phenomena and Its Practical Application

In front of the windows of booking offices, post offices, and banks, at the counters of large stores, and at the timeclocks in factories, waiting lines are formed, at least at certain hours, of the kind that we studied in our last example, in which people experience irritating and seemingly interminable delays before being served.

But it is not only human beings who form such lines. The production orders piling up on a manager's desk, calls reaching a telephone exchange, and faulty machines awaiting repair in a factory also constitute waiting-line phenomena.

As we discovered in our last example, it is usually possible in a problem of this kind to distinguish between *entries* or *arrivals* of animate or inanimate clients on the one hand, and on the other hand, *stations* which perform a particular service. The laws of the arrivals and of the durations of service, which can be drawn up by statisticians, enable us to define the system and to obtain useful results, such as the average waiting time of the customers and the average period of inactivity of the stations. The economic solution of a problem presented by waiting-line phenomena frequently lies in the optimal number of stations corresponding to the minimal total cost of the customers' waiting time and of the idleness of the stations. Thus it often appears as a compromise between the value, often subjective, that is attached to the waiting time of the clients and the increased costs of an improved service.

The study of waiting-line phenomena can become very complicated if we introduce priorities for certain customers, or if we endeavor to define the *transitory regime*, rather than the *permanent regime*, which in most cases becomes more or less established after the lapse of a certain period.

On the other hand, for a number of classic laws corresponding to the rhythm of the entries and the durations of service, we have at our disposal standard models, the use of which is often facilitated by the existence of an appropriate nomogram.

For the sake of an example, let us consider what happens when the arrivals follow Poisson's law, and a solitary station gives times of service corresponding to an exponential law.

If λ and μ are, respectively, the average rate of arrival and the average number of services per unit of time, the *intensity of traffic* or *utilization factor* is $\psi = \lambda/\mu$, and the waiting system will not get out of hand as long as $\lambda/\mu < 1$.

Let us suppose that at a time t there are n units in the waiting line, including the one that is being served; the probability of this eventuality can be represented as $p_n(t)$. Let us now seek the probability that there will always be n units at time $t + \Delta t$, this probability being represented as $p_n(t + \Delta t)$, and Δt being a very short interval of time.

In what follows we shall, of course, assume that the first hypothesis of the three given earlier in the chapter, with regard to Poisson's law, is verified here.

By definition (third hypothesis of Poisson's law), the probability of one arrival during time Δt is $\lambda \cdot \Delta t$; equally, the probability of one service being completed in Δt is $\mu \cdot \Delta t$. In accordance with the second hypothesis, there can never be more than one arrival or one departure during the brief interval Δt. The complementary probabilities, that there will be neither an arrival nor a departure are, respectively,

$$1 - \lambda \cdot \Delta t \qquad \text{and} \qquad 1 - \mu \cdot \Delta t.$$

Two cases have, therefore, to be considered immediately:

(a) There is no new arrival or departure during the interval Δt, and the compound probability will accordingly be

$$p_n(t) \cdot (1 - \lambda \cdot \Delta t)(1 - \mu \cdot \Delta t) = p_n(t)[1 - (\lambda + \mu) \cdot \Delta t + \lambda\mu \cdot \Delta t^2].$$

(b) There is a new arrival and also a completion of service during Δt; when the compound probability becomes

$$p_n(t) \cdot \lambda \cdot \Delta t \cdot \mu \cdot \Delta t = p_n(t) \cdot \lambda\mu \cdot \Delta t^2.$$

These, however, are not the only ways in which $p_n(t + \Delta t)$ can be formulated. There may be n units at time $t + \Delta t$ if there were $n + 1$ at time t, and one unit has left without another arriving, in which case the probability becomes

$$p_{n+1}(t) \cdot (1 - \lambda \cdot \Delta t) \cdot \mu \cdot \Delta t = p_{n+1}(t)[\mu \cdot \Delta t - \lambda\mu \cdot \Delta t^2].$$

Finally, there will still be n units at time $t + \Delta t$ if there were $n - 1$ at time t, and if a new unit has entered without another leaving during Δt; in this case the probability will be

$$p_{n-1}(t) \cdot \lambda \cdot \Delta t \cdot (1 - \mu \cdot \Delta t) = p_{n-1}(t)[\lambda \cdot \Delta t - \lambda\mu \cdot \Delta t^2].$$

Let us observe that the products $\lambda \cdot \mu \cdot \Delta t^2$ are negligible compared with $\lambda \cdot \Delta t$ or $\mu \cdot \Delta t$; for example, if $\Delta t = 1/100$, then $\lambda \cdot \Delta t$ and $\mu \cdot \Delta t$ are of the order of $1/100$, whereas $\lambda \cdot \mu \cdot \Delta t^2$ is of the order of $1/10{,}000$. In consequence, the sum of the probabilities corresponding to the various ways in which $p_n(t + \Delta t)$ can be represented is reduced to

$$p_n(t + \Delta t) = p_n(t) \cdot [1 - (\lambda + \mu) \cdot \Delta t] + p_{n+1}(t) \cdot \mu \cdot \Delta t + p_{n-1}(t) \cdot \lambda \cdot \Delta t$$

or, again,

$$\frac{p_n(t + \Delta t) - p_n(t)}{\Delta t} = \lambda \cdot p_{n-1}(t) - (\lambda + \mu) \cdot p_n(t) + \mu \cdot p_{n+1}(t).$$

The left member of this equation is the derivative of $p_n(t)$, when Δt approaches zero, so that we can write

$$p_n'(t) = \lambda \cdot p_{n-1}(t) - (\lambda + \mu) \cdot p_n(t) + \mu \cdot p_{n+1}(t).$$

In this problem we are concerned with the permanent regime, so that $p'_n(t)$ is clearly nil, since the probabilities of the presence of n units in the system are then stable, whatever the value of n. We find that this simple application of the hypotheses pertaining to Poisson's process leads to a recurring formula connecting the $p_n(t)$ terms

$$\lambda \cdot p_{n-1}(t) - (\lambda + \mu) \cdot p_n(t) + \mu \cdot p_{n+1}(t) = 0,$$

which is valid for $n > 0$. It could easily be shown that it does not apply for $n = 0$ and that, in this particular case, we have

$$-\lambda p_0(t) + \mu p_1(t) = 0.$$

In succession, therefore,

$$p_1 = \psi p_0$$

for the particular equation which concerns them; then, by using the general formula for $n > 1$, we have

$$\mu p_2 = (\lambda + \mu) p_1 - \lambda p_0,$$

that is,

$$p_2 = (1 + \psi) p_1 - \psi p_0,$$

or

$$p_2 = (1 + \psi)\psi p_0 - \psi p_0 = \psi^2 p_0, \quad \text{etc.}$$

Let us write the successive relations between the p_n terms

$$\begin{aligned} p_0 &= p_0, \\ p_1 &= \psi p_0, \\ p_2 &= \psi^2 p_0, \\ &\vdots \\ p_n &= \psi^n p_0. \end{aligned}$$

Then let us add them member to member

$$\sum_0^n p_i = [1 + \psi + \psi^2 + \cdots + \psi^n] p_0.$$

If we make n approach infinity, we know by definition that

$$\sum_0^\infty p_i = 1;$$

in addition, the geometric progression of common ratio 0 and base 1 has as its sum

$$\frac{1}{1-\psi};$$

whence,

$$1 = \frac{1}{1-\psi} \cdot p_0$$

and

$$p_0 = 1 - \psi.$$

It is at once apparent that

$$p_n = \psi^n(1-\psi).$$

Let us calculate the average number $\bar{n}$ (or expected value) of units in the system

$$\begin{aligned} \bar{n} = \sum_0^\infty n \cdot p_n &= \sum_0^\infty n \cdot \psi^n(1-\psi) \\ &= (1-\psi)\sum_0^\infty n \cdot \psi^n \\ &= (1-\psi)[\psi + 2\psi^2 + 3\psi^3 + \cdots] \\ &= \psi(1-\psi)[1 + 2\psi + 3\psi^2 + \cdots]. \end{aligned}$$

The last bracket represents the derivative of

$$\psi + \psi^2 + \psi^3 + \cdots = \frac{1}{1-\psi},$$

that is to say,

$$\frac{1}{(1-\psi)^2}.$$

Finally,

$$\bar{n} = \psi(1-\psi) \cdot \frac{1}{(1-\psi)^2} = \frac{\psi}{1-\psi}.$$

Let us take $\bar{\nu}$ for the number of units in the waiting line (excluding the unit being served). At every instant $\nu = n - 1$, if $n > 0$. The quotient of the average number of units in the system $\bar{n}$ divided by the average number of services per unit time μ obviously provides the average flow time of the average number of units, $\bar{n}/\mu$. The quotient of the average number of units in the waiting line $\bar{\nu}$ divided by the average rate of arrivals, λ, gives us the waiting time of the average number of units, $\bar{\nu}/\lambda$. Since the regime is permanent, these two quantities are equal,

$$\frac{\bar{n}}{\mu} = \frac{\bar{\nu}}{\lambda}.$$

This deduction enables us to calculate $\bar{\nu}$,

$$\bar{\nu} = \frac{\lambda}{\mu} \cdot \bar{n} = \psi \cdot \bar{n} = \frac{\psi^2}{1 - \psi},$$

as well as the average waiting time in the line,

$$\bar{t}_f = \frac{\bar{\nu}}{\lambda} = \frac{1}{\lambda} \frac{\psi^2}{1 - \psi} = \frac{1}{\mu} \frac{\psi}{1 - \psi}.$$

Example. Let us consider the single window of an occasional bank, such as can be found on market days in very small French towns. A solitary employee performs all the services required, and the window remains continuously open from 7:00 a.m. to 1:00 p.m. It has been discovered that the average number of clients is 54 during the day, and that the average service time is five minutes per person. We can, therefore, at once calculate

$$\lambda = 54/6 = 9 \quad \text{persons per hour,}$$
$$\mu = 60/5 = 12 \quad \text{services per hour.}$$

As a result,

$$\psi = \frac{\lambda}{\mu} = \frac{3}{4},$$

$$\bar{n} = \frac{\psi}{1 - \psi} = \frac{\frac{3}{4}}{1 - \frac{3}{4}} = 3,$$

$$\bar{\nu} = \frac{\psi^2}{1 - \psi} = \frac{\frac{9}{16}}{1 - \frac{3}{4}} = \frac{9}{16} \times \frac{4}{1} = \frac{9}{4},$$

$$\bar{t}_f = \frac{\bar{\nu}}{\lambda} = \frac{\frac{9}{4}}{9} = \frac{1}{4}.$$

These calculations show that the average number of clients in the system (including the one being served) is 3, that the average number of clients in the waiting line (excluding the one being served) is $\frac{9}{4} = 2.25$,[2] and that the average waiting time is 15 minutes.

A fuller study of the phenomenon would enable us to determine the probabilities that there would be more than N persons in the system, that the waiting time would be greater than T, and so on, where N and T are numbers chosen in advance.

Let us now consider a system in which the rate of arrival and the average number of services per unit of time are, respectively, λ and μ, but in which there are S stations. When the number n of units in the system is less than S, all the units are served simultaneously without every station being used, a condition which gives an overall rate of service equal to $n\mu$. On the other hand, if n is greater than or equal to S, all the stations are operating, and the overall rate of service is $S\mu$.

Under these conditions, the recurring formulas given above for the case of a permanent regime are now modified as

$$\begin{aligned} n = 0: &\quad -\lambda p_0 + \mu p_1 = 0, \\ 1 \leqslant n < S: &\quad -(\lambda + n\mu)p_n + \lambda p_{n-1} + (n+1)\mu p_{n+1} = 0, \\ n \geqslant S: &\quad -(\lambda + S\mu)p_n + \lambda p_{n-1} + S\mu p_{n+1} = 0. \end{aligned}$$

A method similar to that used earlier enables us to obtain

$$p_n = p_0 \frac{\psi^n}{n!}, \qquad \text{if} \quad 1 \leqslant n < S,$$

$$p_n = p_0 \frac{\psi^n}{S!\, S^{n-S}}, \qquad \text{if} \quad n \geqslant S,$$

and also

$$p_0 = \left[\frac{\psi^S}{S!(1 - \psi/S)} + \sum_{n=0}^{S-1} \frac{\psi^n}{n!} \right]^{-1}$$

$$\bar{\nu} = \frac{\psi^{S+1}}{SS!(1 - \psi/S)^2} \cdot p_0 ;$$

$$\bar{n} = \bar{\nu} + \psi;$$

$$\bar{t}_f = \frac{\bar{\nu}}{\lambda} = \frac{\psi^L}{SS!\mu(1 - \psi/S)^2} \cdot p_0.$$

The average number of unused stations is $\bar{\rho} = S - \psi$.

[2] We have $\bar{\nu} = n - 1$ if $n > 0$, but $\bar{\nu} = \bar{n} - 1 + p_0 = n - \psi = 3 - \frac{3}{4} = \frac{9}{4}$.

For $S = 2$ and $\psi = 1.777 \ldots$, the given values for the Lavenbloc problem, we at once find

$$p_0 = \left[\frac{(1.777)^2}{2!(1 - 1.777/2)} + 1 + \frac{1.777}{1!}\right]^{-1} = 0.0582,$$

$$\bar{t}_f = \frac{(1.777)^2}{2 \cdot 2!\, 0.9(1 - 1.777/2)^2} \times 0.0582 = 4.00 \text{ min.},$$

$$\bar{\rho} = 2 - 1.777 = 0.222.$$

As a result,

$$C_2 = 0.222 \times 480 \times 3/60 + 768 \times 4 \times 6/60 = 312.5 \text{ F},$$

since in one day the windows (stations) are open for 480 minutes and serve 768 workers (units). This agrees very well with the earlier result of 312.57 F.

CHAPTER 5

SHIPMENTS OF COFFEE

(Transport Network. The Ford-Fulkerson Algorithm)

About half of the excellent coffee grown in Mexico is sold abroad, and a large firm of Mexican exporters has stocks of the commodity stored at the ports of Veracruz, Tampico, Tuxpan, and Campechy, for which orders have been received for shipments to the French ports of Dunkirk, Bordeaux, Saint-Nazaire, and Le Havre. Of these stocks 120 tons are stored at Veracruz and 100 tons at each of the other three ports. The amounts to be delivered are 100 tons to Dunkirk, 80 to Bordeaux, 90 to Saint-Nazaire, and 150 to Le Havre.

Various freighters sail between the Mexican and French ports, and their tonnage capacities are shown in Table 5.1. For example, the

TABLE 5.1

		Port of destination			
Port of origin		Dunkirk E	Bordeaux F	Saint-Nazaire G	Le Havre H
Veracruz	A	70	30	20	0
Tampico	B	50	40	10	0
Tuxpan	C	0	20	40	80
Campechy	D	0	20	40	80

freighter from Veracruz to Dunkirk has space for 70 tons; on the other hand, there is no ship from this port to Le Havre or, if there is, it has no space available, which means that the transport capacity from A to H is nil. It will be observed that the total transport capacity of the ships exceeds the total orders and that the capacity of each ship leaving a particular port is at least equal to the tonnage which is stored there.

Assuming the transport costs to be the same between any two of these ports, our aim will be to satisfy the orders to a maximal degree. To add a touch of sophistication to the problem, we shall suppose that certain of these orders are to receive priority: the 80 tons to be delivered to Bordeaux and the 150 tons consigned to Le Havre. However, as we shall discover, this constraint will not in any way modify the process of optimization.

A diagram or *graph* of the problem can easily be drawn in this manner:

(1) Each point of origin is connected by an oriented arrow or *arc* to the points of destination, and this arc bears a number representing the *capacity*, in other words, the tonnage that can be carried by this route. No arc will be drawn from a point of origin to a point of destination if the transport capacity between them is nil (e.g., Veracruz and Le Havre).

(2) An auxiliary point O is connected to each port of origin by an arc bearing the tonnage stored at the port.

(3) Each port of destination is connected to an auxiliary point Z by an arc bearing the order to be delivered at this port.

In this way we obtain the transport network of Fig. 5.1 where the

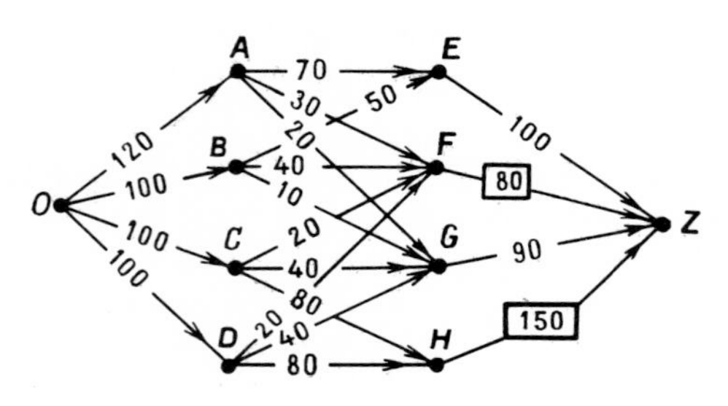

FIG. 5.1

numbers in boxes represent priorities, and our problem now consists of finding the maximal quantity, or maximal *flow*, that can be carried from O to Z.

In the first place, we shall look for a *complete* flow such that every route from O to Z includes at least one *saturated* arc. The procedure for doing this is extremely simple. Starting with any flow, we examine it to discover whether there is a route which does not contain any saturated arc: if there is, we increase the flow through this route by one unit, and so on, until all the routes of the same type eventually include at least one saturated arc. In this case, we shall first saturate the priorities. To satisfy the demand at H, we saturate arc HZ. We give the route $ODHZ$ a flow of 80, which saturates DH, the route $OCHZ$ a flow of 70, which only saturates HZ. By proceeding in this manner we shall obtain, for example, Fig. 5.2 (for there are other valid solutions), in which the double arrows represent saturated arcs.

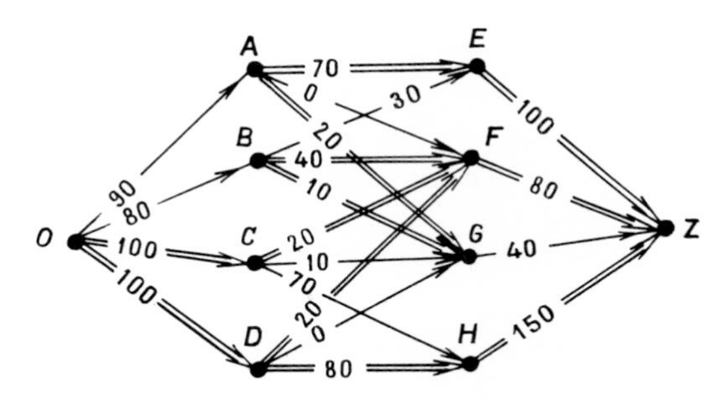

Fig. 5.2

It can easily be verified that every route contains at least one saturated arc, and also that the flow entering the network is equal to the flow leaving it. In the suggested solution, the orders at E, F, and H are satisfied, but not the order at G.

We must now improve the flow, and to do this we shall place a plus sign at O and a $+O$ at all the points connected to it by a nonsaturated arc, in this case A and B. Generalizing this, we can say that if a point X has just been marked, a $+X$ will be placed at all the points connected to X by a nonsaturated arc, and a $-X$ will be placed at the point of origin of each arc ending at X in which the flow is not nil.

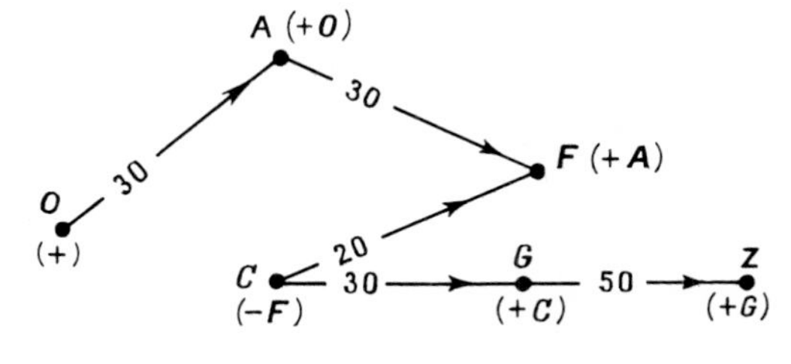

Fig. 5.3

When this procedure leads to the marking of Z, the flow is not maximal. In the example given, we shall mark A and B with $+O$ (OA and OB are not saturated); then F with $+A$ (AF is not saturated); E with $+B$ (BE is not saturated); C and D with $-F$ (CF and DF carry flows which are not nil); G with $+C$ or $+D$ (CG or DG are not saturated); Z with $+G$ (GZ is nonsaturated).

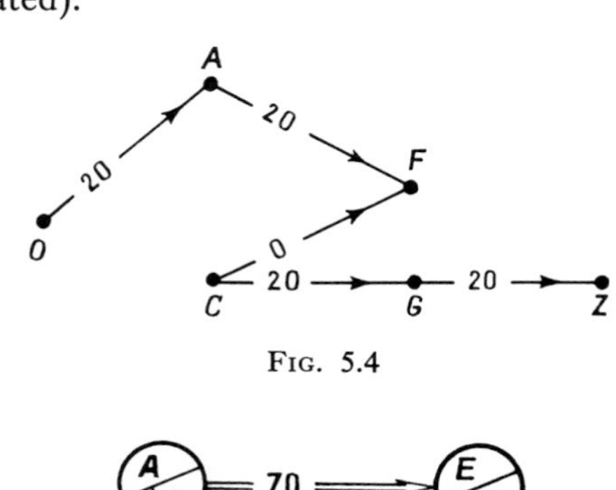

FIG. 5.4

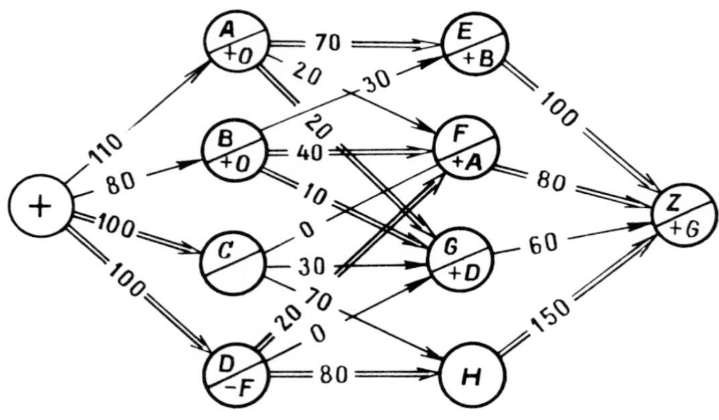

FIG. 5.5

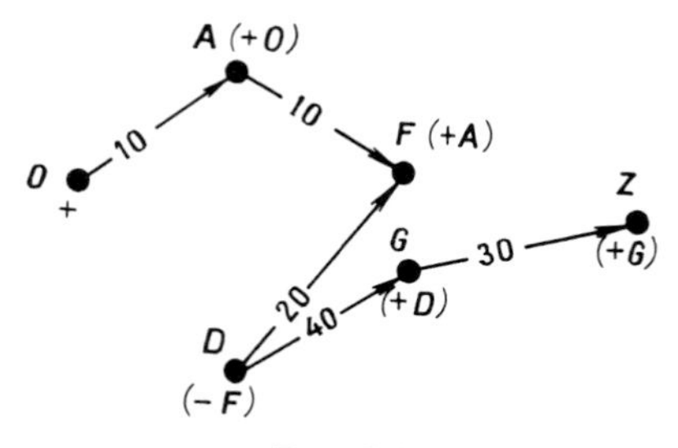

FIG. 5.6

Let us now take one of the marked sequences: O, $A(+O)$, $F(+A)$, $C(-F)$, $G(+C)$, $Z(+G)$, as shown in Fig. 5.3. If their origin is marked with a $+$, the arcs will carry the flow which can be added to them when account has been allowed for the previous distribution. For example, OA carries 30, since $120 - 90 = 30$; if it is marked with a $-$, the arcs will carry the same total as previously.

It can easily be seen (Fig. 5.4) that 20 can be added to the flow from O to F, provided CF is reduced by 20 and this amount is repaid to the flow from C to Z. From these changes, we obtain a new figure, in which the flow entering the network will still equal the flow leaving it (Fig. 5.5), and in which the flow has been improved.

In this new figure, we can still mark point Z, and the flow is therefore not maximal. In fact, it is sufficient to write: O, $A(+O)$, $F(+A)$, $D(-F)$, $G(+D)$, $Z(+F)$, which at once enables us to draw Fig. 5.6, where the smallest number is 10; whence, the development shown in Fig. 5.7.

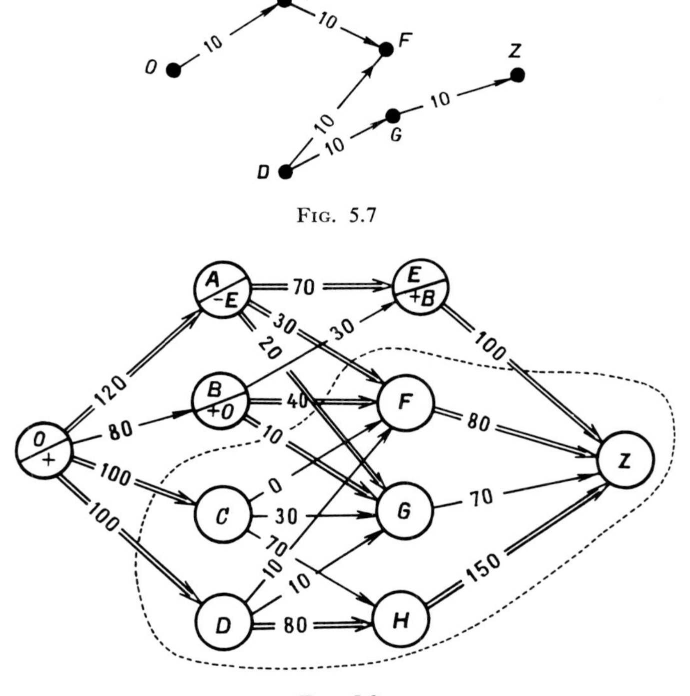

FIG. 5.7

FIG. 5.8

Finally, we obtain Fig. 5.8, in which it is impossible to mark point Z, and we have now discovered the maximal flow.

The distribution obtained from Fig. 5.8 provides the solution of the problem: only the order for St. Nazaire cannot be completely met, and this deficiency originates at Tampico.

All the freighters leaving Veracruz will fill their available cargo space: 70 tons for Dunkirk, 30 tons for Bordeaux, and 20 tons for St. Nazaire. In the same way, the ships leaving Tampico for Bordeaux and St. Nazaire will fill the available tonnage of 40 and 10 tons respectively; only the one sailing to Dunkirk will carry 30 instead of the required 50 tons.

None of the vessels leaving Tuxpan will carry their full cargo: those for St. Nazaire and Le Havre will carry 30 and 70 tons respectively, while the one for Bordeaux will not carry any coffee. Finally, the ships leaving Campechy will carry 10, 10, and 80 tons to Bordeaux, St. Nazaire, and Le Havre respectively, only the last one filling its available space completely.

By comparing the lines and columns of Table 5.2, we conclude that the 20 tons missing from the consignment to St. Nazaire are still on the docks at Tampico and, as the table shows, there is no method of remedying this situation.

In Table 5.3, line A can be immediately filled in, and leads to line B, with the resulting deduction, based on column E, that 20 tons have been

TABLE 5.2

	E	F	G	H	
A	(70)	(30)	(20)	0	120
B	30	(40)	(10)	0	80
C	0	0	30	70	100
D	0	10	10	(80)	100
	100	80	70	150	

TABLE 5.3

	E	*F*	*G*	*H*	sat.	
A	70	30	20	0	120	left at docks
B	30	40	10	0	/////// + 20	
C	0	·		·	+ 100	avail.
D	0	·		·	+ 100	avail.
	100 (sat.)	— 10 (sat. by priority)	— 60	— 150 (sat. by priority)	sat. if possible	

S_1	*F*	*H*		S_2	*F*	*H*	
C	10	80	(+ 10)	*C*	0	80	(+ 20)
D	0	70	(+ 30)	*D*	10	70	(+ 20)
S_3	***F***	***H***		**S_4**	***F***	***H***	
C	10	70	(+ 20)	*C*	0	70	(+ 30)
D	0	80	(+ 20)	*D*	10	80	(+ 10)

left at Tampico. If we now turn to columns F and H, which should, if possible, be saturated, so as to satisfy the priorities, we find that there are four valid solutions: S_1, S_2, S_3, and S_4. The treatment by the Ford–Fulkerson algorithm has given us S_4, and the choice of different routes would have led to the other equivalent solutions.

The Ford-Fulkerson Algorithm and Theorem

Let us now try to show that we have, in fact, obtained the optimum by means of the algorithm used for this problem. To do so, let us return to Fig. 5.8 and examine the set of nonmarked points: C, D, F, G, H, and Z.

All the arcs entering this set $\mathscr{E}$ from the marked points are saturated, for otherwise we should have been able to mark at least one of the points of $\mathscr{E}$.

We apply the term *cut of* $\mathscr{E}$ to the set of arcs entering $\mathscr{E}$, provided $\mathscr{E}$ is a set of points which includes Z, but not O. The capacity of a cut is the sum of the capacities of its arcs. Since $\mathscr{E}$ contains Z, every flow necessarily passes through one of the arcs entering it, and hence, flow φ is less than or equal to the capacity of a cut, whatever the latter may be.

Consequently, if we find a flow which is equal to the capacity of a cut, we can be sure that this flow is maximal and the capacity of the cut is minimal.

In the example just treated, we find

$$\varphi = 100 + 80 + 70 + 150 = 400;$$

$$\text{Cut } \mathscr{E} = 100 + 30 + 20 + 40 + 10 + 100 + 100 = 400.$$

The Ford–Fulkerson theorem proves that, for every transport network, $\varphi_{\max}$ = minimal cut.

Remark. The priorities which we introduced have not influenced the procedure of optimization. All that they entailed was that we should start with a complete flow which satisfied them, a condition made possible since the arcs reaching F and H were respectively greater than 80 and 150. These flows can only be increased, and never diminished, by the process of optimization: in fact, no point of destination can be marked, since this would mean that Z is marked, but then one could increase the flow of one of the arcs reaching Z without diminishing the flow of the other arcs ending at it.

CHAPTER 6

MEXICO CITY–ACAPULCO

(A Problem of Assignment)

The trip from Mexico City to Acapulco takes five to six hours by car or bus. The route winds through volcanic mountains and radiant valleys; it takes you south through Taxco and into the sudden tropical heat of Guerrero state. A few hours later, you arrive at Acapulco, finest of Pacific coast resorts.

Thousands of people from Mexico City make this trip every weekend and during vacations. Many travel by bus since several coach lines provide regular service between the two cities. A typical timetable of the service in both directions is given in the accompanying tabulation.

TIMETABLE

Mexico City–Acapulco (6 hours)		
Depart Mexico City	Service line	Arrive Acapulco
06:00	a →	12:00
07:30	b →	13:30
11:30	c →	17:30
19:00	d →	01:00
00:30	e →	06:30

Acapulco–Mexico City (6 hours)

Arrive Mexico City	Service line	Depart Acapulco
11:30	1 ←——	05.30
15:00	2 ←——	09:00
21:00	3 ←——	15:00
00:30	4 ←——	18:30
06:00	5 ←——	00:00

The problem concerning us here is one that confronts the bus company providing this service: namely, the accommodation of bus crews. For in addition to maintaining its schedules, the company must find a way to minimize the time spent by the crews away from home. This is necessary because the crews are paid for the hours during which they wait for return trips as well as for the time they work. It is also presumed psychologically advantageous to unite crews with their families as soon as possible. In addition, there are physiological constraints requiring each crew to rest at least four hours before making the return trip. Finally, no crew is to wait more than 24 hours for a return trip.

Given these conditions, we can state the problem as follows: Where should the bus crews live and which "lines" should they work so that the total time spent by them waiting for return journeys is minimal. The dream of all the crews is to live in Acapulco, but the company manager seems insensible to the charms of the Pacific.

Let us suppose, for example, that a crew living in Mexico City works line *c* to Acapulco and line 2 on the return trip. According to the timetable, they arrive at 17:30 and depart at 09:00 after a $15\frac{1}{2}$-hour wait. Similarly, we proceed to draw up two tables of time lost in waiting for return trips. In Table 6.1 we suppose that all the crews live in Mexico City and in Table 6.2, that they all live in Acapulco.

From these two tables we shall form Table 6.3. Each entry in this table consists of the smaller of the two numbers occupying corresponding squares in Tables 6.1 and 6.2. We have eliminated numbers equal

TABLE 6.1

CREWS LIVING IN MEXICO CITY

	1	2	3	4	5
a	17.5	21	3	6.5	12
b	16	19.5	1.5	5	10.5
c	12	15.5	21.5	1	6.5
d	4.5	8	14	17.5	23
e	23	2.5	8.5	12	17.5

TABLE 6.2

CREWS LIVING IN ACAPULCO

	1	2	3	4	5
a	18.5	15	9	5.5	0
b	20	16.5	10.5	7	1.5
c	0	20.5	14.5	11	5.5
d	7.5	4	22	18.5	13
e	13	9.5	3.5	0	18.5

TABLE 6.3

	1	2	3	4	5
a	17.5	15	9	5.5	12
b	16	16.5	10.5	5	10.5
c	12	15.5	14.5	11	5.5
d	4.5	8	14	17.5	13
e	13	9.5	8.5	12	17.5

to or less than 4 so as to take into account the constraint of the crews' four-hour rest period. For example, if there is a choice between *a*1 (living in Mexico City) and 1*a* (living in Acapulco), we shall choose *a*1, giving a wait of $17\frac{1}{2}$ hours instead of $18\frac{1}{2}$ hours. On the other hand, in choosing between 3*b* and *b*3, we must select 3*b* because *b*3 would give a rest period of less than four hours.

Let us use the term *assignment* to mean the designation of a crew to a particular "line" or service such as *a*1, 2*a*, *a*3, etc. Obviously, we can assign only one crew to a line and vice versa. Hence, any possible solution to this problem of assignment can be demonstrated by use of a table consisting of the numbers 0 and 1 and having only a single 1 in any line or column; the number 1 represents a chosen assignment. For example, the solution shown in Table 6.4 corresponds to services 2*a*, *b*1, 5*c*, *d*3,

TABLE 6.4

EXAMPLE OF A POSSIBLE SOLUTION

	1	2	3	4	5
a	0	1	0	0	0
b	1	0	0	0	0
c	0	0	0	0	1
d	0	0	1	0	0
e	0	0	0	1	0

and *e*4, which can be verified by referring to the earlier tables. Thus, three crews would live in Mexico City and two in Acapulco and the total loss of time would be

$$15 + 16 + 5.5 + 14 + 12 = 62.5 \text{ hours}$$

For a table of five lines and five columns, there are

$$1 \times 2 \times 3 \times 4 \times 5 = 120$$

possible solutions. A table having six lines and six columns would have

$$1 \times 2 \times 3 \times 4 \times 5 \times 6 = 720$$

possible solutions to calculate and classify. In a table of 20 lines and 20 columns, the number of possible solutions would become 2.4329×10^{23}, a quantity requiring 4.63 million billion centuries for complete evaluation if one minute were allowed for calculating each solution.

Problems involving more than six assignments cannot, except in very special cases, be solved by enumeration of the solutions. A special procedure or algorithm must be employed. We shall use the *Hungarian method*, named after the celebrated Hungarian mathematician, König.

The fundamental principle of the Hungarian method is easy to grasp (although there are certain rigorous demonstrations of proof which have been deliberately omitted here), and it states that the optimal solution (or solutions) of a problem of assignment remains unaltered if all the elements of a line (or column) are decreased (or increased) by a quantity c of the table c_{ij} of times.[1] This is obvious since a solution can contain only one element equal to 1 in each line and column (see Table 6.4). Hence, the above operation decreases (or increases) the total sum (time lost or costs, whichever is being considered) by the quantity c, but cannot modify the optimal solution.

We now apply the Hungarian method to find the optimal assignments for each bus crew. In order to obtain the 1's of an optimal solution in a table analagous to Table 6.4, we must first cause zeros to appear in Table 6.5 (a reproduction of Table 6.3).

Stage I. Obtaining Zeros

We subtract from all the elements in a column the smallest element in that column and form the table

$$C_{ij}^{(1)} = c_{ij} - \min_{i} c_{ij}$$

where i represents the line and j the column (for example, c_{14} is the element of line 1 in column 4). For convenience, we will now use numbers to indicate the lines instead of the letters used earlier.

This procedure of subtraction enables us to obtain at least one zero per column. In Table 6.5, we subtract the quantity 4.5 from all the elements in column 1, the quantity 8 from those in column 2, and so on,

[1] In other problems the c_{ij} elements may represent costs, for example, instead of times.

TABLE 6.5

	1	2	3	4	5
1	17.5	15	9	5.5	12
2	16	16.5	10.5	5	10.5
3	12	15.5	14.5	11	5.5
4	4.5	8	14	17.5	13
5	13	9.5	8.5	12	17.5

TABLE 6.6

	1	2	3	4	5
1	13	7	0.5	0.5	6.5
2	11.5	8.5	2	0	5
3	7.5	7.5	6	6	0
4	0	0	5.5	12.5	7.5
5	8.5	1.5	0	7	12

TABLE 6.7

	1	2	3	4	5
1	12.5	6.5	0	0	6
2	11.5	8.5	2	0	5
3	7.5	7.5	6	6	0
4	0	0	5.5	12.5	7.5
5	8.5	1.5	0	7	12

thereby obtaining Table 6.6, that is, $C_{ij}^{(1)}$. Next, we treat the lines in the same way as the columns so as to obtain $C_{ij}^{(2)}$ (Table 6.7) such that

$$C_{ij}^{(2)} = c_{ij}^{(1)} - \min_i c_{ij}^{(1)}.$$

We observe that this table has at least one zero in each line and column.

Stage II. Seeking an Optimal Solution

With the zeros of $C_{ij}^{(2)}$, let us seek a solution in which the total time (or total cost in other problems) has a null value, that is, an assignment in which all the $C_{ij}^{(2)}$ elements of the solution are zeros. If this is possible, we have found an optimal solution, and if not, we go on to stage III.

To find such a solution, let us consider the line, or one of the lines, containing the fewest zeros. We draw a box around one of the zeros in this line and then cross out the other zeros in the same line and column as the one we have encased (Table 6.8). From among the remaining lines we now seek the one with the fewest zeros and repeat the same procedure, continuing until we can no longer encase any zeros.

In Table 6.8, we encase c_{24}, then c_{35}, then c_{53}, crossing out c_{13} and c_{14} (we could have equally well retained c_{13} and eliminated c_{53}). Finally, we encase c_{41} and cross out c_{42}, although we could equally well reverse the operation. It is now obvious that we have

TABLE 6.8

	1	2	3	4	5
1	12.5	6.5	~~0~~	~~0~~	6
2	11.5	8.5	2	[0]	5
3	7.5	7.5	6	6	[0]
4	[0]	~~0~~	5.5	12.5	7.5
5	8.5	1.5	[0]	7	12

not obtained a solution of null value; in fact, if we complete the assignment by choosing c_{12}, the value of the solution would be: $6.5 + 0 + 0 + 0 + 0 = 6.5$. We must therefore proceed to stage III but before doing so, we have to verify that the relations retained in Table 6.8 constitute a maximal linking, that is, that we have assigned the maximal possible number of zeros.

The reader will appreciate that verification can be carried out by the method for finding the maximal flow explained in Chapter 5. By treating the encased zeros as saturated arcs, and the crossed-out zeros as arcs with a null flow in a transport network, we obtain Fig. 6.1.

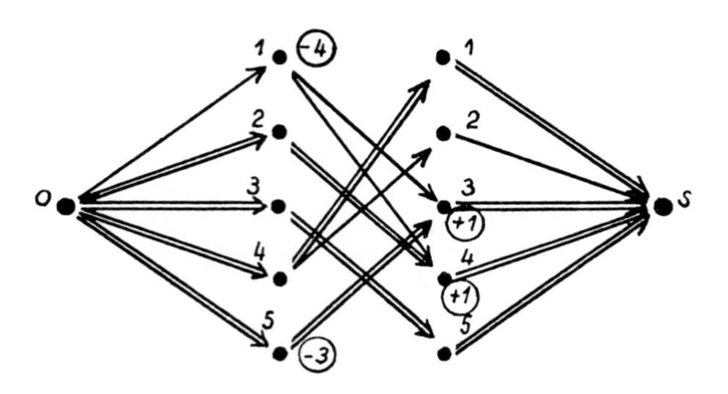

Fig. 6.1

It will be seen that the Ford–Fulkerson procedure does not allow us to mark S; the linking provided by Table 6.8 is therefore maximal.

Stage III. Finding the Minimal Number of Lines and Columns Which Contain All the Zeros

(a) Mark a cross (×) next to each line in Table 6.9 that does not contain an encased zero.

(b) Similarly, mark each column containing an encased zero in one or more of the marked lines.

(c) Mark each line that has an encased zero in a marked column.

(d) Repeat (b) and (c) until there are no more lines or columns to be marked.

Thus, in Table 6.9 we first mark line 1 which results in marking columns 3 and 4, and consequently, lines 2 and 5. As we shall see

TABLE 6.9

	1	2	3	4	5	
1	12.5	6.5	~~0~~	~~0~~	6	×
2	11.5	8.5	2	[0]	5	×
3	7.5	7.5	6	6	[0]	
4	[0]	~~0~~	5.5	12.5	7.5	
5	8.5	1.5	[0]	7	12	×
			×	×		

in stage IV, this procedure will enable us to obtain the minimal number of lines and columns containing all the encased or crossed-out zeros.

Stage IV. Completion of Stage III

Draw a straight line through each unmarked line of the table and each marked column. Now we have the minimal number of lines and columns which contain all encased or canceled zeros. In Table 6.10, we must draw lines through lines 3 and 4 and columns 3 and 4.

TABLE 6.10

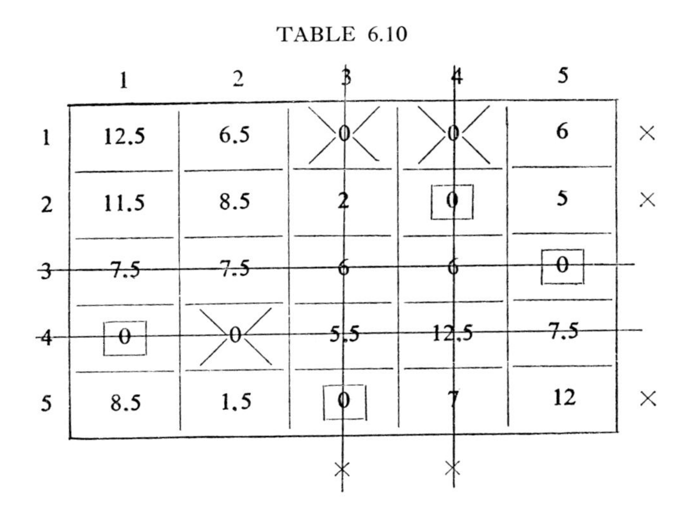

	1	2	3	4	5	
1	12.5	6.5	~~0~~	~~0~~	6	×
2	11.5	8.5	2	[0]	5	×
3	7.5	7.5	6	6	[0]	
4	[0]	~~0~~	5.5	12.5	7.5	
5	8.5	1.5	[0]	7	12	×
			×	×		

Stage V. Removing Certain Zeros

Let us examine the partial table c of the elements not traversed by a line, and let us *subtract* the smallest number in it from the elements of the columns which are *not crossed out*, and *add* this number to the elements of the lines which *are crossed out.*[2] In our example the smallest element not traversed by a line is $c_{52} = 1.5$. After subtracting it from the elements of columns 1, 2, and 5, and adding it to those of lines 3 and 4, we obtain Table 6.11.

TABLE 6.11

	1	2	3	4	5
1	11	5	0	0	4.5
2	10	7	2	0	3.5
3	7.5	7.5	7.5	7.5	0
4	0	0	7	14	7.5
5	7	0	0	7	10.5

Stage VI. Obtaining the Optimal Solution or Commencing a New Cycle

In the table $C_{ij}^{(3)}$, obtained in stage V, we seek an optimal solution according to the method explained in stage II. Here we find a ready solution, that is, an assignment of one, and only one zero to each line and each column (Table 6.12). We now have $c_{41}^{(3)} + c_{52}^{(3)} + c_{13}^{(3)} + c_{24}^{(3)} + c_{35}^{(3)} = 0$ which corresponds to $4.5 + 9.5 + 9 + 5 + 5.5 = 33.5$ hours in the initial table (Table 6.5).

As in Table 6.4, the solution can finally be expressed in 1's and 0's, where the 1's represent the chosen assignment (Table 6.13).

If we had not found a solution at this stage, we would have been obliged to repeat stages III–V and in the event of a further failure, to repeat stage II–V until we were successful. Finally, the solution

[2] It amounts to the same thing if we subtract the number from the elements of the table which are not crossed by a line, and add it to those which are crossed by both a vertical and horizontal line.

TABLE 6.12

	1	2	3	4	5
1	11	5	[0]	⨯0	4.5
2	10	7	2	[0]	3.5
3	7.5	7.5	7.5	7.5	[0]
4	[0]	⨯0	7	14	7.5
5		[0]	⨯0	7	10.5

TABLE 6.13

	1	2	3	4	5
a	0	0	1	0	0
b	0	0	0	1	0
c	0	0	0	0	1
d	1	0	0	0	0
e	0	1	0	0	0

(in this case, it is the only one) that gives a minimal waiting time equal to 33.5 hours is shown in the following tabulation.

Crew	Residence	Service number	Waiting time (hours)
1	Mexico City	*d*1	4.5
2	Acapulco	2*e*	9.5
3	Acapulco	3*a*	9.0
4	Mexico City	*b*4	5.0
5	Acapulco	5*c*	5.5
		Total:	33.5

Similar calculations would enable us to find the *maximal* waiting time which is $83\frac{1}{2}$ hours. There is a difference of 50 hours between the best and the worst solution and there are 118 intermediate solutions (not all different; thus, 2*a*, *b*1, 5*c*, *d*4, and *e*3 is equivalent to 2*a*, *b*1, 5*c*, *d*3, and *e*4). Who dares to assume that the optimal solution could be found by intuition and a brief consideration of the timetable, especially if it included two or three additional services? All that now remains is to hope that you will be able to join the lucky crews in Acapulco on your next vacation.

König's Theorem

It was in 1916 that the Hungarian mathematician König made known the theorem on which the algorithm for solving problems of assignment has been based.[3] Most proofs of this theorem are lengthy and complicated, and although the Ford–Fulkerson algorithm[4] is of a much later date, it provides an effective method[5] of proving König's theorem.

Given a matrix $[M]$ of the order (m, n) in which certain coefficients are zero and others are undefined, we call (L) the set of m lines $L_1, L_2, \ldots, L_m$ and (C) the set of n columns $C_1, C_2, \ldots, C_n$.

A *support* of $[M]$ is a set of rows (lines and/or columns) such that their suppression eliminates all the zeros in the matrix. The set of lines or the set of columns constitutes a support which is not, in general, minimal. If a support is composed of p lines $L_{i1}, \ldots, L_{ip}$ and q columns $C_{j1}, \ldots, C_{jq}$, we have $p + q \leqslant \min(m, n)$, since a support is, at most, composed of $\min(m, n)$ rows.

For the sake of an example, let us consider matrix 1 where $L_1, \ldots, L_4$ and $C_1, \ldots, C_5$ are supports. The smallest among them contains four rows, but it is possible to find a support with an even smaller number of rows: C_1, L_3, L_4.

[3] Some writers credit Frobenius with an earlier proof in 1912, while Kuhn claimed that the properties proved by König were given by Egervary. See the Bibliography.

[4] This algorithm and the corresponding theorem are the basis of the anecdote which introduces Chapter 5.

[5] We thank Y. Malgrange, Engineer, SERETE, Paris, for suggesting this proof.

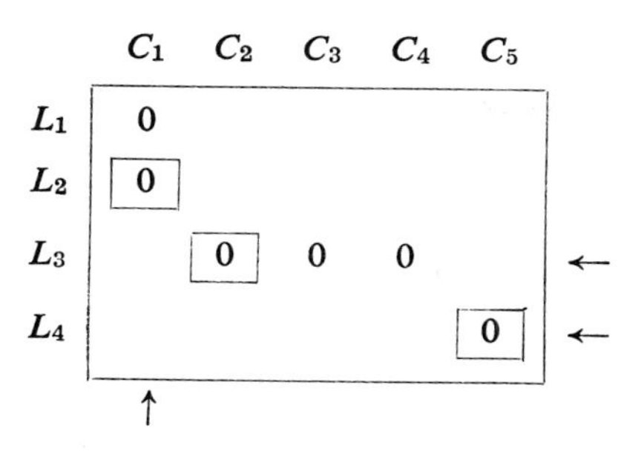

MATRIX 1

We use the term *dissemination index* of a matrix $[M]$ for the minimal number of rows $D(M)$ of a support. For matrix 1, it is easy to show that $D(M) = 3$; hence, $D(M) \leqslant \min(m, n)$.

A set of k zeros of the matrix forms a *linking* of k lines and k columns if these k zeros are at the intersection of k separate lines and columns. Thus, the encased zeros of matrix 1 form a linking

$$L_2C_1 - L_3C_2 - L_4C_5 .$$

No line and no column appears twice in this expression.

A maximal linking is one containing the maximal number of zeros; this number is called the *squaring index* of $[M]$ and is represented as $Q(M)$.

König's theorem can be enunciated as

$$D(M) = Q(M).$$

In other words, the minimal number of rows in a support is equal to the maximal number of zeros in a linking. For matrix 1, $D(M) = Q(M) = 3$.

With every matrix $[M]$ we can associate a transport network formed by the following procedure:

(a) An entry O is connected by an arc OC_j to the n points $C_1 ,..., C_n$ (if $n \geqslant m$) or by an arc OL_j to the m points $L_1 ,..., L_m$ (if $m > n$), the capacity of each of these arcs being 1.

(b) An exit Z is connected by an arc L_iZ to the m points $L_1 ,..., L_m$ (if $m \leqslant n$) or by an arc C_iZ to the n points $C_1 ,..., C_n$ (if $n < m$), the capacity of each of these arcs again being 1.

(c) Each zero L_iC_j of the matrix is represented by an arc C_jL_i (if $m \leqslant n$) or by an arc L_iC_j (if $n < m$), each arc having an infinite capacity.

Example. The transport network associated with matrix 1 is shown in Fig. 6.2. Finding a maximal linking in the matrix is equivalent to determining the maximal flow in the associated network. $Q(M)$ is the value of the maximal flow.

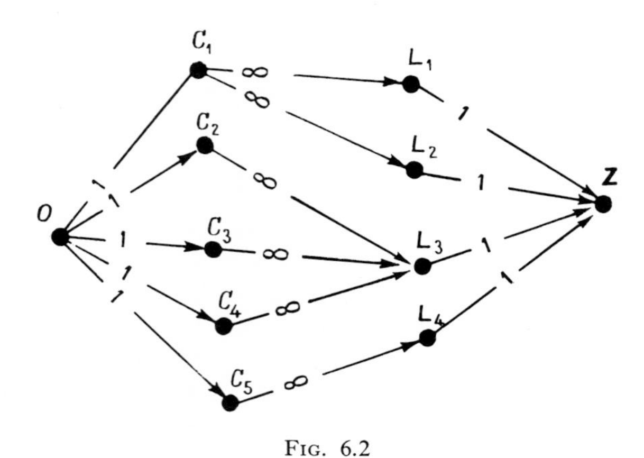

FIG. 6.2

A zero L_iC_j of the matrix is, in fact, represented by an arc C_jL_i. If a flow with a value of 1 passes along this arc, we shall also have a flow of this value for OC_j and L_iZ, which will both be saturated. In other words, each line and each column can only be assigned once and we can immediately see that if $m \leqslant n$, the total value of the flow capable of entering Z is less than or equal to m, since the point Z forms a cut[6] of the network.

We shall show that with each support we can associate a cut with a capacity equal to the number of rows in the support, and that, inversely, with each cut of finite capacity we can associate a support in which the number of rows equals the capacity of the cut. Thus, $D(M)$ equals the minimal capacity of a cut, and by the Ford–Fulkerson theorem, minimal cut equals maximal flow; hence,

$$Q(M) = D(M).$$

(1) Let us first prove that with each support we can associate a cut with a capacity equal to the number of rows in the support. To do so, let us take the support formed by the set (L^+) of the lines

[6] The concept of a cut was defined in the preceding chapter.

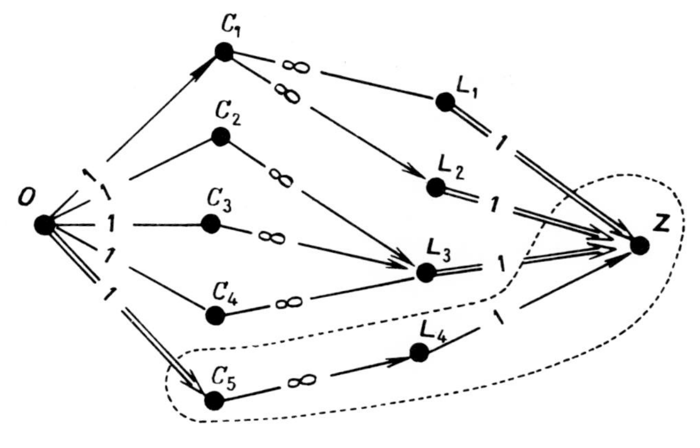

FIG. 6.3

$L_{i1}, \ldots, L_{ip}$ and the set (C^+) of the columns $C_{i1}, \ldots, C_{iq}$. For example, for matrix 1,

$$(L^+) = (L_1, L_2, L_3), \qquad (C^+) = (C_5).$$

Let us call (L^-) and (C^-), respectively, the sets of the lines and columns which do not belong to the support.

After suppressing (L^+) and (C^+), the matrix formed by the lines (L^-) and the columns (C^-) does not contain any zero.

In the associated network, there is no arc which connects a vertex of (C^-) to a vertex of (L^-). In our example,

$$(L^-) = (L_4)$$

$$(C^-) = (C_1, C_2, C_3, C_4);$$

L_4 is not joined to any of the vertices C_1, C_2, C_3, and C_4.

Let $\mathscr{E}$ be the set of vertices formed by the point Z, the vertices of (L^-), and the vertices of (C^+). Here,

$$\mathscr{E} = (Z, L_4, C_5).$$

This set of vertices defines a cut $C(\mathscr{E})$ whose incoming arcs are all arcs entering $\mathscr{E}$ from a point external to $\mathscr{E}$. It follows that:

(a) The only arcs leaving a point outside $\mathscr{E}$ and ending at Z are those with an origin (L^+). For each vertex L_i of (L^+), there is one and only one arc L_iZ with a capacity of 1. If (L^+) contains p vertices, where p is the number of lines of the support (here, $p = 3$), the total capacity of these arcs is equal to p.

(b) The vertices of (L^-) are not connected with any vertex of (C^-); hence, there is no arc entering $\mathscr{E}$ that is terminally connected to the vertices of (L^-). In the present case, there is no incoming arc ending at L_4.

(c) Every vertex of (C^+) is connected by an arc with a capacity of 1 to the vertex O. If (C^+) contains q points, and q is the number of columns of the support (in this case, $q = 1$), the total capacity of the arcs entering $\mathscr{E}$ and terminating at the vertices of (C^+) is therefore equal to q. Thus, the capacity of the cut is $p + q$ (in this case, $3 + 1 = 4$).

(2) Let us now prove that every cut with a finite capacity has an associated support. To do this, let us take any cut that includes Z but excludes O. This cut contains a certain number of vertices L, the set of which is (L^-), and also a certain number of vertices C, the set of which will be called (C^+). If the capacity of this cut is finite, it means that there is no arc connecting a vertex of (L^-) with a vertex of (C^-) formed from the vertices not included in (C^+). In fact, in the contrary case, there would be at least one entering arc with an infinite capacity, and contrary to the assumption, the capacity of the cut would not be finite.

Hence, the submatrix formed by the lines corresponding to the vertices of (L^-) and by the columns corresponding to those of (C^-), after the suppression of the other lines and columns, does not contain any zero. Thus, all the zeros of $[M]$ are included in the lines and columns of (L^+) and (C^+), the set of which is therefore a support. Moreover, as before, the number of rows of the support is equal to the capacity of the cut.

Let us therefore call $C(\mathscr{E}')$ a minimal cut. With this cut is associated a minimal support, the number of rows in which is $D(M)$, equal to the capacity of the cut. By the Ford–Fulkerson theorem, the minimal cut is equal to the maximal flow so that the maximal flow is also $D(M)$. Now the value of this maximal flow is equal to the maximal number of zeros in a linking, namely $Q(M)$.

Thus, $D(M) = Q(M)$, and König's theorem is proved.

USE OF KÖNIG'S THEOREM FOR PROBLEMS OF ASSIGNMENT

Where the question of cost is not involved, a problem of assignment consists of finding the maximal linking. For example, given a problem in which n machines are to be operated by m workers, each worker must be assigned to a machine he knows how to operate. We take $X_1, X_2, \ldots, X_n$ to represent the workers and $Y_1, Y_2, \ldots, Y_m$ to represent the machines and we join X_i to Y_j in the graph of Fig. 6.4, if worker X_i is able to operate machine Y_j.

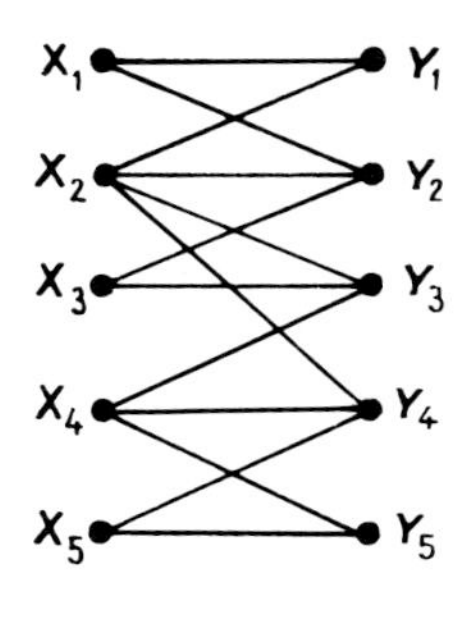

FIG. 6.4

With this graph we can associate matrix 2 in which all the M_{ij} elements are equal to 1 if there is an arc X_iY_j.

A maximal assignment will be a linking of the X_i and Y_j elements in such a way that only one worker will be assigned to a machine and

$[M] =$

	Y_1	Y_2	Y_3	Y_4	Y_5
X_1	**1**	1			
X_2	1	1	**1**	1	
X_3		**1**	1		
X_4			1	**1**	1
X_5				1	**1**

MATRIX 2

the maximal number of machines will be utilized. To find such a linking, the following procedure is used:

(1) Choose the line (or one of the lines) containing the fewest 1's and draw a box around one number 1.

(2) Cross out the line and column containing the encased 1.

(3) Repeat these two steps for the remainder of the matrix until all the lines and columns containing 1's are crossed out.

Here, for example, we obtain the linking X_1Y_1, X_2Y_3, X_3Y_2, X_4Y_4, X_5Y_5 (there exist others). This is a maximal linking which enables us to assign all n workers. This result does not always occur but when it does, the linking is said to be *saturating*.

When the question of cost intervenes in a problem of assignment, it is necessary to find a saturating linking of minimal cost; this is when König's theorem is utilized.

In such a case, we begin with a matrix of the costs $[C]$ in which each element c_{ij} represents the cost of assigning X_i to Y_j (matrix 3).

(1) We show that the problem is not changed if we subtract a constant u_i from the cost of a line i or/and a constant v_j from the cost of a column j.

Example. We take matrix 3 to represent matrix $[C]$. For example, let

$$u_i = \min_j(c_{ij})$$

and

$$v_j = \min_i(c_{ij} - u_i).$$

$[C] =$						u_i
	3	5	7	2	1	1
	4	6	7	3	1	1
	2	1	3	4	5	1
	6	3	2	7	8	2
	5	4	3	1	9	1
v_j	1	0	0	0	0	

MATRIX 3

$[C_1'] =$

1	4	6	1	0
2	5	6	2	0
0	0	2	3	4
3	1	0	5	6
3	3	2	0	8

MATRIX 4

We obtain matrix 4 or $[C_1']$ with elements

$$c'_{ij} = c_{ij} - (u_i + v_j).$$

Let us consider the two arbitrarily selected linkings

$$\gamma_1 = (X_1Y_1, X_2Y_2, X_3Y_3, X_4Y_4, X_5Y_5)$$

and

$$\gamma_2 = (X_1Y_5, X_2Y_4, X_3Y_3, X_4Y_2, X_5Y_1);$$

the equivalent total costs are (matrix 3):

$$C(\gamma_1) = 3 + 6 + 3 + 7 + 9 = 28,$$

$$C(\gamma_2) = 1 + 3 + 3 + 3 + 5 = 15,$$

and we find

$$\Delta = C(\gamma_1) - C(\gamma_2) = 28 - 15 = 13.$$

We verify that this difference Δ remains unchanged if we consider the costs of matrix 4:

$$C'(\gamma_1) = 1 + 5 + 2 + 5 + 8 = 21$$

and

$$C'(\gamma_2) = 0 + 2 + 2 + 1 + 3 = 8,$$

whence,

$$\Delta' = C'(\gamma_1) - C'(\gamma_2) = 21 - 8 = 13 = \Delta;$$

indeed, since we are dealing with a linking,

$$C'(\gamma_1) = C(\gamma_1) - \Big[\sum_i u_i + \sum_j v_j\Big]$$

and

$$C'(\gamma_2) = C(\gamma_2) - \Big[\sum_i u_i + \sum_j v_j\Big],$$

whence,

$$\begin{aligned} \Delta' &= C'(\gamma_1) - C'(\gamma_2) \\ &= C(\gamma_1) - C(\gamma_2) - \sum_i u_i + \sum_i u_i - \sum_j v_j + \sum_j v_j \\ &= C(\gamma_1) - C(\gamma_2) = \Delta. \end{aligned}$$

(2) In addition, whatever the value of c_{ij}, it can be shown that if

$$u_i + v_j \leqslant c_{ij} ,$$

then, for every linking γ,

$$C(\gamma) \geqslant \sum_i u_i + \sum_j v_j ,$$

which does not imply any particular method of calculating the u_i and v_j elements.

It follows that (a) if we find quantities u_i and v_j such that

$$u_i + v_j \leqslant c_{ij}$$

for each i and each j, and (b) if there is a linking γ with

$$C(\gamma) = \sum_i u_i + \sum_j v_j ,$$

then $C(\gamma)$ is minimal, and

$$S = \sum_i u_i + \sum_j v_j$$

is maximal.

We now see that if, for certain values of u_i and v_j, the graph formed by the arcs such that

$$c_{ij} = u_i + v_j \qquad \text{or} \qquad [c'_{ij} = c_{ij} - (u_i + v_j) = 0]$$

having a saturating linking γ, that is, if all the lines and columns of the matrix are assigned, we have

$$C(\gamma) = c_{i_1 j_1} + \cdots + c_{i_n j_n} = (u_{i_1} + v_{j_1}) + \cdots + (u_{i_n} + v_{j_n})$$

and, as each line and column is assigned once and only once,

$$C(\gamma) = (u_{i_1} + v_{j_1}) + \cdots + (u_{i_n} + v_{j_n}) = \sum_i u_i + \sum_j v_j = S.$$

Hence, we have found an assignment with a minimal cost.

(3) Let us consider the example of matrix 3. The auxiliary graph formed of arcs such that $c_{ij} = 0$ (matrix 4) is the one shown in Fig. 6.5.

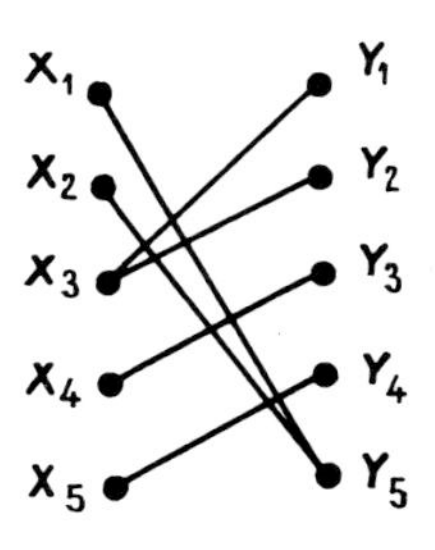

Fig. 6.5

Its associated matrix is matrix 5 which contains only the zeros of matrix 4. Let us now seek a maximal linking of matrix 5. We obtain, for example,

$$\gamma_1' = (X_1 Y_5\,,\, X_3 Y_2\,,\, X_4 Y_3\,,\, X_5 Y_4),$$

a linking which is not saturating since only four lines and columns are assigned. To complete the saturation, we still have to assign line 2 and column 1. We obtain

$$\gamma_1 = \{\gamma_1'\,,\, X_2 Y_1\} = \{X_1 Y_5\,,\, X_2 Y_1\,,\, X_3 Y_2\,,\, X_4 Y_3\,,\, X_5 Y_4\},$$

$$C(\gamma_1) = 1 + 4 + 1 + 2 + 1 = 9,$$

$$S_1 = \sum_i u_i + \sum_j v_j = 1 + 1 + 1 + 2 + 1 + 1 = 7,$$

and we have

$$S_1 < C(\gamma_1).$$

	1	2	3	4	↓ 5
1					[0]
2					0
→ 3	0	[0]			
→ 4			[0]		
→ 5				[0]	

Matrix 5

Our problem now consists of finding the new values of u_i and v_j $(u_i + v_j \leqslant C_{ij})$ which enable us to increase S and, as a result, to discover a new linking γ_2 such that $C(\gamma_2) < C(\gamma_1)$. To do this, let us look for a support of the graph of Fig. 6.5. From König's theorem this support contains four rows, since the linking γ_1' contained four oriented pairs $X_i Y_j$. Using the same method employed for the problem of assignment without cost, we find rows

$$X_3, \quad X_4, \quad X_5, \qquad \text{and} \quad Y_5$$

Returning to matrix $[C_1']$, let us consider matrix $[K']$, obtained by suppressing the lines and columns of the support.

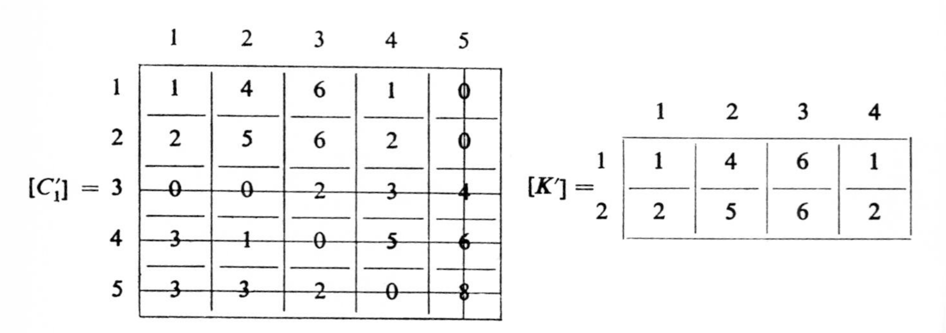

$[C_1'] =$

	1	2	3	4	5
1	1	4	6	1	0
2	2	5	6	2	0
3	0	0	2	3	4
4	3	1	0	5	6
5	3	3	2	0	8

$[K'] =$

	1	2	3	4
1	1	4	6	1
2	2	5	6	2

Fig. 6.6

Let k be the smallest element of $[K']$ (in this case $k = 1 = C'_{11} = C_{14}$); it is positive, since $[K']$ does not contain any 0. Let us assume

$$u'_i = u_i + k,$$

if line i *is not* a row of the support, and

$$v'_j = v_j - k,$$

if column j *is* a row of the support.

We obtain the following values:

$$u'_1 = u_1 + k = 1 + 1 = 2; \qquad u'_2 = u_2 + k = 1 + 1 = 2;$$

$$u'_3 = u_3 = 1; \qquad u'_4 = u_4 = 2; \qquad u'_5 = u_5 = 1;$$

$$v'_1 = v_1 = 1; \qquad v'_2 = v_2 = 0; \qquad v'_3 = v_3 = 0; \qquad v'_4 = v_4 = 0;$$

$$v'_5 = v_5 - k = 0 - 1 = -1.$$

whence we obtain the new matrix $[C'_2]$, in which

$$c'_{ij} = c_{ij} - (u'_i + v'_j)$$

We see that, in matrix $[C'_1]$, we have subtracted $k = 1$ from the elements of $[K']$ and added $k = 1$ to the elements situated at the intersection of a line and a column of the support (matrix 6).

We now have

$$S_2 = (2 + 2 + 1 + 2 + 1) + (1 + 0 + 0 + 0 - 1) = 8 \quad \text{and} \quad S_2 > S_1 .$$

$[C_2] =$

					u'_i
0	3	5	0	0	2
1	4	5	1	0	2
0	0	2	3	5	1
3	1	0	5	7	2
3	3	2	0	9	1
1	0	0	0	−1	v'_1

Matrix 6

Indeed, since the support $D(M) = Q(M)$ contains I lines and J columns, we find

$$S_2 = S_1 + k(n - I - kJ)$$
$$= S_1 + k[n - (I + J)],$$

and since

$$I + J = Q(M) < n,$$

then

$$k[n - (I + J)] > 0.$$

The value of König's theorem for solving problems of assignment has thus been made clear.

Figure 6.7 and its associated matrix (matrix 7) show the following linking:

$$\gamma_2 = (X_1Y_1\,,\, X_2Y_5\,,\, X_3Y_2\,,\, X_4Y_3\,,\, X_5Y_4),$$

with

$$C(\gamma_2) = 3 + 1 + 1 + 2 + 1 = 8 = S_2\,.$$

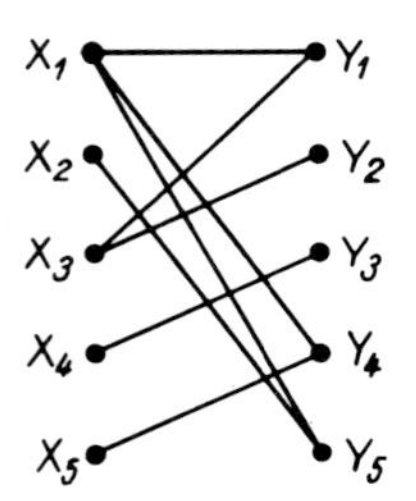

FIG. 6.7

0			0	0
				0
0	0			
		0		
			0	

MATRIX 7

We have thus obtained a maximal assignment. If the linking were not saturating, we would have to calculate new values u_i'' and v_j''.

Application to Cyclic Problems

The Hungarian method has been applied to various cyclic problems, notably, the celebrated problem of the traveling salesman: given n towns, A, B,..., N and either their respective distance apart or the transportation costs between them, find the most economic route which must start and end at A, and pass through each of the other towns once and only once.

The practical difficulty of this problem will be appreciated from the fact that for ten towns, there are

$$\tfrac{1}{2}9! = \tfrac{1}{2}(9 \cdot 8 \cdot 7 \cdot 6 \cdot 5 \cdot 4 \cdot 3 \cdot 2 \cdot 1) = 181{,}440$$

separate routes possible and, for 31 towns, more than 10^{30} different itineraries.

The problem may be treated as a linear program with integral numbers. Gomory's algorithm should, theoretically, be capable of providing a solution, but the programming for this method soon leads to calculations beyond the scope of most present-day computers.

The problem of the traveling salesman is akin to problems of assignment, in as much as:

(1) We have at our disposal a matrix of costs containing as many lines and columns as there are towns; we can state $C_{ii} = \infty$ since, by assumption, we do not remain in any one town.

(2) We seek an assignment of the lines to the columns, but this assignment must be such that the sequence of the indices of the lines and columns forms a complete circuit.

Some writers, such as Flood and Dantzig, have suggested methods which solve particular cases, but no general solution has so far been found. We shall, therefore, limit our survey to two classic examples so as to demonstrate both the effectiveness and limitations of these methods.

First Example. We are given matrix 8, representing the transportation costs between five towns A_1, A_2, A_3, A_4, and A_5.

$[C_{ij}] =$	1	2	3	4	5	u_i
1	∞	5	6	10	8	3
2	5	∞	5	12	12	2
3	6	5	∞	8	10	3
4	10	12	8	∞	6	3
5	8	12	10	6	∞	3
v_j	3	2	3	3	3	

MATRIX 8

As in the problem of assignment, the solution is not altered if we subtract $u_i + v_j$ from each coefficient C_{ij}, thereby obtaining matrix 9 for which

$$c'_{ij} = c_{ij} - (u_i + v_j).$$

Dantzig has shown that, in a case of symmetry, the problem is not changed if we state

$$c_{i_1 i_2} = c_{i_2 i_3} = c_{i_3 i_1} = \infty$$

for each series of distinct indices i_1, i_2, i_3.

$[C'_{ij}] =$	1	2	3	4	5
1	∞	[0]	0	4	2
2	0	∞	[0]	7	7
3	0	0	∞	[2]	4
4	4	7	2	∞	[0]
5	[2]	7	4	0	∞

MATRIX 9

Hence we transform:

$$c'_{54} = 0 \quad \text{into} \quad c''_{54} = \infty,$$
$$c'_{42} = 0 \qquad\qquad c''_{42} = \infty,$$
$$c'_{25} = 0 \qquad\qquad c''_{25} = \infty.$$

$[C''_{ij}] =$

	1	2	3	4	5	u'_i
1	∞	0	0	4	2	
2	0	∞	0	7	∞	
3	0	0	∞	2	4	
4	4	∞	2	∞	0	
5	2	7	4	∞	∞	+ 2
v'_j				+ 2		

MATRIX 10

We thereby obtain matrix 10 and can state

$$u'_5 = u_5 + 2,$$
$$u'_4 = v_4 + 2,$$

whence we obtain matrix 11.

$[C'''_{ij}] =$

	A_1	A_2	A_3	A_4	A_5
A_1	∞	[0]	0	2	2
A_2	0	∞	[0]	5	∞
A_3	0	0	∞	[0]	4
A_4	4	∞	2	∞	[0]
A_5	[0]	5	2	∞	∞

MATRIX 11

The assignment given by the encased zeros solves the problem of the traveling salesman, since we have obtained a complete cricuit:

$$A_1 \rightarrow A_2 \rightarrow A_3 \rightarrow A_4 \rightarrow A_5 \rightarrow A_1 .$$

Second Example. Let us now consider matrix 12, obtained after first calculating the u_i and v_j elements.

	A_1	A_2	A_3	A_4	A_5	A_6
A_1	∞	0	0	2	4	[1]
A_2	0	∞	[0]	1	5	3
A_3	[0]	0	∞	2	5	3
A_4	2	[1]	2	∞	0	0
A_5	4	5	5	[0]	∞	0
A_6	1	3	3	0	[0]	∞

MATRIX 12

The method used above does not enable us to obtain new zeros leading to a solution of the problem. On the other hand, it can be seen that the circuit

$$A_1 \quad A_6 \quad A_5 \quad A_4 \quad A_2 \quad A_3 \quad A_1$$

provides a solution since we must have at least two positive coefficients, and the most economical choice is obviously to take the two coefficients with a value of 1.

In discussing these two examples, our aim was simply to show the difficulties that arise as soon as the concepts of circuits and cycles make their appearance.

CHAPTER 7

225,000 BOTTLES THE NEXT DAY!

(A Transport Problem. Algorithm of the Steppingstone)

It is a year since the craze for *Euphoria* was taken up by Frenchmen, and especially by Parisians, who never like to see provincials becoming the arbiters of taste. What, then, is this *Euphoria*, a beverage which is rapidly becoming a menace to our habits of intemperance?

The drink really originated in 1975, when a young chemical engineer and dietician discovered the properties of R 178, a substance which remains a mystery to laymen, but which provides all the pleasures of intoxication without any of the ill effects.

Patents were taken out and a large company was formed to manufacture R 178, but almost at once strikes broke out in Burgundy and Champagne and all the chief wine-producing districts of France. Roads were barricaded, the Chamber of Deputies was surrounded, the effigy of the inventor was publicly burned. But can anything stop progress? When the Minister of Finance finally imposed a very high tax on the new beverage, the various public services combined to assist in the development of this miraculous drink which was to be of such benefit to the Treasury.

In due course, the company perfected *Euphoria*, which was a mixture of water, coloring material, scents, a small quantity of the inevitable chlorophyl, and carbonic gas, and it was launched with enormous fanfare. Three factories were built in the Paris region to satisfy the newly acquired taste of ten million Parisians. After some months of heroic resistance, the owners of bars, public houses, liquor shops, taverns, nightclubs, restaurants, and snack bars were all forced to capitulate to the new craze, and orders for *Euphoria* multiplied.

To meet the growing demand, five depots or warehouses were opened; these delivered the cases of *Euphoria* to the public houses, which had sent in their orders two days previously. In this way, the depots were able to notify the Supervisor of Supplies of the total requirements for the following day. Figure 7.1 shows the geographical positions of the three factories *A*, *B*, and *C*, as well as those of the five depots *a*, *b*, *c*, *d*, and *e*. Because of the different distances and varied transport costs, the cost of transporting a bottle of *Euphoria* varies according to the factory supplying it and the depot to which it is consigned. The arcs of Fig. 7.1 show the unit costs of transport.

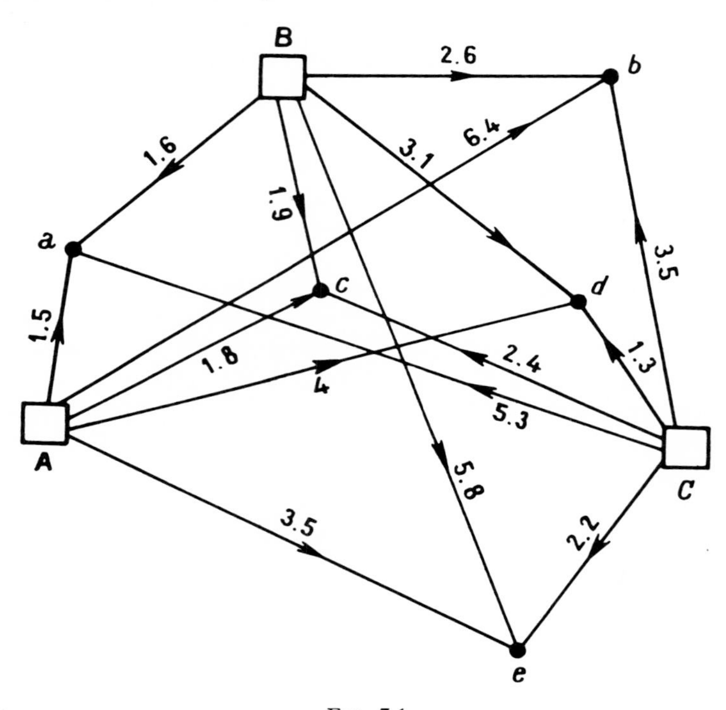

FIG. 7.1

On this 5th of July 1975, the supervisor was in possession of the following information, the numbers representing thousands of bottles:

Production: $A = 90$; $B = 75$; $C = 35$; total: 200.

Demand: $a = 40$; $b = 35$; $c = 70$; $d = 30$; $e = 50$; total: 225.

According to these figures, 25,000 unfortunate Parisians would have to replace their favorite beverage with a small Vouvray. However, it is not their plight which interests us, but the measures adopted by the supervisor. In the Middle Ages a merchant who could perform division was looked on as something of a scientist, but we are in the year 1975 and it is now normal practice for a man such as the supervisor to have recourse to operations research.

His task is to organize the deliveries so that their cost will be minimal, a process repeated daily, since both production and demand vary from day to day. His first operation is to construct Table 7.1 with the unit costs taken from Fig. 7.1, the demand and available supplies being added at the end of the columns and lines.

TABLE 7.1

	a	*b*	*c*	*d*	*e*	
A	1.5	6.4	1.8	4	3.5	90
B	1.6	2.6	1.9	3.1	5.8	75
C	5.3	3.5	2.4	1.3	2.2	35
F	50	50	50	50	50	25
	40	35	70	30	50	

But because the demand is greater than the available supplies, he introduces a fictitious factory F from which the transport costs are to be much higher than the real costs; by doing this, he ensures that the optimal solution will only include 25,000 bottles originating from this factory. The unit cost of transport from F to any of the depots is fixed at 50.

To obtain a solution (Table 7.2), we need only ensure that the quantities in the lines add up to the corresponding supplies, and that the sum of the quantities in the columns is equal to the demand of the respective depots. But the number of possible solutions is enormous, and we have no reason to suppose this particular one is the best and will give the minimal cost. How, then, is the supervisor to proceed?

Fortunately, the supervisor has retained certain basic properties learned in the course of his professional training. He has been taught that, in a problem of this kind, constituted by a table of m lines and n columns, the optimal solution *must include at least* $(m - 1)(n - 1)$ *null quantities*.

TABLE 7.2

	a	*b*	*c*	*d*	*e*	
A	15	20	40	15	0	90
B	16	9	20	0	30	75
C	9	2	7	10	7	35
F	0	4	3	5	13	25
	40	35	70	30	50	

Consequently, it is useless to try to hit on an optimal solution by chance, or to depend solely on one's mental ability. The optimal solution is, in fact, one of the set of solutions containing $(m - 1)(n - 1)$ zeros. If one knows such a solution, often referred to as a *basic solution*, one can then progressively diminish the total cost, using a procedure which we shall explain, but ensuring that every solution includes the required number of zeros. By so doing, we are certain to obtain the optimal solution.

Table 7.3 shows how a basic solution is constructed. From the northwest corner (marked by an arrow), obtain the first line by saturating columns a and b, and place the remainder in the first square of column c. Next, saturate column c, then line B, column d, line C, and, finally, column e; line F will be automatically saturated. By this procedure, we are certain to obtain a solution with at least $(m - 1)(n - 1)$ zeros.

Here, $m = 4$, $n = 5$, and $(m - 1)(n - 1) = 3 \times 4 = 12$, and we can see that Table 7.3 contains twelve zeros (it would still have been a basic

TABLE 7.3[a]

↘	*a*	*b*	*c*	*d*	*e*	
A	40	35	15	0	0	90
B	0	0	55	20	0	75
C	0	0	0	10	25	35
F	0	0	0	0	25	25
	40	35	70	30	50	

[a] Total cost: 5455 F (excluding the 25,000 fictitious bottles).

solution if there had been more than twelve). The total cost corresponding to this solution is 5455 F.

Before seeking a better solution, we shall now designate the lines and columns by numbers. To improve a solution, we use *marginal reasoning*. What will happen, for example, if we add one unit to an empty square, and what effect will it have on the cost ? Suppose, for instance, we add one unit to square (3, 1), third line, first column; we must subtract 1 from square (3, 4) to preserve the total of line 3, add one in square (2, 4) to leave the total in column 4 the same, and so on, leading to the subtraction of 1 in (2, 3), the addition of 1 in (1, 3) and, finally, the subtraction of 1 in (1, 1). Referring to Table 7.1, we discover that the above procedure has resulted in a variation of cost amounting to

$$5.3 - 1.3 + 3.1 - 1.9 + 1.8 - 1.5 = 5.5 \text{ centimes.}$$

The proposed change is, therefore, useless since it would increase the transport cost of a bottle by 5.5 centimes. But if we make a systematic calculation of the marginal costs for all the void squares in the basic

TABLE 7.4

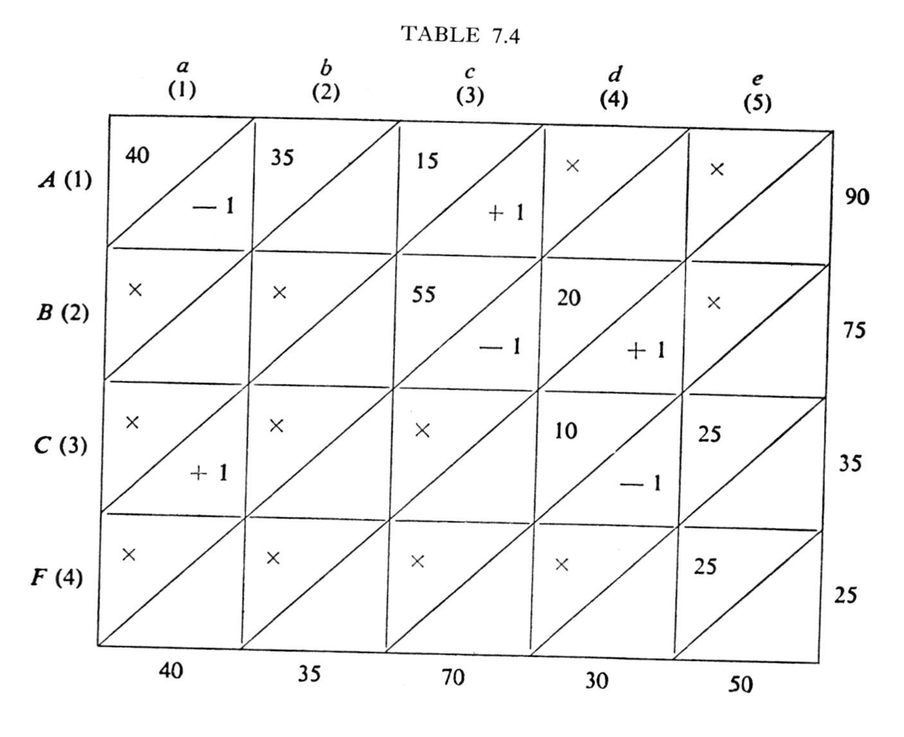

	a (1)	*b* (2)	*c* (3)	*d* (4)	*e* (5)	
A (1)	40 / − 1	35	15 / + 1	×	×	90
B (2)	×	×	55 / − 1	20 / + 1	×	75
C (3)	× / + 1	×	×	10 / − 1	25	35
F (4)	×	×	×	×	25	25
	40	35	70	30	50	

solution, forming each time a circuit or *stairway* closing on itself, we obtain

$$\delta_{14} = 4 - 3.1 + 1.9 - 1.8 = 1$$
$$\delta_{15} = 3.5 - 2.2 + 1.3 - 3.1 + 1.9 - 1.8 = -0.4$$
$$\delta_{21} = 1.6 - 1.9 + 1.8 - 1.5 = 0$$
$$\delta_{22} = 2.6 - 1.9 + 1.8 - 6.4 = -3.9 \leftarrow$$
$$\delta_{25} = 5.8 - 2.2 + 1.3 - 3.1 = 1.8$$
$$\delta_{31} = 5.3 - 1.3 + 3.1 - 1.9 + 1.8 - 1.5 = 5.5$$
$$\delta_{32} = 3.5 - 1.3 + 3.1 - 1.9 + 1.8 - 6.4 = -1.2$$
$$\delta_{33} = 2.4 - 1.3 + 3.1 - 1.9 = 2.3$$
$$\delta_{41} = 50 - 50 + 2.2 - 1.3 + 3.1 - 1.9 + 1.8 - 1.5 = 2.4$$
$$\delta_{42} = 50 - 50 + 2.2 - 1.3 + 3.1 - 1.9 + 1.8 - 6.4 = -2.5$$
$$\delta_{43} = 50 - 50 + 2.2 - 1.3 + 3.1 - 1.9 = 2.1$$
$$\delta_{44} = 50 - 50 + 2.2 - 1.3 = 0.9.$$

TABLE 7.5

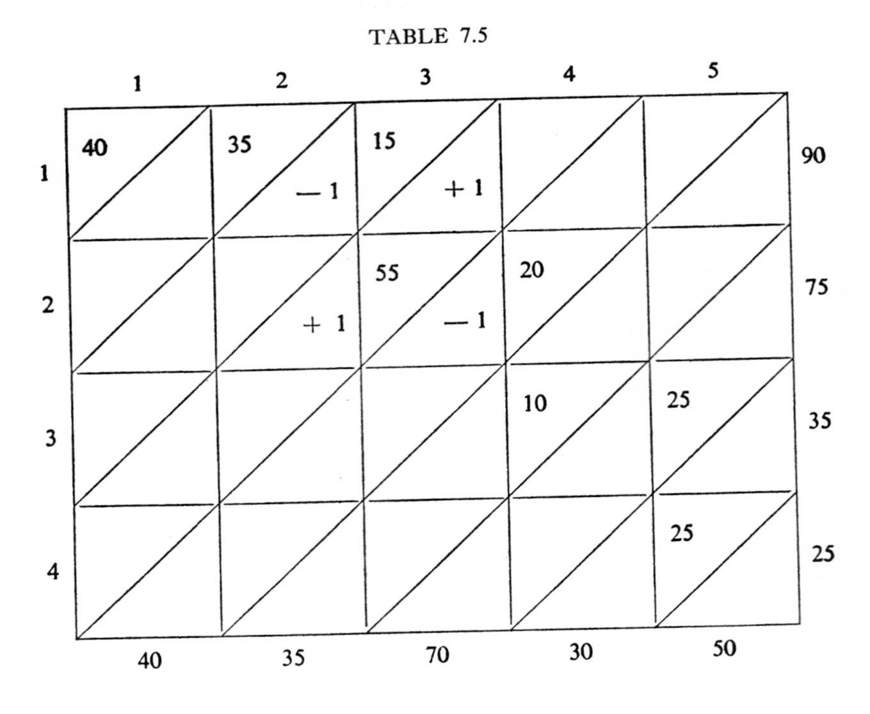

	1	2	3	4	5	
1	40	35 — 1	15 + 1			90
2		+ 1	55 — 1	20		75
3				10	25	35
4					25	25
	40	35	70	30	50	

It will be noticed that each marginal cost is designated by the number of the line and column in which we place a unit. Some of them are negative, in particular δ_{22}, which has the highest negative value, -3.9.

To pass from one basic solution to another, we must "empty" one of the squares and fill a void square with the corresponding quantity.

In Table 7.5 we discover that if we add one unit to square (2, 2), we must subtract one from (2, 3), add one to (1, 3), and subtract one from (1, 2). Squares (1, 2) and (2, 3) contain negative signs; we can only subtract the smaller quantity in these squares, and choose 35. Finally, we add 35 in (2, 2) and (1, 3), and subtract 35 in (1, 2) and (2, 3). The new basic solution which we obtain is given in Table 7.6. The total transport costs have diminished by $3.9 \times 35 = 136.5$, that is 1365 F. For Table 7.6 this is equal to $5455 - 1365 = 4090$ F.

In Table 7.6 we repeat the same procedure by first calculating the marginal costs

$$\begin{array}{ll} \delta_{12} = 2.9 & \delta_{32} = 2.7 \\ \delta_{14} = 1 & \delta_{33} = 2.3 \\ \delta_{15} = -0.4 \leftarrow & \delta_{41} = 2.4 \\ \delta_{21} = 0 & \delta_{42} = 1.4 \\ \delta_{25} = 1.8 & \delta_{43} = 2.1 \\ \delta_{31} = 5.5 & \delta_{44} = 0.9 \end{array}$$

There is only one negative marginal cost δ_{15} and when we consider the sequence of changes corresponding to it, we find that the maximum possible displacement is 20 units. We then obtain Table 7.7, for which the total cost has diminished by $0.4 \times 20 = 80$ F; hence, the cost is now $4090 - 80 = 4010$ F.

Starting with Table 7.7, we now obtain the new marginal costs

$$\begin{array}{ll} \delta_{12} = 3.9 & \delta_{32} = 2.3 \\ \delta_{14} = 1.4 & \delta_{33} = 1.9 \\ \delta_{21} = 0 & \delta_{41} = 2 \\ \delta_{24} = 0.4 & \delta_{42} = 1 \\ \delta_{25} = 2.2 & \delta_{43} = 1.7 \\ \delta_{34} = 5.1 & \delta_{44} = 0.9 \end{array}$$

This time, there are no negative marginal costs, so that the total cost cannot be reduced any further. Hence, the solution giving a total cost of

TABLE 7.6

COST: 4090 F

	1	2	3	4	5	
1	40		50 −1		+1	90
2		35	20 +1	20 −1		75
3				10 +1	25 −1	35
4					25	25
	40	35	70	30	50	

4010 F is the optimal one. It is not the only one, since there is a nil marginal cost, and every exchange beginning with (2, 1) gives a solution, though with the same cost as the above.

Figure 7.2 shows the diagram for the optimal system of transportation. Obviously, the distribution is only valid for the day we have been considering, and a fresh calculation must be made daily. In the simple case which we chose, an experienced calculator could obtain the result in a matter of an hour. On the other hand, with a more complex problem of this type, several hours or even days might be needed for a solution, which is why the algorithm for problems of this type has been programmed to a computer. After the addition of the data for the day, requiring only the perforation of a few cards, a result can then be very quickly obtained, and even when there are numerous points of origin and of destination, the time needed for an answer is still acceptable.

Criticism might be directed at the procedure followed by the supervisor in "starving" depot *e*, which only receives half its requirements,

TABLE 7.7

Cost: 4010 F

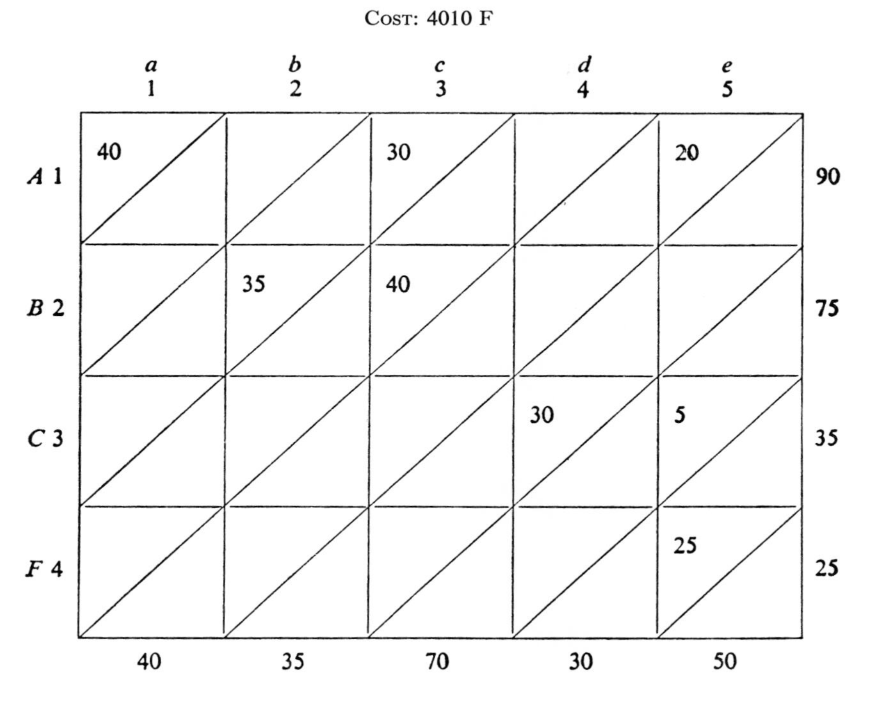

	a 1	*b* 2	*c* 3	*d* 4	*e* 5	
A 1	40		30		20	90
B 2		35	40			75
C 3				30	5	35
F 4					25	25
	40	35	70	30	50	

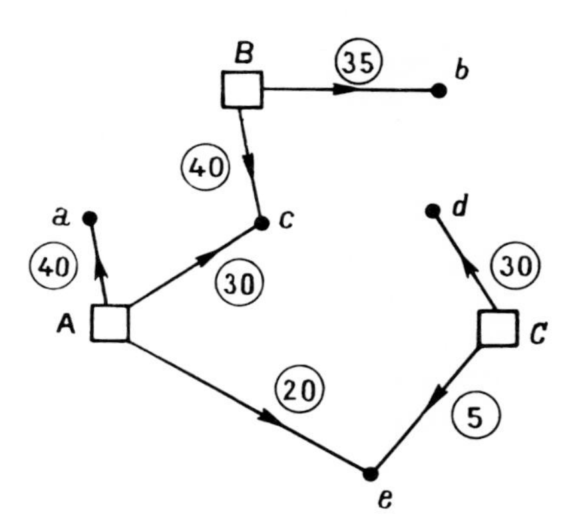

Fig. 7.2

whereas the needs of the other depots are fully met. It need scarcely be pointed out that a different rule might have been followed: an equal sharing of the deficit between the depots, or a procedure corresponding to the economic policy adopted.

The reader may find it interesting to work out the solution (Table 7.8) for the following distribution:

$$a = 36, \quad b = 31, \quad c = 62, \quad d = 27, \quad e = 44.$$

TABLE 7.8

	a	*b*	*c*	*d*	*e*	
A	36		18		36	90
B		31	44			75
C				27	8	35
	36	31	62	27	44	200

The cost in this case is 4103 F, which is 2.3% above the minimum, though the distribution provided is more equitable to the customers.

Transport Problems

A transport problem can always be expressed by the table of transport costs between the points of origin and destination. If we are given the table or *matrix of transport costs* (Table 7.9), any solution of the problem

TABLE 7.9

	Destination				
Origin	Client 1	Client 2	Client 3	Client 4	Available supplies
Depot 1	2	5	4	5	60
Depot 2	1	2	1	4	80
Depot 3	3	1	5	2	60
Customer demand	50	40	70	40	200

can be represented by another table (Table 7.10), in which all the quantities to be transported from a given origin to a given destination are shown.

TABLE 7.10

	1	2	3	4
1	x_{11}	x_{12}	x_{13}	x_{14}
2	x_{21}	x_{22}	x_{23}	x_{24}
3	x_{31}	x_{32}	x_{33}	x_{34}

The quantities x_{11}, x_{12}, x_{13}, and x_{14} to be dispatched from depot 1 to clients 1, 2, 3, and 4 are entered in the first line; similarly, those dispatched from depots 2 and 3 are shown in the second and third lines. The twelve symbols x_{11} to x_{34} are, in fact, the unknows of the problem, and their values must satisfy certain relations, known as the *constraints*.

(I) the quantities dispatched from any depot must equal the available stock at this depot

$$\begin{aligned} x_{11} + x_{12} + x_{13} + x_{14} &= 60, \\ x_{21} + x_{22} + x_{23} + x_{24} &= 80, \\ x_{31} + x_{32} + x_{33} + x_{34} &= 60. \end{aligned} \tag{I}$$

(II) The quantities dispatched to a particular customer must equal the demand of this customer

$$\begin{aligned} x_{11} + x_{21} + x_{31} &= 50, \\ x_{12} + x_{22} + x_{32} &= 40, \\ x_{13} + x_{23} + x_{33} &= 70, \\ x_{14} + x_{24} + x_{34} &= 40, \end{aligned} \tag{II}$$

and, in addition, the constraints must minimize the total transport cost, known as the *economic function*, which can be expressed as

$$\begin{aligned} Z = 2x_{11} + 5x_{12} + 4x_{13} + 5x_{14} \\ +x_{21} + 2x_{22} + x_{23} + 4x_{24} \\ + 3x_{31} + x_{32} + 5x_{33} + 2x_{34}. \end{aligned}$$

All the equations, as well as the function Z, are of the first degree in relation to each of the variables; they completely define the problem, which belongs to the more general class of *linear programs*, as we shall see later.

But the linear program here is a special case: the constraints are expressed by equalities, which indicates that it should not be solved by one of the general methods used for more complex problems in which the constraints are in the form of inequalities. This is why the algorithm described in connection with the problem of *Euphoria*, known as the *steppingstone* method, is to be preferred here.

Let us observe that this new example includes seven constraints; but they are not independent, since the sums of the right members of (I) and (II) are equal. There are, therefore, only six independent equations that represent the constraints. Expressed in a more general form, this means that if there are m lines and n columns in the matrix of costs, the number of independent constraints is equal to $m + n - 1$.

If the problem can be solved, we shall find at least one nonzero variable in each column and in each line, that is, *at least* four nonzero variables in the present case; in more general form, there will be m such nonzero variables, if $m > n$, and n such nonzero variables if $n > m$. See Fig. 7.3.

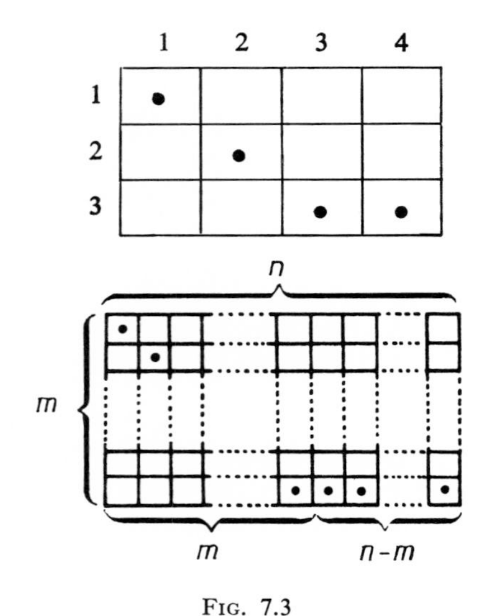

FIG. 7.3

	1	2	3	4	
1	50	10			60
2		30	50		80
3			20	40	60
	50	40	70	40	

Let us now apply the rule of the "northwest corner" to try to obtain a basic solution (that is to say, one which satisfies the two systems of equations, without for the moment concerning ourselves with minimizing the function Z), and let us assume that, as in this case (Fig. 7.4),

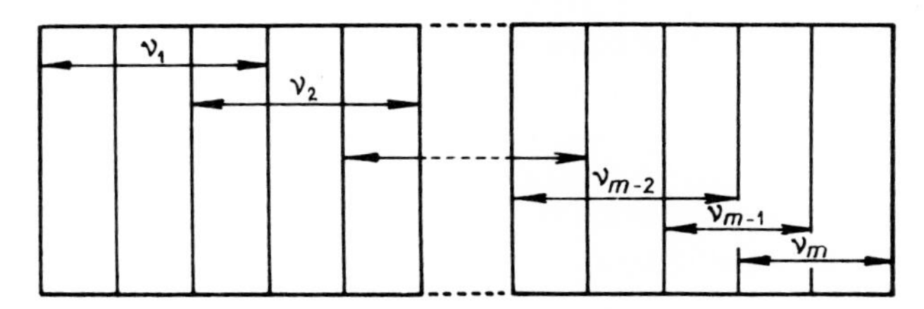

FIG. 7.4

there is always a coincidence of columns in the last occupied square of a line and the first occupied square of the next line, a condition which ensures that the maximal number of squares is filled.

The saturation of line 1 enables us to fill ν_1 squares and to saturate $\nu_1 - 1$ columns; the saturation of line 2 enables us to fill ν_2 squares and to saturate $\nu_2 - 1$ columns, and so on. Finally, the saturation of line m allows us to fill ν_m squares and to saturate ν_m columns.

In all, we have saturated m lines and n columns, so that

$$(\nu_1 - 1) + (\nu_2 - 1) + \cdots + (\nu_{m-1} - 1) + \nu_m + m = m + n$$

or, alternatively,

$$\sum_i \nu_i - (m - 1) + m = m + n$$

and

$$\sum_i \nu_i = m + n - 1.$$

Thus, the greatest number of squares that can be filled is $m + n - 1$. We conclude that the least number of squares containing zeros will be

$$mn - (m + n - 1) = (m - 1)(n - 1),$$

and the greatest number will be $n(m - 1)$ or $m(n - 1)$, depending on whether $n > m$ or $m > n$.

Furthermore, to return to our example, six equations allow us to express six of the variables as functions of the other variables. In particular, let us take as variables those of the basic solution, provided by the rule of the northwest corner

$$\begin{aligned}
x_{11} &= 50 - x_{21} - x_{31}, \\
x_{12} &= 10 - x_{13} - x_{14} + x_{21} + x_{31}, \\
x_{22} &= 30 + x_{13} + x_{14} - x_{21} - x_{31} - x_{32}, \\
x_{23} &= 50 - x_{13} - x_{14} - x_{24} + x_{31} + x_{32}, \\
x_{33} &= 20 + x_{14} + x_{24} - x_{31} - x_{32}, \\
x_{34} &= 40 - x_{14} - x_{24}
\end{aligned}$$

If we substitute these values in function Z, we obtain

$$\begin{aligned}
Z = 440 + 0 \cdot x_{13} + 4 \cdot x_{14} + 2 \cdot x_{21} \\
+ 6 \cdot x_{24} + 0 \cdot x_{31} - 5 \cdot x_{32}.
\end{aligned}$$

Let us now calculate the δ_{ij} quantities in the way already explained:

$$\delta_{13} = 0, \quad \delta_{14} = 4, \quad \delta_{21} = 2, \quad \delta_{24} = 6, \quad \delta_{31} = 0, \quad \delta_{32} = -5.$$

We observe that the δ_{ij} elements are the same as the coefficients, in the expression of Z, of the x_{ij} quantities which do not appear in the basic solution chosen. Indeed, Z is equal to 440 here, since all the x_{ij} elements that do not appear in the basic solution are zero.

We are not concerned with the positive δ_{ij} quantities, which would yield higher values for Z, nor with the zero ones, which would yield equivalent solutions. On the contrary, the sole negative δ_{ij} will give us a lower value for Z. The inspection of the expressions yielding the variables chosen for the basic solution as a function of the other variables shows that we can make x_{33} equal to 0 by taking as our maximum $x_{32} = 20$, which decreases the economic function by $5 \times 20 = 100$.

TABLE 7.11

	1	2	3	4
1	50	10		
2		10	70	
3		20		40

Table 7.11 provides the new solution, with $Z = 340$. As before, we now obtain

$$Z = 340 + 0 \cdot x_{13} - 1 \cdot x_{14} + 2 \cdot x_{21} + 1 \cdot x_{24} + 5 \cdot x_{31} + 5 \cdot x_{33}.$$

In consequence, since

$$x_{12} = 10 - x_{13} - x_{14} + x_{21} + x_{31},$$
$$x_{32} = 20 + x_{14} + x_{24} - x_{31} - x_{33},$$

and

$$x_{34} = 40 - x_{14} - x_{24},$$

we can take for our maximum $x_{14} = 10$, whence we obtain a new reduction of $1 \times 10 = 10$ in the economic function and Table 7.12.

TABLE 7.12

$Z = 330$

	1	2	3	4
1	50			10
2		10	70	
3		30		30

It is easy to calculate

$$Z = 330 + 1 \cdot x_{12} + 1 \cdot x_{13} + 1 \cdot x_{21} + 1 \cdot x_{24} + 4 \cdot x_{31} + 5 \cdot x_{33},$$

which shows that the problem has been solved since Z cannot be diminished any further.

The method we have just used on a problem in which $m = 3$ and $n = 4$ is valid whatever the values of m and n.

If there are $m + n - 1$ independent equations, it is possible to express the same number of variables as a function of the

$$mn - (m + n - 1) = (m - 1)(n - 1)$$

other equations and of the constant second members, whence we can express Z in the form

$$Z = K + \sum_i \sum_j \delta_{ij} x_{ij},$$

where the i and j quantities indicate the $(m - 1)(n - 1)$ variables that remain when we have chosen $m + n - 1$ variables to form a basic solution by the northwest-corner rule. The presence of the δ_{ij} terms then allows us, with the same justification, to apply the algorithm of the steppingstone.

We shall not study the general case where the rule of the northwest corner produces more than $(m - 1)(n - 1)$ zeros, but we shall briefly treat an example.

With the same table of costs as before, let us consider a modification of the available supplies (Table 7.13). In this case the rule of the northwest corner gives us Table 7.14 which, instead of six, contains seven nil

TABLE 7.13

	1	2	3	4	
1	2	5	4	5	50
2	1	2	1	4	90
3	3	1	5	2	60
	50	40	70	40	200

variables, and could have contained eight with available supplies of 50, 40, and 110.

The calculation of the δ_{ij} quantities is now more complicated than when there were only $(m - 1)(n - 1)$ nil variables. In the case of δ_{12} there is no difficulty: any units removed from square (1, 2) must be placed in (1, 1), and this can only be compensated for by transferring the same number of units from (2, 2) to (2, 1), whence

$$\delta_{12} = 5 + 1 - 2 - 2 = 2.$$

TABLE 7.14

$Z = 410$

	1	2	3	4
1	50			
2		40	50	
3			20	40

But in the case of δ_{13}, though the displaced units must come from (1, 1), the compensating adjustment may be made either from (3, 2) to (2, 1) or from (3, 3) to (3, 1), so that there are alternative values for δ_{13} :

$$\delta'_{13} = 4 + 1 - 2 - 1 = 2. \qquad \delta''_{13} = 4 + 3 - 2 - 5 = 0.$$

Again, if we take δ_{31}, we find

$$\delta'_{31} = \underset{(3,1)}{3} - \underset{(3,3)}{5} + \underset{(2,3)}{1} - \underset{(2,2)}{2} + \underset{(1,2)}{5} - \underset{(1,1)}{2} = 0,$$

$$\delta''_{31} = \underset{(3,1)}{3} - \underset{(3,3)}{5} + \underset{(1,3)}{4} - \underset{(1,1)}{2} = 0,$$

$$\delta'''_{31} = \underset{(3,1)}{3} - \underset{(3,4)}{2} + \underset{(1,4)}{5} - \underset{(1,1)}{2} = 4.$$

The calculations are, therefore, longer than with the assumption of only one possible δ_{ij} quantity for each empty square. In the present example we should soon find that one of the δ_{32} terms is the only negative one, with a value of -5 and the possibility of a displacement of 20 units, that is, a decrease of 100 in the economic function.

The solution is given by Table 7.15, in which all the elements are positive; it is therefore optimal.

Remark 1. If we wish to avoid calculating numerous δ_{ij} terms when the rule of the northwest corner has caused more than $(m - 1)(n - 1)$ nil variables to appear in the problem, we can always come back to a basic solution having that exact number of variables without being too far removed from the optimum. For example, if we place the maximum of units totaling 130 in the squares with the lowest cost (1) of Table 7.3, we shall obtain Table 7.16.

TABLE 7.15

$Z = 310$

	1	2	3	4
1	50			
2		20	70	
3		20		40

This basic solution, adopted as a result of elementary economic reasoning, is decidedly superior to that of Table 7.14. In addition, it includes six nil variables only, and there is only a single series of δ_{ij} terms to be calculated. We find that $\delta_{22} = -1$ and by displacing 20 units we discover the optimum (Table 7.15) which, of course, can only be checked by calculating all the δ_{ij} quantities.

TABLE 7.16

$Z = 330$

	1	2	3	4
1	30			20
2	20		70	
3		40		20

Remark 2. In problems depending on the algorithm of the steppingstone, it is possible to obtain several negative δ_{ij} elements, and it is then only logical to choose the one which, when multiplied by the displaced quantity, gives the greatest decrease of the economic function.

Remark 3. It is possible to approach the optimum (and even sometimes obtain it directly) before applying the steppingstone method, by another method which, as can easily be proved, leads to a basic solution. This is Houthakker's method, based on the search for *mutually preferable* costs. Another equally satisfactory method is that of Balas–Hammer.

Transport problems are of fundamental importance in such fields as the petroleum industry, metallurgy, etc., and once the algorithm of the steppingstone has been programmed to a computer, it is possible to solve them for every short management period that may be considered.

An Algorithm for a High Number of Costs

A variety of methods can be used to solve transport problems if the number of costs is not too high. Basically, these depend on programming the matrix of costs to a computer, so that each line and column can be explored by the machine. But the time needed for a solution increases very rapidly in proportion to the dimensions of the problem.

For instance, with a matrix of 500×1000, or 500,000 relations, there will not be more than 1499 variables to be determined, but with each iteration of the calculations the number of δ_{ij} quantities to be found reaches 498,501. It will be appreciated that even a very large computer would be unable to solve such a problem in a reasonable time by the steppingstone method.

The procedure that we shall now describe very briefly[1] depends on the following steps:

(1) to program only the costs of relations that are economically acceptable[2];

(2) to carry out the first allocation of the quantities to be transported so as to obtain a basic solution by considering the lowest costs in accordance with the concept discussed in Remark 1;

(3) to optimize step by step the *dual costs*, as they are termed in this procedure.

For an example let us take the matrix shown in Table 7.17, which shows not only the transport costs, but also, on the right, the available supplies at the points of origin 1, 2, and 3, and at the bottom, the demands at the destinations 11, 12, 13, and 14.

Stage I. To find an *initial basic solution*, we classify the costs in increasing order and then allocate the maximal quantities in this order, taking into account the limitations imposed both by the availability and the demands. The classification and allocation for the present example are shown in Tables 7.18 and 7.19.

[1] We wish to thank A. Le Garff for this algorithm, which he developed in July 1961.

[2] Under normal circumstances no one would consider supplying Paris with gasoline from Marseilles, when there are refineries situated much nearer at Basse-Seine, Dunkirk, and even in Alsace.

TABLE 7.17

	11	12	13	14	Available supplies
1	100	100	0	1	9
2	25	20	15	19	11
3	15	30	4	100	8
Demand	6	9	5	8	

TABLE 7.18

Column	13	14	13	11	13	14	12	11	12	14	11	12
Line	1	1	3	3	2	2	2	2	3	3	1	1
e_{ij}	0	1	4	15	15	19	20	25	30	100	100	100
x_{ij}	5	4	0	6	0	4	7	0	2	0	0	0

TABLE 7.19

	11	12	13	14	
1			5	4	9
2		7		4	11
3	6	2			8
	6	9	5	8	

It is clear that a basic solution is obtained, since the technique of allocation (except in cases of degeneracy[3]) depends on saturating a line *or* a column at each step, with the exception of the last one when, due to the equality between the total available supplies and the total demand, we are led to saturate a line *and* a column simultaneously. The number

[3] To avoid saturating both a line and a column simultaneously before the final step in a case of degeneracy, all that is required is to add $+\epsilon$ to the corresponding element of the column of availabilities.

of allocations is, therefore, clearly $m + n - 1$, if there are m lines and n columns in the table of costs.

STAGE II. Our aim is now, if possible, to improve the initial basic solution obtained in stage I.

With this object, we calculate (Table 7.20) the dual costs in the following manner. We take $v_j = 0$ for the maximal cost allocated, and

TABLE 7.20

	11	12	13	14	$u_i \downarrow$
1			0	1	2
2		20		19	20
3	15	30			30
$v_j \rightarrow$	−15	0	−2	−1	

with this assumption we can at once calculate all the u_i and v_j elements from the fact that, for the allocated costs, we must have $c_{ij} = u_i + v_j$, and because a total of $m + n - 1$ squares have been filled.

The result of this method of calculating the dual costs is that the u_i and v_j elements which correspond to the maximal allocated cost are the maxima of their respective column and line.

The optimal solution will not have been obtained in stage I if there is at least one c_{ij} element corresponding to a nil x_{ij} (that is, to a nonallocated square) such that $c_{ij} < u_i + v_j$, where the terms of the right member have been found in the preceding calculation.[4] In addition, it can be proved that

$$c_{ij} - (u_i + v_j) = \delta_{ij},$$

where the δ_{ij} quantities are the marginal costs which we used for the algorithm of the steppingstone.

[4] It should be realized that this method of calculating the u_i and v_j elements was adopted merely because it is convenient for the purpose of the proof, and that any other method might have been used.

If c_{mn} represents the last allocated cost (Table 7.21), and if we consider a c_{pq} element situated farther to the right on the line of the c_{ij} quantities, we have from the construction of the table,

$$c_{pq} \geqslant c_{mn} .$$

TABLE 7.21

Column					
Line					
c_{ij}		c_{mn}		c_{pq}	
x_{ij}		$x_{mn} \neq 0$			

Now in Table 7.20, $u_p \leqslant u_m$ and $v_q \leqslant v_n$ so that

$$u_p + v_q \leqslant u_m + v_n = c_{mn} ,$$

that is to say,

$$\delta_{pq} = c_{pq} - (u_p + v_q) \geqslant c_{pq} - c_{mn}$$

and

$$\delta_{pq} \geqslant 0.$$

From this we deduce that the c_{pq} elements beyond c_{mn} can be discarded in our search for a matrix representing the total mimimal cost. Every $c_{pq} \geqslant c_{mn}$ will therefore be eliminated from now on, and our search for negative δ_{ij} elements will be restricted to the $x_{ij} = 0$ terms which precede the last allocated cost.

Table 7.22 shows that in our example there are only two negative δ_{ij} elements, and we now look for the permutations which provide their value. To do this, we scan the table of initial allocations ($x_{ij} \neq 0$) and mark on a line of reference the successive numbers of the lines and columns of the squares which constitute the chain of permutation. For $\delta_{3,13} = -24$ the chain will be found to be

$$(3, 13) \rightarrow (3, 12) \rightarrow (12, 2) \rightarrow (14, 2) \rightarrow (14, 1) \rightarrow (13, 1).$$

TABLE 7.22

Column	13	14	13	11	13	14	12	11	12	14	11	12
Line	1	1	3	3	2	2	2	2	3	3	1	1
c_{ij}	0	1	4	15	15	19	20	25	30	100	100	100
x_{ij}	5	4	0	6	0	4	7	0	2	0	0	0
u_i			30		20			20				
v_j			—2		—2			—15				
$u_i + v_j$			28		18			5				
δ_{ij}			—24		—3			20				

This allows a decrease in the total cost of $2 \times 24 = 48$; see Table 7.23.

TABLE 7.23

Column	13	14	11	14	12	12
Line	1	1	3	2	2	3
c_{ij}	0	1	15	19	20	30
x_{ij}	5	4	6	4	7	2

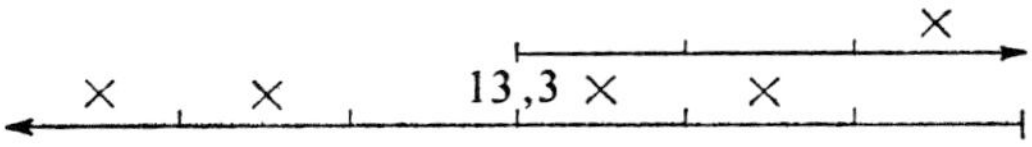

×

× × 13,3 × ×

The chain corresponding to $\delta_{2,13} = -3$ is

$$(2, 13) \to (2, 14) \to (14, 1) \to (13, 1);$$

this allows a decrease of the total cost by $4 \times 3 = 12$; see Table 7.24.

We shall therefore choose the first chain, and obtain the improved solution of Table 7.25.

TABLE 7.24

Column	13	14	11	14	12	12
Line	1	1	3	2	2	3
c_{ij}	0	1	15	19	20	30
x_{ij}	5	4	6	4	7	2

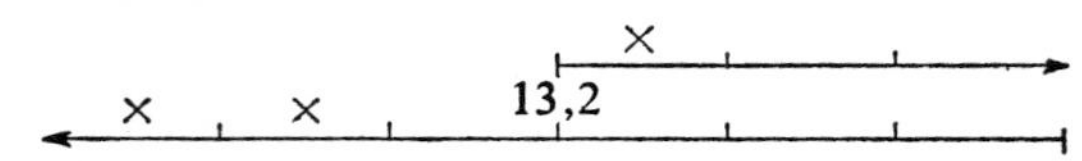

TABLE 7.25

	11	12	13	14
1			3	6
2		9		2
3	6		2	

TABLE 7.26

	11	12	13	14	u_i
1			0	1	2
2		20		19	20
3	15		4		6
v_j	9	0	−2	−1	

STAGE III. Starting with Table 7.25 we calculate the new dual costs (Table 7.26). We no longer possess the property that the costs corresponding to the maximal allocated cost are themselves maximal, but this is not of importance for the remainder of the problem.

We again find that two δ_{ij} elements are negative (Table 7.27). For the first one, $\delta_{2,13} = -3$, the corresponding chain is

$$(2, 13) \rightarrow (2, 14) \rightarrow (1, 14) \rightarrow (1, 13)$$

TABLE 7.27

Column	13	14	13	11	13	14	12	11	12
Line	1	1	3	3	2	2	2	2	3
c_{ij}	0	1	4	15	15	19	20	25	30
x_{ij}	3	6	2	6	0	2	9	0	0
u_i					20			20	6
v_j					—2			9	0
$u_i + v_j$					18			29	6
δ_{ij}					—3			—4	24

TABLE 7.28

Column	13	14	13	11	14	12
Line	1	1	3	3	2	2
c_{ij}	0	1	4	15	19	20
x_{ij}	3	6	2	6	2	9

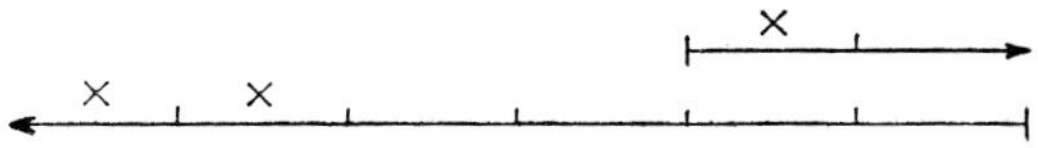

TABLE 7.29

Column	13	14	13	11	14	12
Line	1	1	3	3	2	2
c_{ij}	0	1	4	15	19	20
x_{ij}	3	6	2	6	2	9

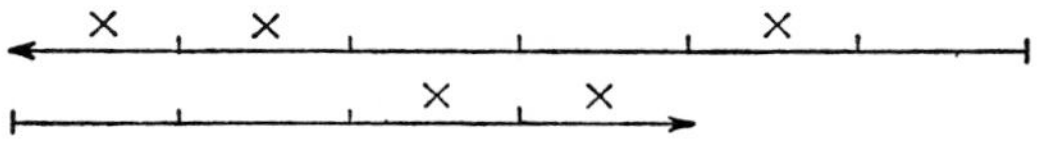

with a gain of $2 \times 3 = 6$; see Table 7.28. For the second, $\delta_{2,11} = -4$, the chain is

$$(2, 11) \to (2, 14) \to (1, 14) \to (1, 13) \to (3, 13) \to (3, 11)$$

with a gain of $2 \times 4 = 8$; see Table 7.29. Our new solution is given in Table 7.30.

TABLE 7.30

	11	12	13	14
1			1	8
2	2	9		
3	4		4	

TABLE 7.31

					u_i
			0	1	11
	25	20			25
	15		4		15
v_j	0	—5	—11	—10	

TABLE 7.32

Column	13	14	13	11	13	14	12	11	12
Line	1	1	3	3	2	2	2	2	3
c_{ij}	0	1	4	15	15	19	20	25	30
x_{ij}	1	8	4	4	0	0	9	2	0
u_i					25	25			15
v_j					—11	—10			—5
$u_i + v_j$					14	15			10
δ_{ij}					1	4			20

Now we return to the commencement of stage III in order to calculate the dual costs (Table 7.31), stopping as soon as all the δ_{ij} elements are positive (Table 7.32). If we find any nil elements, we shall be forced to examine equivalent solutions.

The time saved by the use of this algorithm is considerable. Using the method of the steppingstone there would have been five iterations with 36 δ_{ij} quantities to be calculated and 16 allocations to be examined. With the procedure we have used here only two iterations were required with nine δ_{ij} quantites and four allocations.

Moreover, in order to explain the new method we purposely avoided using previous examples; had we chosen those of Tables 6.1 and 6.8, only one iteration would have been needed.

CHAPTER 8

WHEN SHOULD I SELL MY GOLONDRINA?

(Replacement of Depreciating Equipment. Investments and Discounting)

The Golondrina is a European-style automobile which is very popular in Mexico. Startling acceleration, smoothness of the swallow (hence its name), 140 kilometers an hour on the freeways and, in spite of all this, no sign of overheating when climbing Insurgentes Avenue at 1 km/c (one kilometer per cigarette) in the rush hour. One of our friends owned a Golondrina and was thinking of replacing it by a new one. At what date was it advisable to make the change?

The purchase price (henceforth represented as A_0) is 35,000 pesos for a new Golondrina. As with other cars, it is not difficult to estimate the cost of maintenance, repairs, and insurance, as well as the quarterly depreciation $A_0[1 - \varphi(t)]$, giving a *residual value* of $A_0\varphi(t)$. For vehicles with normal use, the mileage does not appreciably affect the resale price, although it naturally has a marked influence on the running costs and repairs. Table 8.1 shows both the depreciation and the

TABLE 8.1

Number of months	6	12	18	24	30	36	42	48	54	60
Depreciation $A_0[1 - \varphi(t)]$	5570	12,250	14,185	17,500	20,280	22,625	24,650	26,250	27,000	28,810
Cumulative cost $\psi(t)$	620	1500	2740	4500	6985	10,500	16,000	24,500	34,000	46,500

cumulative costs for the Golondrina at six-monthly periods. It should be observed that in Mexico the resale price is little affected by the season, since there is no real winter.

When deciding about a resale, two criteria are available: the cost per month or the cost per kilometer. Of course, the desire to impress one's neighbor or to provide a pleasant surprise for one's wife may also be valid criteria in Mexico just as anywhere else, but these lead to studies which would defy even the most experienced worker in operations research. On the other hand, the first two criteria can form the basis of a study open to anyone prepared to undertake some simple calculations.

What method should we adopt to find the minimal monthly cost? (Equally, we could find this per kilometer, although it would involve more calculation.)

If A_0 is the purchase price, the resale price can be expected to show a regular monthly decrease. Let us use $A_0\varphi(t)$ for the resale price after a period t, where $\varphi(t)$ is a function representing the variation in the residual value. Sometimes it is true, in the case of cars, there is a sharp drop from 1 to $1 - k$ at the very beginning of the curve: a day after the purchase, the automobile has lost an appreciable amount of its value. On the other hand, the opposite phenomenon occurs when automobiles are in short supply and there is a waiting list for purchasers.

The usual shape of the curve $\varphi(t)$ is that shown in Fig. 8.1. The

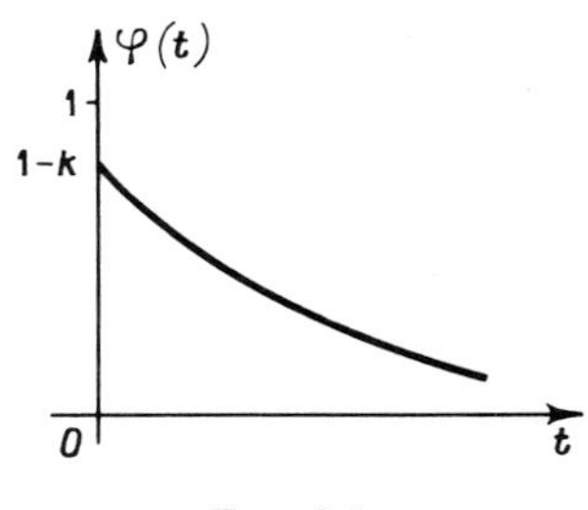

Fig. 8.1

cumulative expenses of repairs, maintenance, and driving costs, which will be represented by another function $\psi(t)$, have curves similar to the one in Fig. 8.2.

For a period t, the total cost is therefore,

$$\Gamma(t) = A_0 - A_0\varphi(t) + \psi(t). \tag{1}$$

How, it may be asked, can we compare the expense incurred with two vehicles of different characteristics and different purchase prices?

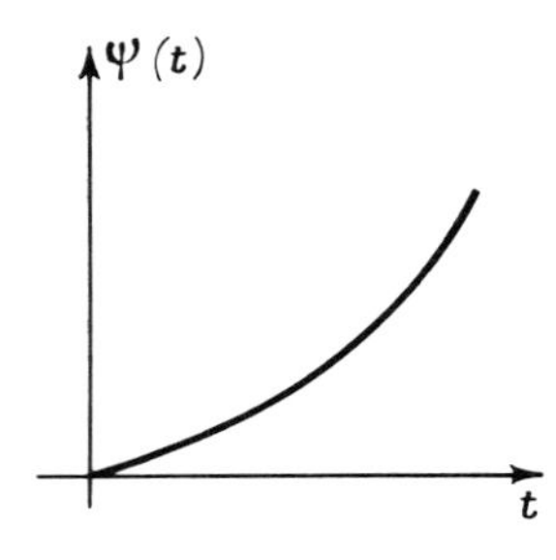

FIG. 8.2

To make the comparison, let us rid ourselves of any emotional criteria with regard to the possession of this asset, and regard it from a purely economic standpoint. The quantity which enables us to form an economic comparison between two or more vehicles of a different make, or used for different purposes, is that of the average monthly cost of each, calculated over the period between their purchase and their resale or relegation to the scrap heap. The criterion usually chosen is the quantity

$$\gamma(t) = \frac{\Gamma(t)}{t} = \frac{A_0[1 - \varphi(t)] + \psi(t)}{t}, \tag{2}$$

so that if we are concerned with the optimal date of resale for a particular vehicle it is logical to choose one which will minimize the average monthly cost.

Since we already know the depreciation and cumulative costs for the Golondrina, we can easily obtain Table 8.2 by means of the simple formulas given earlier, and from this table we discover that the optimal period of ownership is 30 months.

TABLE 8.2

Number of months (t)	6	12	18	24	30	36	42	48	54	60
Depreciation $A_0[1 - \varphi(t)]$	5570	12,250	14,185	17,500	20,280	22,625	24,650	26,250	27,000	28,810
Cumulative cost $\psi(t)$	620	1500	2740	4500	6985	10,500	16,000	24,500	34,000	46,500
$\Gamma(t)$	6190	13,750	16,925	22,000	27,265	33,125	40,650	50,750	61,000	75,310
$\gamma(t) = \Gamma(t)/t$	1031	1146	940	916	909	920	968	1057	1129	1255

With the values obtained in Table 8.2, it is easy to draw the curve $\gamma(t)$ shown in Fig. 8.3, which clearly reveals to what an extent the average cost depends on the period of use.

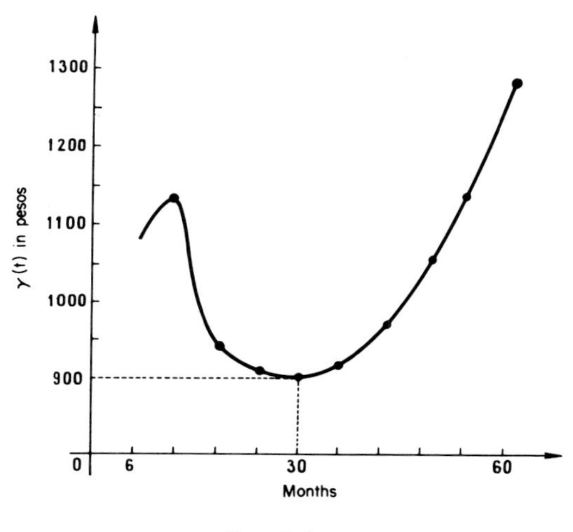

FIG. 8.3

However, from our knowledge of our Mexican friend, we can be sure that he will not wait 30 months before buying a new car, for he is very attached to his wife, and she greatly appreciates a handsome new automobile. With little doubt, he will provide her with the satisfaction of a new Golondrina after a year, and in doing so his finacial sacrifice will amount to

$$(1146 - 900) \cdot 12 = 246 \times 12 = 2952 \text{ pesos},$$

or about 3000 pesos. But, to be valid, this result assumes the purchase of a car of the same type, which would obviously not always be true. Thus, to make a strict comparison between two resale policies, we should take account of all the cars which will be bought later; an impossible undertaking, since the cost of these unknown vehicles cannot be reckoned. This is why, in practice, we accept a calculation based on the period of use of the present automobile without being concerned with the one which will replace it.

In such cases, economists are interested in two quantities: the *temporal marginal cost* (or variation of the monthly cost), and the average cost. These are

$$\Gamma'(t) \qquad \text{and} \qquad \frac{\Gamma(t)}{t},$$

where $\Gamma'(t)$ represents the *derivative*, in the mathematical sense of the term. Since the values are given for six-monthly periods for the Golondrina, this derivative or temporal variation is easily calculated by the formula

$$\frac{\Gamma(t) - \Gamma(t-1)}{6}.$$

Common sense urges us to follow the rule: sell the car when the variation of cost per unit of time is greater than the average cost. But, as this is not obvious, and the proof is a simple one, we shall explain it by means of the concept of marginal cost or variation of the average cost.

If I sell my car today (time $t - 1$), the average cost will be

$$\frac{\Gamma(t-1)}{t-1};$$

if I sell it a period later (time t), it will be $\Gamma(t)/t$. As long as

$$\frac{\Gamma(t)}{t} < \frac{\Gamma(t-1)}{t-1},$$

it is to my advantage to keep my car. The above expression can also be written

$$\frac{\Gamma(t-1)}{t-1} - \frac{\Gamma(t)}{t} > 0,$$

$$\Gamma(t-1) - (t-1)\,\Gamma(t) > 0$$

or

$$\Gamma(t)/t > \Gamma(t) - \Gamma(t-1);$$

whence the rule.

In Mexico, however, there is a very high rate of interest on loans, sometimes exceeding 10%, due, among other reasons, to the venturesome spirit of the people of this country. Would it not be useful to rework the problem by introducing a rate of interest?

Spending 100 pesos today and 100 pesos in a year's time is not the same thing in a country with a high borrowing rate. To obtain a valid comparison, we must find what sum will today be equivalent to 100 pesos in a year's time. With a rate of interest amounting to α, it would be necessary to invest $100/(1 - \alpha)$ pesos to obtain 100 pesos a year hence.

We shall, accordingly, compare the policies of resale at 6, 12 months, and so on, by bringing all the expenses back to the time of purchase—by *discounting*. We shall use formulas where the tax will, for instance, be 5% a quarter, and where t will represent the number of quarters which have elapsed. With an introduced rate, the *depreciation* will be

$$A_0\left[1 - \frac{\varphi(t)}{(1.05)^t}\right] \qquad \text{(instead of } A_0[1 - \varphi(t)]\text{);}$$

while the *running costs* (calculated quarterly) will amount to

$$\frac{\psi(t) - \psi(t-1)}{(1.05)^t} \qquad [\text{instead of } \psi(t) - \psi(t-1)].$$

Table 8.3 gives the new values obtained for $\Gamma(t)$ and $\gamma(t)$ by means

TABLE 8.3

Number of months	6	12	18	24	30	36	42	48	54	60
$\Gamma(t)$ discounted	7530	15,630	20,430	24,420	29,240	34,090	40,890	46,390	53,950	61,920
$\gamma(t)$ discounted	1255	1302	1135	1017	974	948	973	966	999	1032

of the formulas which take discounting into account. Figure 8.4 shows the curve of $\Gamma(t)$ for both cases, and it will be seen that the optimal discounted cost is higher and that the optimal period before resale is increased by six months.

According to modern econonomics, a car which has been kept for 12 months and the same car kept for 18 months constitute *separate* assets, and we are obliged to take discounting into consideration except where the rate is very low. From Table 8.3, we find that the optimal period of use is 36 months.

This shows that the sacrifice of our Mexican friend in buying a new car to please his wife was considerably higher if discounting is taken into account, and amounted to

$$(1302 - 948) \cdot 12 = 354 \times 12 = 4248 \text{ pesos.}$$

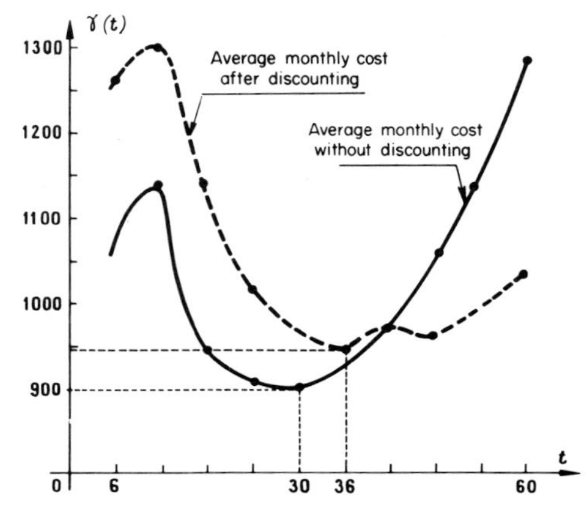

FIG. 8.4

Thus, the marginal cost of a decision which is not optimal can be evaluated, and in the last analysis this is what is important.

It can be useful to know the overall cost of a car per kilometer, and in calculating this the detailed expenses must all be taken into account, so that an analytical study proves difficult and we have to be satisfied with approximate formulas. Here is one drawn up applicable to France[1]:

$$p = \frac{EC}{100} + \frac{HQ + T}{V} + \frac{A + R - Z}{K} + F$$
$$+ \frac{U}{K}(12G + X + I + Y) + \frac{PN}{K},$$

where

A is the purchase price of the vehicle, including taxes and delivery charges;

C is the gasoline consumption per 100 km in liters;

E is the purchase price of a liter of fuel;

F is the cost of mechanical repairs, cleaning, and polishing;

G is the monthly rent of a garage;

H is the price of a liter of motor oil;

I is the annual interest on the capital invested in the purchase and reconditioning of the car (the latter only in the case of job-lots);

[1] From *Auto Journal*, Dec. 1 (1961).

K is the mileage in km chosen as the basis for calculating the resale price;
N is the number of tires required for K;
P is the price of a tire;
Q is the capacity in liters of oil of the sump, to which, if necessary, should be added the amount of oil needed between oil changes;
R is the cost of repairs which have already been paid for or are to be expected during normal use (in the case of a new car $R = 0$);
T is the cost of greasing and related maintenance;
U is the period of use decided upon, expressed in years;
V is the mileage in km between oil changes;
X is the annual insurance premium;
Y is the special annual tax imposed on cars in France;
Z is the residual value of the car at the time of resale.

It is possible to establish more complicated formulas which take account of cumulative effects and discounting. The variations in the running cost per kilometer for different annual mileages are shown in Fig. 8.5. These curves are intended for the case of the Golondrina, but almost all cars would have similar ones. In observing them, we should note the considerable decrease in the running cost per kilometer as a function of the period of use.

To obtain a complete picture, we should, in fact, introduce a number of other factors. Used-car dealers are well aware that the residual value

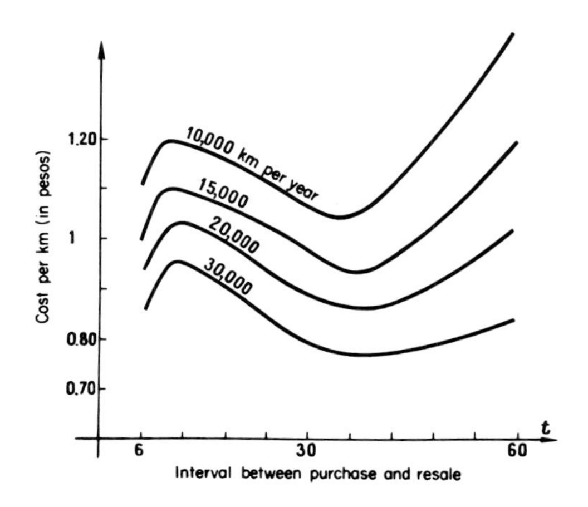

FIG. 8.5

does not only depend on the age of the vehicle or on the mileage: the quotation for certain makes includes a value which takes account of material and psychological factors. Again, one vehicle has been carefully driven, another has been treated without any regard for the mechanism. One car will have been regularly and conscientiously maintenanced, another will be in an advanced stage of disintegration. There are indeed people who maintain that the mere fact that the last owner was a woman is sufficient reason to reduce its resale value. But such views are expressed by ungallant and ill-intentioned persons, and we refuse to subscribe to their opinions.

Investments and Discounting

The problems of investment, which we shall, as far as possible, treat from a commercial standpoint, raise awkward questions about which economists are not always in agreement.

A businessman obviously cannot control the commercial area external to his particular venture: he is subject to numerous constraints, such as prices over which he can have but a small influence. If today he should decide to make an investment, he not only immobilizes a part of his capital, but he also freezes it by acquiring material, which is immediately subject to the effects of obsolescence due to the rapid increase of progress.

He also undertakes risks, the most serious being that he may go bankrupt due to the uncertainty of the future. How is he to evaluate these risks? Should he assume that *nature* will be systematically hostile, and that competition is a fight to the finish?

Again, the businessman has a social role to play. His investment, with that of others, is a basic factor in economic growth, and contributes to employment. Is he, or is he not, to take these factors into account when weighing his decisions? We shall examine some of these questions later, especially in Chapter 14, but we shall prudently leave others undiscussed.

For the moment let us simply consider the case of a businessman who has the choice between two types of equipment with different purchase prices and varying returns.

(1) Machine A is supposed to last four years. It costs 50,000 F, maintenance amounts to 2000 F a year, and its residual value is 10,000 F.

Its output is 10,000 articles a year, selling at 10 F each; the cost of raw materials, tooling, and labor amounts to 70% of this price.

(2) Machine B is supposed to last six years and costs 65,000 F. Its maintenance costs are represented by an arithmetical progression with a base of 2000 F and an annual difference of 1000 F. Its residual value is 15,000 F, and it can produce 14,000 examples of the same article a year.

We can draw the curves of the cumulative profits relating to the two machines. These curves (Fig. 8.6) are such that they intersect (with linear variations in the intervals) at time 1.36 for a cumulative revenue of $-10{,}820$. At this point curve B, which was previously below curve A, crosses it and henceforth dominates it. Again by linear interpolation, B recovers its costs after 1.64 years and A recovers them after 1.75 years.

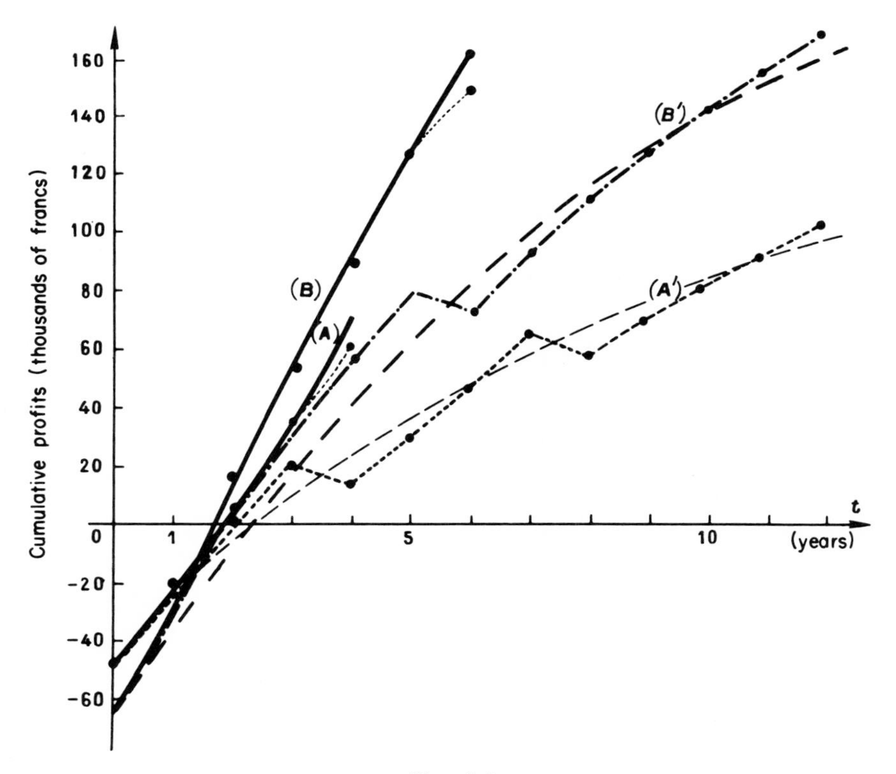

Fig. 8.6

What conclusions are we to draw from these facts? Not many, and this mainly for two reasons:

(a) The durations of the two investments are not the same.

(b) Our representation takes no account of the discount rate, and spending a Franc today is not the same thing as spending a Franc a year, two years, or six years from now.

It should at once be obvious that we cannot compare two machines with different life expectancies, for this would be to assume that our business ceases as soon as one of them is out of service, whereas it continues as long as the other is functioning. Hence, we must assume either that production continues indefinitely, at least with a very large number of periods, new machines of the same type replacing those that are scrapped, or that it continues with an adequate horizon which could be the common multiple of the two periods. Accordingly, in the present problem we could choose a horizon of 24 years, but we shall select one of 12 years in order to simplify our calculations.

We shall next choose a rate of discount of 10% (again to simplify our calculations), although in practice the size of the rate is obviously of fundamental importance. We shall have:

Discounted profit $B(i)$ from machine A

$$-50{,}000 + \frac{29{,}000}{1.1} + \frac{28{,}000}{(1.1)^2} + \frac{27{,}000}{(1.1)^3} + \frac{26{,}000 - 40{,}000}{(1.1)^4} + \frac{29{,}000}{(1.1)^5}$$

$$+ \frac{28{,}000}{(1.1)^6} + \frac{27{,}000}{(1.1)^7} + \frac{26{,}000 - 40{,}000}{(1.1)^8} + \frac{29{,}000}{(1.1)^9}$$

$$+ \frac{28{,}000}{(1.1)^{10}} + \frac{27{,}000}{(1.1)^{11}} + \frac{36{,}000}{1\,(1.1)^{12}} = 100{,}351.$$

Discounted profit $B(i)$ from machine B

$$-65{,}000 + \frac{40{,}000}{1.1} + \frac{39{,}000}{(1.1)^2} + \frac{38{,}000}{(1.1)^3} + \frac{37{,}000}{(1.1)^4} + \frac{36{,}000}{(1.1)^5}$$

$$+ \frac{35{,}000 - 50{,}000}{(1.1)^6} + \frac{40{,}000}{(1.1)^7} + \frac{39{,}000}{(1.1)^8} + \frac{38{,}000}{(1.1)^9}$$

$$+ \frac{37{,}000}{(1.1)^{10}} + \frac{36{,}000}{(1.1)^{11}} + \frac{50{,}000}{(1.1)^{12}} = 168{,}949.$$

For equipment A, the average annual profit with discounting is

$$100{,}351/12 = 8362.60 \text{ F},$$

and for equipment B,

$$168{,}949/12 = 14{,}079.10 \text{ F}.$$

For every 100 F of capital invested the discounted profit is 16.72 F for machine A and 21.66 F for machine B. For each article manufactured the profit is 0.84 F for A and 1 F for B.

Naturally, any choice based on such criteria between machine A and machine B assumes the immediate sale of the total production of each over the twelve years in question.

Let us now assume that we know the current rate of interest i (again 10%), and have drawn the curve (C) of the return (R)

$$R(I) = i(B + I),$$

as a function of the initial investment I for a number of different machines. In particular, for the totals of $B + I$ respectively equal to 150.35 (50 + 100.35) and 233.95 (168.95 + 65), expressed in thousands of Francs, the abscissas of 50 and 65 will correspond to the ordinates of 15.03 and 23.39.

If, from a point of the curve, we draw a straight line with a slope $i = 0.1$, it will cut the abscissa at a point whose distance from the

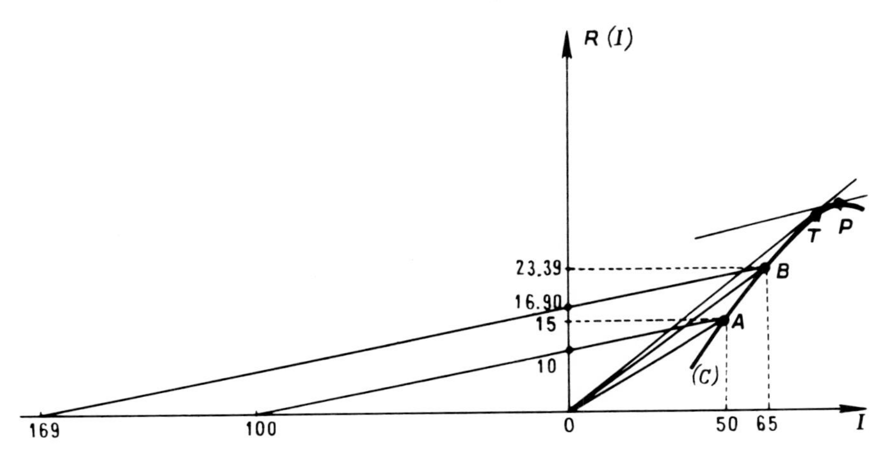

FIG. 8.7

origin is equal to the discounted profit $B(I, i)$, corresponding to the investment I and the rate of discount i.

The profitability, for each point A, B, and so on, is the gradient of the straight lines OA, OB, etc. Thus, for point A ($I = 50$), we have

$$r_A = 15/50 = 0.30$$

and for point B ($I = 65$) we have

$$r_B = 23.39/65 = 0.36 \text{ etc.}$$

The side of curve (C) which is concave usually faces the axis of the investments, and if we draw a tangent to it from the origin, we obtain point T for which the profitability is maximal. Point P, which gives the maximal discounted profit, is beyond T at the point where the tangent parallel to the direction of slope i touches the curve.

To the left of T both profit and profitability increase with the investment; between T and P the profit continues to increase, but the profitability diminishes.

In asking ourselves whether we should choose T rather than a point somewhere between T and P we pass beyond the bounds of the criterion for the business alone. The choice of T, giving the maximal profitability, unfortunately implies Malthusian consequences that would not result from a wider operation with a higher discounted profit.[2]

Renewal of Machinery Subject to Depreciation

When we considered the optimal resale date for the Golondrina, we took $\varphi(t)$ for a function of the time, such that the depreciation is expressed by $A_0[1 - \varphi(t)]$, and $\psi(t)$ for the cumulative expenses of running the car. It frequently happens that $\varphi(t)$ can be treated as a decreasing exponential $e^{-\lambda t}$ and that $\psi(t)$ can be expressed in the form

$$\psi(t) = k_0(e^{\mu t} - 1).$$

In this case the average discounted cost can be expressed

$$\gamma(t) = \frac{1}{t}[A_0(1 - e^{-\lambda t}) + k_0(e^{\mu t} - 1)].$$

[2] On this subject see P. Masse, *Le choix des investissements*, Dunod, Paris.

The derivative of this expression,

$$\gamma'(t) = \frac{(A_0\lambda e^{-\lambda t} + k_0\mu e^{\mu t})t - [A_0(1 - e^{-\lambda t}) + k_0(e^{\mu t} - 1)]}{t^2},$$

disappears when its numerator is zero, that is, for

$$\frac{1 - e^{-\lambda t}(1 + \lambda t)}{1 - e^{\mu t}(1 - \mu t)} = \frac{k_0}{A_0}.$$

To solve this equation for t when A_0, k_0, μ, and λ are known, we can make use of a nomogram such as the one shown in Fig. 8.8; this is very easy to employ.

In the problem of the Golondrina we can ascertain that

$$\varphi(t) \approx e^{-0.029t};$$

indeed, if the depreciation is of the form

$$A_0[1 - e^{-\lambda t}],$$

the ratios of the values for the depreciations to A_0 give $1 - e^{-\lambda t}$, and we can verify (Table 8.4) that $\lambda t \approx 0.029t$.

In the same way it would be seen that $\psi(t)$ can be expressed as

$$\psi(t) = 1470(e^{0.058t} - 1).$$

In these conditions we have

$$\frac{A_0}{k_0} = \frac{35{,}000}{1470} \approx 24 \quad \text{and} \quad \frac{\lambda}{\mu} = \frac{0.029}{0.058} = 0.5.$$

TABLE 8.4

Period	6	12	18	24	30	36	42	48	54	60
Depreciation	5.570	12,250	34,185	17,500	20,280	22,625	24,650	26,250	27,000	28,810
Divided by $A_0 = 35{,}000$	0.159	0.350	0.405	0.500	0.579	0.646	0.704	0.750	0.780	0.823
$e^{-t\lambda}$	0.841	0.650	0.595	0.500	0.421	0.354	0.296	0.250	0.220	0.177
λt	0.163	0.431	0.520	0.700	0.87	1.04	1.22	1.39	1.50	1.70
$0.029t$	0.174	0.348	0.522	0.696	0.87	1.04	1.22	1.39	1.57	1.74

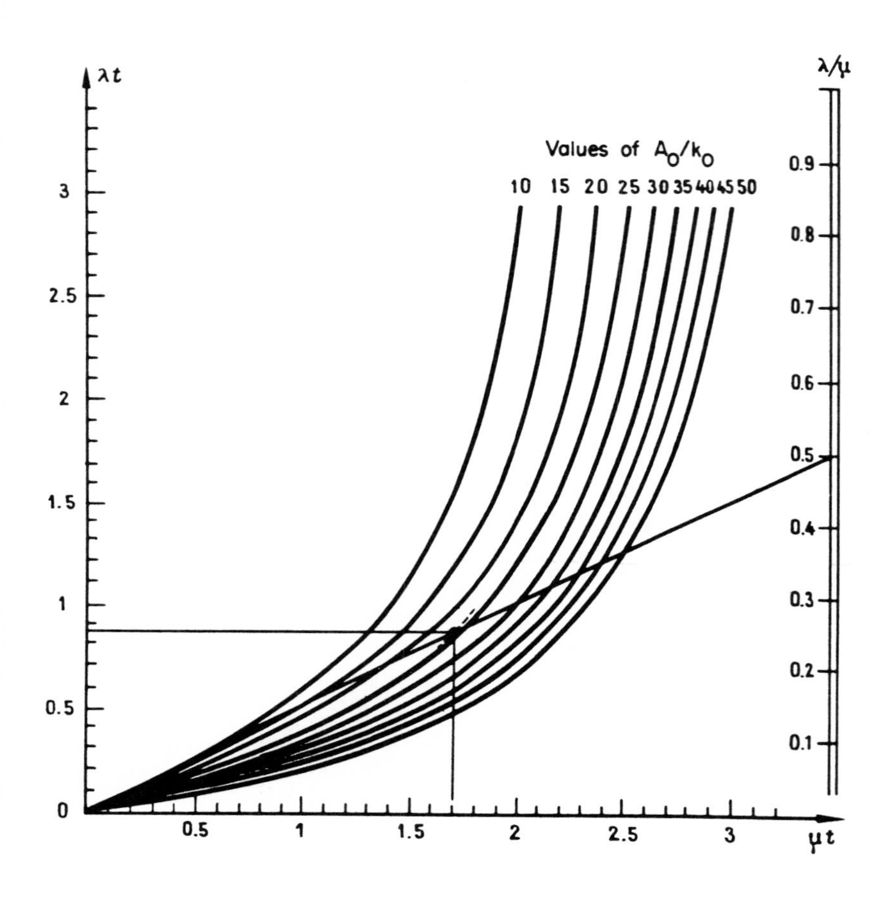

Fig. 8.8

Let us now refer to the nomogram and join the value 0.5 on the scale λ/μ to the origin. If we examine its intersection with the curve corresponding to the value 24 of A_0/k_0, we find that the abscissa of this intersection corresponds to $\mu t \approx 1.71$ and that $\lambda t \approx 0.85$. From this we deduce that

$$t \approx \frac{1.71}{0.058} \approx \frac{0.85}{0.029} \approx 29.$$

This result is nearly the same as that obtained by our earlier calculations; the advantage of this method lies in the brevity of the calculations.

In the case of a discounting of the costs with a rate α it can be proved that machinery (assumed to possess no residual value) should be discarded at time n, as soon as the maintenance cost at time $n + 1$ exceeds the quotient of

$$\frac{A_0 + C_1 + C_2\alpha + \cdots + C_n\alpha^{n-1}}{1 + \alpha + \alpha^2 + \cdots + \alpha^{n-1}},$$

where $C_1, C_2, \ldots, C_n$ are the expenditures agreed upon at the beginning of periods $1, 2, \ldots, n$.

In the case of the Golondrina we can state

$$C_n = \psi(n) - \psi(n - 1),$$

with $n = 1, 2, 3, \ldots$, for $t = 6, 12, 18, \ldots$. We must also take the residual value into account, which leads us to find C_{n+1} such that

$$C_{n+1} > \frac{[A_0\varphi(n)]/(1 + \alpha)^n + C_1 + C_2\alpha + \cdots + C_n\alpha^{n-1}}{1 + \alpha + \alpha^2 + \cdots + \alpha^{n-1}}.$$

It can easily be seen that

$$C_6 < \frac{35{,}000 \cdot \dfrac{0.421}{(1.05)^5} + 620 + 880(1.05) + 1240(1.05)^2 + 1760(1.05)^3 + 2485(1.05)^4}{1 + 1.05 + \cdots + (1.05)^4}$$

$$\approx 4470;$$

as a result, $C_6 = 3515$. On the other hand, we conclude that

$$C_7 > \frac{35{,}000 \dfrac{0.354}{(1.05)^6} + 620 + 880(1.05) + \cdots + 2485(1.05)^4 + 3515(1.05)^5}{1 + 1.05 + \cdots + (1.05)^5}$$

$$\approx 3190,$$

$$C_7 = 5500.$$

The application of the general result clearly leads to the same conclusion as our special calculation: the Golondrina should be sold when n is equal to 6, that is, after 36 months.

CHAPTER 9

KEEP AN EYE ON THOSE TIRES!

(The Theory of Restocking)

The *Mercury Company* has a fleet of 40 tanker trucks for delivering its petroleum products. Each of these trucks is a ten-wheeler and the company has decided to make a survey of all the tires in order to forecast their probable wear. These tires are expensive and the company does not wish to keep an unnecessarily large stock on hand; however, it would be regrettable if deliveries had to be held up for lack of tires. That at least is the opinion of the management, although it might not be shared by an exasperated motorist, held up for mile after mile behind a Mercury truck, whose driver seems to have forgotten that he is not the only one on the road.

The tires are examined by an expert who can evaluate their condition and mileage at a glance. He knows that 20% wear means that the tire has 6000 km use, 40% means 12,000 km, 60% means 18,000 km, 80% means 24,000 km, and a worn-out tire has a mileage of 30,000 km. For various reasons, however, not all the tires have a life of 30,000 km. Indeed, a survey carried out over a period of several years shows that out of every 100 tires used on the trucks, 5 have to be replaced before 6000 km, 10 between 6000 and 12,000, 25 between 12,000 and 18,000, 30 between 18,000 and 24,000, and 30 between 24,000 and 30,000 km. From these statistics it is possible to draw a *curve of survival* showing the number, or preferably the percentage, of tires which are still in service after the particular mileage required.

The management draws up a weekly forecast for the employment of the tankers, and sufficient tires must be ordered to replace those worn out by use or accidental deterioration. It has been found that a tanker averages 2000 km a week, which gives a weekly mileage of 80,000 km for the fleet and 800,000 km for the tires used. What should be the rhythm or *rate of restocking* adopted? Solving this problem requires quite simple mathematics, as we shall show.

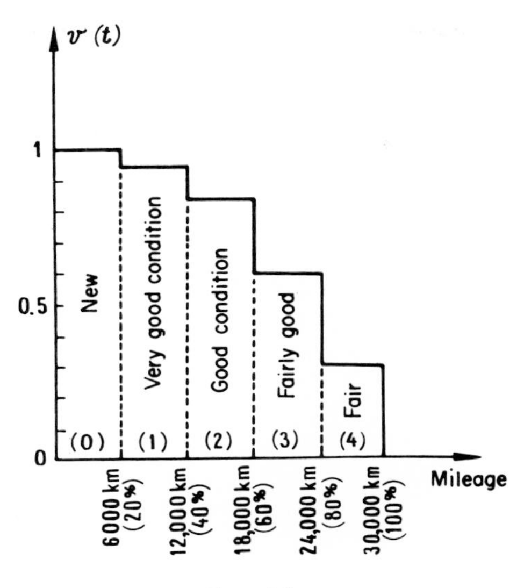

FIG. 9.1

To begin with, we shall assume that the tire "population" is homogeneous and that the statistics obtained from the past will apply to the future; thus, the percentages given in Fig. 9.1 are probabilities which correspond to the stated mileages. The condition of a tire will be shown by a curve of survival and, due to the assumption of homogeneousness, the graph can be graduated in weeks along the time axis (Fig. 9.2). The probability that a tire will last more than 4 weeks is 0.95, more than 10 weeks 0.60, more than 14 weeks 0.30, more than 15 weeks 0. It is because the company's examination of the tires takes place every three weeks, and also to reduce the number of operations for the reader, that the law of probability is given in classes with intervals of three weeks.

Before we begin our calculations, let us explain how to evaluate the survival probability of a tire which is already partially worn. Let us take $v(A)$ for the probability of survival at time A of a new tire which was put into service at $t = 0$, and $v(t + A)$ for that of the survival of the same tire at time $t + A$. Let us now take $v_A(t)$ for the *conditional probability* that a tire which was put into service at $t = 0$, but with a previous use equal to $v(A)$, will last until time t. From an elementary property of probability, we know that

$$v(t + A) = v(A) \cdot v_A(t),$$

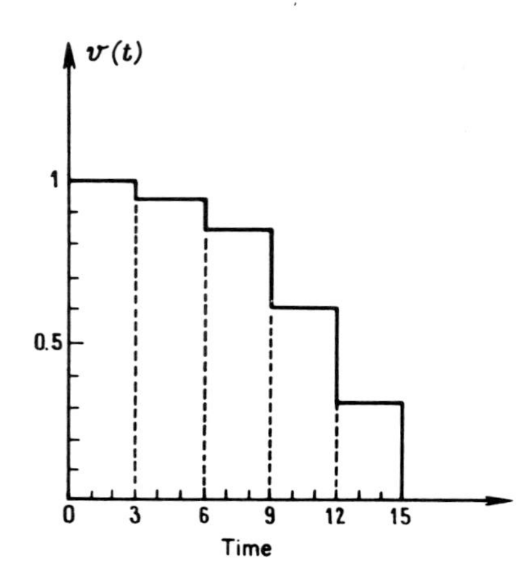

FIG. 9.2

since the probability of its surviving at time $t + A$ must equal the probability of its survival until A multiplied by the probability, under these conditions, of its further survival during time t.

Let us, as an example, calculate the probability that a tire which has 40% of wear (considered, for exactitude, at the beginning of the seventh week) will last another three weeks. We find

$$v_7(4) = \frac{v(4+7)}{v(7)} = \frac{v(11)}{v(7)} = \frac{0.60}{0.85} = 0.706,$$

whereas for a new tire we should have

$$v(4) = 0.95.$$

For convenience of calculation, Fig. 9.2 will be converted into a table (Table 9.1).

Let us now assume that the supervisor in charge has divided all the tires at time 0 into the following classes (R) according to their degree of use

$$N_{(0)} = 130, \qquad N_{(1)} = 90, \qquad N_{(2)} = 80, \qquad N_{(3)} = 60, \qquad N_{(4)} = 40,$$

where $N_{(0)}$ represents the number of new tires (class 0), $N_{(1)}$ the number of tires in very good condition, and so on.

TABLE 9.1

Class by wear	t week	$v(t)$
	0	1
0	1	1
	2	1
	3	0.95
1	4	0.95
	5	0.95
	6	0.85
2	7	0.85
	8	0.85
	9	0.60
3	10	0.60
	11	0.60
	12	0.30
4	13	0.30
	14	0.30
	15	0
	> 15	0

Thus, if no replacements were to take place, at time t this population of tires would be reduced to

$$N_{(0)} \cdot v(t) + N_{(1)} \cdot \frac{v(\ + 3)}{v(3)} + N_{(2)} \cdot \frac{v(t + 6)}{v(6)} + N_{(3)} \cdot \frac{v(t + 9)}{v(9)} + N_{(4)} \cdot \frac{v(t + 12)}{v(12)},$$

that is,

$$N_{(0)} \cdot v(t) + 1.05N_{(1)} \cdot v(t+3) + 1.18N_{(2)} \cdot v(t+6) + 1.67N_{(3)} \cdot v(t+9) + 3.33N_{(4)} \cdot v(t+12).$$

We shall now proceed to establish the equation which will balance the company's restocking with its losses in tires, but as the changes of class can only take place every three weeks, due to the company's method of examination, we shall henceforth take three weeks as our unit of time, so that the previous expression now becomes

$$N_{(0)}v(t) + 1.05N_{(1)} \cdot v(t+1) + 1.18N_{(2)} \cdot v(t+2) + 1.67N_{(3)} \cdot v(t+3) + 3.33N_{(4)} \cdot v(t+4).$$

The reasoning whereby we obtain equations is a simple one. If $r(u)$ is the number of tires replaced until time u, the quantity

$$\rho(u) = r(u) - r(u-1) \qquad (u \geqslant 1)$$

gives the number of replacements during the interval from $u - 1$ to u; hence the function $\rho(t)$ is called the *rate of restocking*.

Like the other tires, in service at $t = 0$ or already replaced, those replaced at time u will be subject to the law of survival $v(t)$, but at time t, the survivors of the replacement at time u will be

$$\rho(u) \cdot v(t-u),$$

since the number put into service at time u was $\rho(u)$, and the time from u to t is $t - u$.

Hence, the total number of tires in use at time t will be the sum of these survivors, from $u = 1$ to $u = t$, obviously increased by those from the first four classes in service at time $t = 0$, that is

$$N'_{(0)} \cdot v(t) + N'_{(1)} \cdot v(t+1) + N'_{(2)} \cdot v(t+2) + N'_{(3)} \cdot v(t+3) + N'_{(4)} \cdot v(t+4) + \sum_{u=1}^{t} \rho(u) \cdot v(t-u), \qquad (1)$$

in which

$$N'_{(0)} = N_{(0)}, \qquad N'_{(1)} = 1.05N_1, \qquad N'_{(2)} = 1.18N_{(2)},$$
$$N'_{(3)} = 1.67N_{(3)}, \qquad N'_{(4)} = 3.33N_{(4)}.$$

Since each tanker has 10 tires, quantity (1) must be equal to 10 times the number of tankers in service at time t; this quantity is given as a function of the time and will be called $f(t)$.

We now obtain the equation

$$N'_{(0)} \cdot v(t) + N'_{(1)} \cdot v(t+1) + N'_{(2)} \cdot v(t+2) + N'_{(3)} \cdot v(t+3) + N'_{(4)} \cdot v(t+4) + \sum_{u=1}^{t} \rho(u) \cdot v(t-u) = f(t). \quad (2)$$

Now we must calculate $\rho(u)$. Clearly,

$$f(0) = N'_{(0)} + N'_{(1)}v(1) + N'_{(2)} \cdot v(2) + N'_{(3)} \cdot v(3) + N'_{(4)} \cdot v(4)$$

and $v(0) = 1$.

For simplification, we will take

$$\mathcal{N}(t) = N'_{(0)} + N'_{(1)}v(t+1) + N'_{(2)} \cdot v(t+2) + N'_{(3)} \cdot v(t+3) + N'_{(4)} \cdot v(t+4). \quad (3)$$

Thus,

$$f(0) = \mathcal{N}(0);$$

and Eq. (2) becomes

$$f(t) = \mathcal{N}(t) + \sum_{u=1}^{t} \rho(u) \cdot v(t-u). \quad (4)$$

From this we obtain

$$f(1) = \mathcal{N}(1) + \rho(1),$$

whence

$$\rho(1) = f(1) - \mathcal{N}(1) \quad (5)$$

and the first restocking $\rho(1)$ has been found.

From Eq. (4), we obtain

$$f(2) = \mathcal{N}(2) + \rho(1) \cdot v(1) + \rho(2) \cdot v(0),$$

whence

$$\rho(2) = f(2) - \mathcal{N}(2) - \rho(1) \cdot v(1), \quad (6)$$

and $\rho(2)$ has been found.

Still using Eq. (4), we successively obtain

$$f(3) = \mathcal{N}(3) + \rho(1) \cdot v(2) + \rho(2) \cdot v(1) + \rho(3) \cdot v(0)$$

$$\rho(3) = f(3) - \mathcal{N}(3) - \rho(1) \cdot v(2) - \rho(2) \cdot v(1), \tag{7}$$

$$f(4) = \mathcal{N}(4) + \rho(1) \cdot v(3) + \rho(2) \cdot v(2) + \rho(3) \cdot v(1) + \rho(4) \cdot v(0).$$

$$\rho(4) = f(4) - \mathcal{N}(4) - \rho(1) \cdot v(3) - \rho(2) \cdot v(2) - \rho(3) \cdot v(1), \tag{8}$$

$$\rho(t) = f(t) - \mathcal{N}(t) - \sum_{u=1}^{t-1} \rho(u) \cdot v(t-u). \tag{9}$$

The reader, perplexed perhaps by the form of the equations, must realize that what we have been using is really no more than bookkeeping: some reflection, in addition to a knowledge of addition and multiplication, is all that has been required.

To proceed, we must now calculate $\mathcal{N}(t)$ for $t = 0, 1, 2, 3, 4$, beginning with the distribution (R) and with (3):

$$\begin{aligned}
\mathcal{N}(0) &= 130 + 90 + 80 + 60 + 40 = 400; \\
\mathcal{N}(1) &= (130)(0.95) + (90)(1.05)(0.85) + (80)(1.18)(0.60) \\
&\qquad + (60)(1.67)(0.30) = 290.5 \approx 290; \\
\mathcal{N}(2) &= (130)(0.85) + (90)(1.05)(0.60) \\
&\qquad + (80)(1.18)(0.30) = 195.5 \approx 195; \\
\mathcal{N}(3) &= (130)(0.60) + (90)(1.05)(0.30) = 106.3 \approx 106; \\
\mathcal{N}(4) &= (130)(0.30) = 39; \\
\mathcal{N}(\geqslant 5) &= 0;
\end{aligned} \tag{10}$$

after 15 weeks, without replacements, all the tires would be worn out.

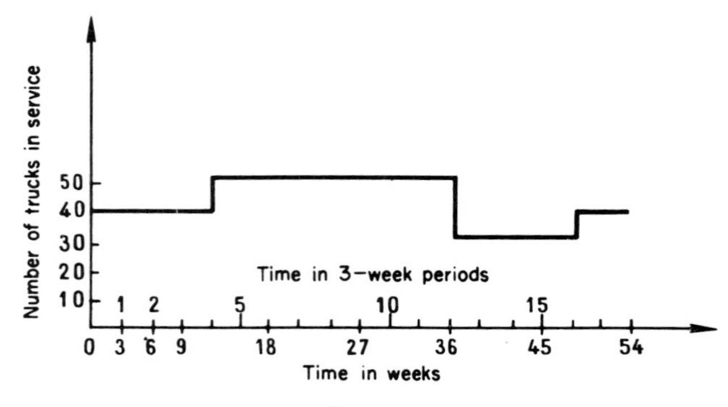

FIG. 9.3

Let us now assume the forecast for the employment of the tankers is that shown in Fig. 9.3, in which a seasonal influence can be discerned. What stocks (t) should be bought in order that the required deliveries can be carried out, assuming new tires are used as replacements? To discover this, we are going to use formulas of the type given in Eq. (9).

$$\rho(1) = f(1) - \mathcal{N}(1) = 400 - 290 = 110;$$

$$\rho(2) = f(2) - \mathcal{N}(2) - \rho(1) \cdot v(1)$$
$$= 400 - 195 - 110 \times 0.95 \approx 100;$$

$$\rho(3) = f(3) - \mathcal{N}(3) - \rho(1) \cdot v(2) - \rho(2) \cdot v(1)$$
$$= 400 - 106 - 110 \times 0.85 - 100 \times 0.95 \approx 105;$$

$$\rho(4) = f(4) - \mathcal{N}(4) - \rho(1) \cdot v(3) - \rho(2) \cdot v(2) - \rho(3) \cdot v(1)$$
$$= 400 - 39 - 110 \times 0.60 - 100 \times 0.85 - 105 \times 0.95 \approx 110.$$

Beginning with period 5, a fresh population of 100 new tires makes its appearance, and we shall then have

$$\rho(5) = 500 - 100 \times 0.95 - 110 \times 0.30$$
$$- 100 \times 0.60 - 105 \times 0.85 - 110 \times 0.95 \approx 118;$$

$$\rho(6) = 500 - 100 \times 0.85 - 100 \times 0.30$$
$$- 105 \times 0.60 - 110 \times 0.85 - 118 \times 0.95 \approx 116;$$
$$- 105 \times 0.60 - 110 \times 0.85 - 118 \times 0.95 \approx 116;$$

$$\rho(7) = 500 - 100 \times 0.60 - 105 \times 0.30$$
$$- 110 \times 0.60 - 118 \times 0.85 - 116 \times 0.95 \approx 132;$$

$$\rho(8) = 500 - 100 \times 0.30 - 110 \times 0.30$$
$$- 118 \times 0.60 - 116 \times 0.85 - 132 \times 0.95 \approx 142;$$

$$\rho(9) = 500 - 118 \times 0.30 - 116 \times 0.60 - 132 \times 0.85$$
$$- 142 \times 0.95 \approx 148;$$

$$\rho(10) = 500 - 116 \times 0.30 - 132 \times 0.60 - 142 \times 0.85$$
$$- 148 \times 0.95 \approx 125;$$

$$\rho(11) = 500 - 132 \times 0.30 - 142 \times 0.60 - 148 \times 0.85$$
$$- 125 \times 0.95 \approx 131;$$

$$\rho(12) = 500 - 142 \times 0.30 - 148 \times 0.60 - 125 \times 0.85$$
$$- 131 \times 0.95 \approx 138.$$

At this point, we shall have to introduce a condition: we shall assume that the choice of the 20 tankers withdrawn from service has been made by some kind of chance draw. Hence, after time 12, restocking should only be carried out for the 30 tankers which are still in use, and we shall take

$$\frac{148 \times 3}{5} = 89; \qquad \frac{125 \times 3}{5} = 75; \qquad \frac{131 \times 3}{5} = 79; \qquad \frac{138 \times 3}{5} = 83$$

for the number of tires put into service in periods 9, 10, 11, 12 and still in use. As a result,

$$\rho(13) = 300 - 89 \times 0.30 - 75 \times 0.60 - 79 \times 0.85 - 83 \times 0.95 \approx 82;$$
$$\rho(14) = 300 - 57 \times 0.30 - 79 \times 0.60 - 83 \times 0.85 - 82 \times 0.95 \approx 82;$$
$$\rho(15) = 300 - 79 \times 0.30 - 83 \times 0.60 - 82 \times 0.85 - 82 \times 0.95 \approx 79;$$
$$\rho(16) = 300 - 83 \times 0.30 - 82 \times 0.60 - 82 \times 0.85 - 79 \times 0.95 \approx 81.$$

We shall stop there. After time 16, 10 tankers have to be put back into service: they will be selected at random from the 20 previously withdrawn from service. This will reintroduce a set of 100 tires whose distribution into classes will correspond to that of the set immediately after time 4. Formulas such as Eq. (10) will be used and the calculations will be resumed.

Fig. 9.4 shows the variations in restocking: we can imagine what

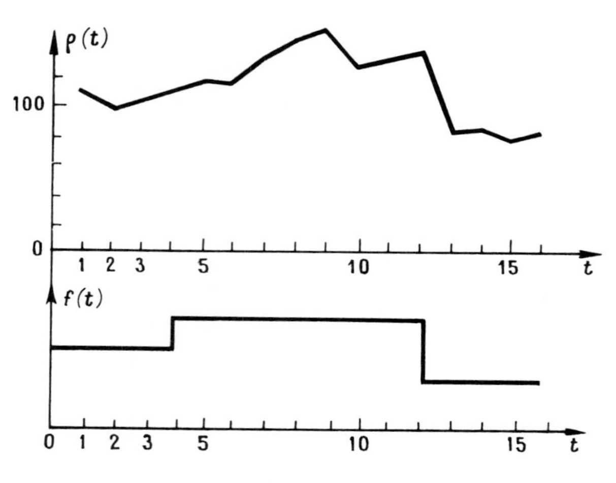

FIG. 9.4

effect the pronounced differences between the two graphs will have on the orders.

It is useful to compare this method of calculation with one based on average values. In doing so, we must first ascertain the expected mileage of a tire. The probability that a tire will survive from 0 to 6000 km is 0.05, from 6000 to 12,000 it is 0.10, from 12,000 to 18,000 it is 0.25, and so on. The average mileage, therefore will be

$$d = 6000 \times 0.05 + 12{,}000 \times 0.10 + 18{,}000 \times 0.25 + 24{,}000 \times 0.30 + 30{,}000 \times 0.30 = 22{,}200 \text{ km}.$$

Since the mileage of a tire is 2000 km a week, the total weekly mileage of all the tires, when 40 tankers are in service, is 800,000 km, so that the number of new tires required per week is 800,000 : 22,200 = 36. The average replacements required for 50 and 30 tankers will also be found, and the results can then be compared with those obtained earlier by the method of recurrence.

Method	Number of tires to restock		
	Periods 1–4	Periods 5–12	Periods 13–16
Calculation by averages	432	1081	324
Recurring method	425	1050	324

Since the results differ so little, why should we not rely on the second and easier method? The reason is because the variations of $\rho(t)$, which are produced by those of $f(t)$, should be followed, and we can only do this by means of the recurring method. It is true that if $f(t)$ remains constant, the value of $\rho(t)$ tends toward a constant which is, in fact, the same as the average value obtained by the second method. But if $f(t)$ shows important variations, the average value of $\rho(t)$ becomes far removed from the correct value.

A curve such as Fig. 9.4 enables a management to have continuous information about consumption and the need for restocking.

As already stated, all that is required for such calculations is a knowledge of the most elementary processes and, if desired, a simple adding machine.

Is Preventive Replacement Justified?

As we saw earlier, wear on a piece of equipment can be effectively shown by the *curve of survival*, obtained from statistics for a large group of similar machines.

If the statistics are sufficiently precise, and if care has been taken to obtain a sufficiently large number of classes representing periods of survival, curve $v(t)$, which is drawn by joining the points of a diagram such as that of Fig. 9.2, presents a form in which breaks are disregarded (Fig. 9.5).

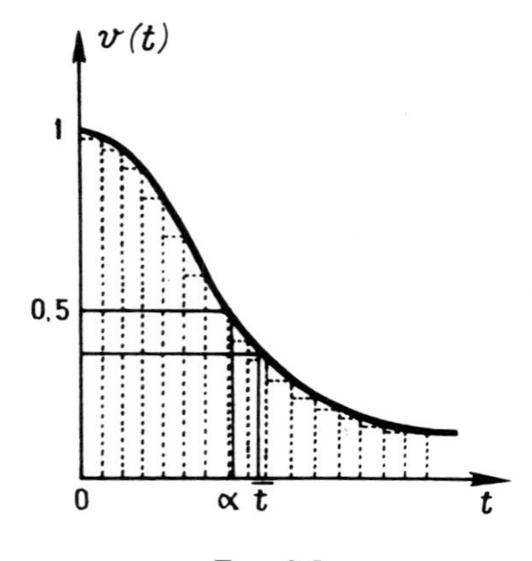

FIG. 9.5

From any particular curve it is easy to find (since it corresponds to the ordinate 0.5) the *median age* α, that is, the period at which one-half of a group of machines of the same type, put into service at the same time 0, are still in working order, as well as the *average age* $\bar{t}$, which is represented by the mean abscissa to the part of the axis subtended by the curve $v(t)$.

Several authors, notably Kelly,[1] have proposed (where α is known for a given curve of survival) the adoption of an auxiliary variable

$$x = \ln(t/\alpha)/\mu,$$

normally distributed, and the discovery of the value of the parameter μ in such a way that the curve corresponding to this law of standard logs

[1] See *Rev. de la SoFRO*, No. 10, L'entretien préventif est-il justifié ? Dunod, Paris.

will coincide, at least for most of its length, with the experimental curve of survival. Under these conditions we obtain

$$\bar{t} = \alpha e^{\mu^2/2} \qquad \text{and} \qquad \sigma_T = \alpha \cdot e^{\mu^2/2} \cdot (e^{\mu^2} - 1)^{1/2}.$$

What is extremely interesting and practical in this research is that the curves for which μ is between 0.3 and 0.6 are those of survival for the class of products subject to *wear* (brake linings, clutch discs, gears), whereas those for which μ is approximately 0.9 represent products subject to *fatigue* (axles, ball-bearings, crankshafts).

The graphs of Fig. 9.6 (see Fig. 9.8a,b) give the shape of the theoretical curves for different values of μ and for $\alpha = 4000$. The dotted area above the intersection of the curves represents the zone of the survival curves for fatigue products; the dotted area below the intersection represents that for products which are subject to wear.

Carrying out preventive replacement means that one will systematically replace particular parts in a series of machines when these parts have reached a survival time θ, in order to reduce the frequency of breakdowns.

If preventive replacement is undertaken, the survival curve for a selected category of parts will be cut off at θ, which has been fixed, and the average survival period of a part from this group will be $\bar{t}_\theta$, which must obviously be less than θ, since, for various causes, some replacements will have to be made before time θ (Fig. 9.7).

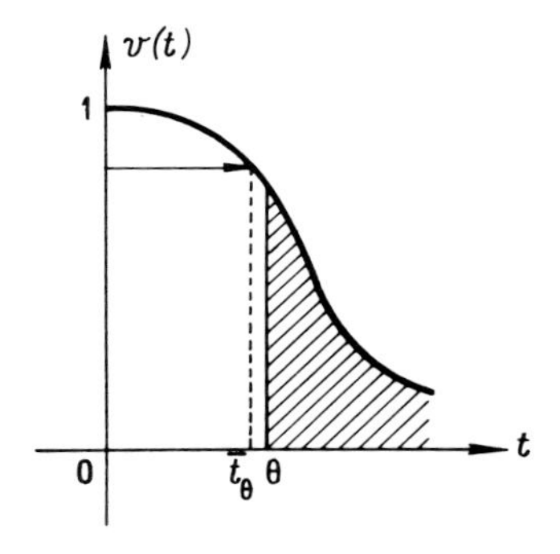

FIG. 9.7

When we study the economic aspect of preventive maintenance, we find that a breakdown caused by the failure of a part in a machine can be expressed as two separate costs:

(a) the price of the part, together with the cost of dismantling, assembling, and testing the machine, represented by p;

(b) the cost due to the breakdown (interruption of production, loss of raw materials, penalties for late delivery, etc.), called P.

Where preventive replacement is not carried out, the sum to be paid, on the failure of a part which lasts an average of $\bar{t}$, is $p + P$; expressed per unit of time this is

$$C_1 = \frac{p + P}{\bar{t}}.$$

If, on the other hand, preventive maintenance is adopted, the cost is always p for replacing a part whose average life is $\bar{t}_\theta$, but P will only be paid if the failure took place before θ, which occurs with a probability of $1 - v(\theta)$. The cost per unit of time is accordingly

$$C_2 = \frac{p + [1 - v(\theta)]P}{\bar{t}_\theta}.$$

Of course, preventive replacement is only justified when

$$C_2 < C_1 \qquad \text{or} \qquad C_2/C_1 < 1.$$

The curves of Figs. 9.8(a) and 9.8(b) represent the values of the function

$$y = 1 - C_2/C_1$$

as a function of x and $\theta/\bar{t}$, in the case where $\mu = 0.3$ [Fig. 9.8(a)], and where $\mu = 0.9$ [Fig. 9.8(b)]. If we endeavor to obtain the maxima of the y curves drawn for different values of p/P, we find that they correspond to the minima of C_2/C_1; the latter are obtained for given values of $\theta/\bar{t}$, that is, of θ, since $\bar{t}$ is known for every part under consideration. For instance, if we have a part such that $\mu \approx 0.3$, $\alpha = 4000$, $\bar{t} = 4200$, and $p/P = 0.1$, we find that $x \approx -2.25$, whence

$$\theta = \alpha \cdot e^{\mu x} \approx 0.51\alpha \approx 2040;$$

thus, we could have obtained $\theta/\bar{t} = 0.48$ at once, if the scale of the θ/t values had been complete.

When μ approximates to 0.3, the y curves reveal clearly defined maxima for values of p/P smaller than 1, and the same phenomenon is found when μ approximates to 0.6, provided p/P is less than 0.5.

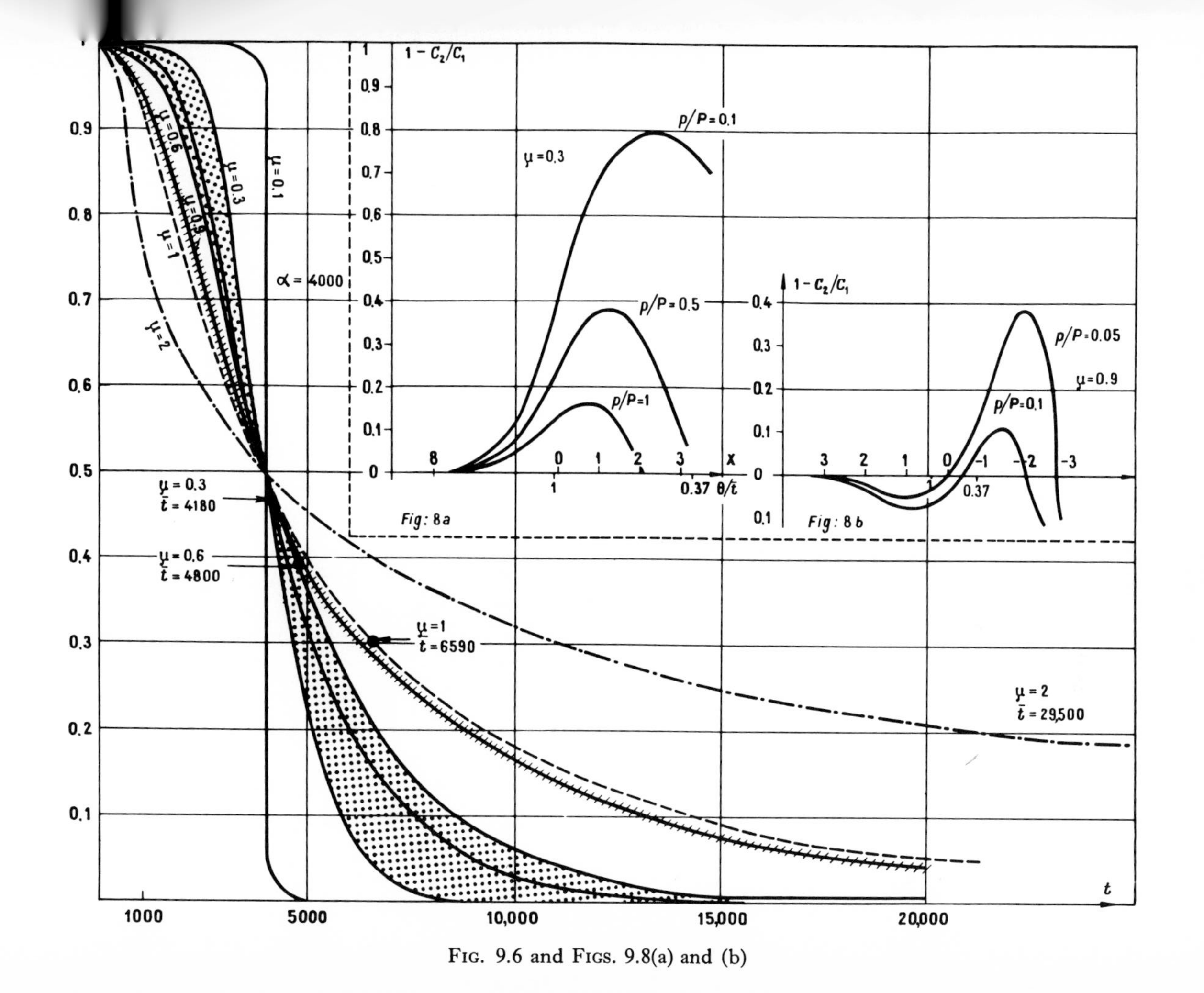

FIG. 9.6 and FIGS. 9.8(a) and (b)

On the other hand, the maxima are not at all distinct for $\mu \approx 0.9$, except possibly when $p/P < 0.05$.

These results can be easily interpreted in terms of preventive replacement:

(a) For parts subject to wear ($0.3 < \mu < 0.6$) there is every reason to practice this policy if p/P is smaller than 0.7 to about 0.5. This is usually the case, since a part in this category is frequently cheap and easily replaced, so that one is generally far from reaching this limit.

(b) For parts subject to fatigue ($\mu \approx 0.9$), on the other hand, it is advisable to practice preventive maintenance only when $p/P < 0.05$. Such parts, however, are usually very expensive, so that the condition regarding p/P is rarely satisfied.

These conclusions are not at all at variance with common sense. It is, indeed, all the less surprising that there should be no advantage in replacing a part subject to fatigue before it fails, when we find that its survival curve is very close to an exponential and that, in consequence, the new part has the same chance of failure as the old one. On the other hand, it is quite normal to replace such comparatively cheap parts as belts, brake linings, or bushes during the life of a machine, in order to avoid untimely interruptions of production. Indeed, it is even possible to develop ideas about the construction or improvement of a machine as the result of such studies.

The owner of a factory should ensure that the manufacturer supplies him with machinery whose parts can be classified in categories with a homogeneous average of survival; such a precaution will enable him to determine times $\theta_1, \theta_2, \ldots, \theta_n$ for preventive replacement, which may, for example, represent multiples of 250 hours. He should also be prepared to pay the extra price needed to ensure that parts subject to fatigue will last as long as the machine itself; often a small increase of price will mean a greatly extended life for such parts, and it will be a considerable satisfaction for the owner to find that the machine can be finally scrapped without having been subject to costly and difficult replacements entailing serious interruptions in production.

CHAPTER 10

STOP THIEF!

(A Rational Use of the Theory of Games of Strategy)

Since the opening of the first *supermercado* in Mexico City some ten years ago, other supermarkets have sprung up for the benefit of housewives ... and also of thieves, who show a particular penchant for self-service stores. The number of thieves in Mexico is probably neither more nor less than elsewhere, but some of them are so clever that it is said they could remove your socks before you have taken off your shoes.

The *Pronto* company runs an ultramodern supermarket in the center of the city, and has organized a system of surveillance which we shall now describe. The store is divided into two areas, A and B; the first, due to the popularity of the goods displayed there, is always crowded, the second has far fewer customers. The management employs two

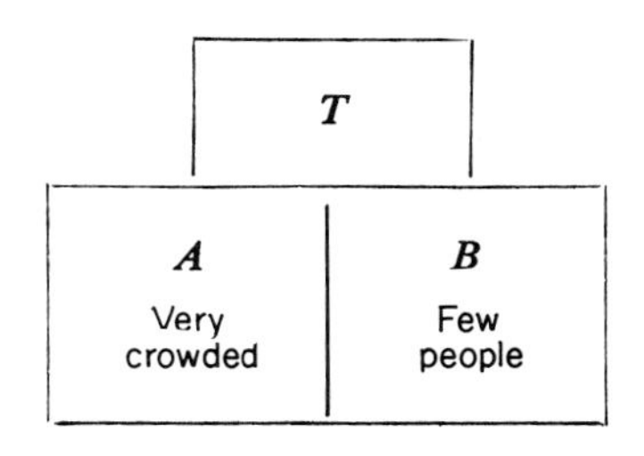

Fig. 10.1

plain-clothes detectives and, in addition, there are TV cameras which photograph both areas from a zone T, where the screens are situated. Thus, the detectives can be in either A, B, or T, whereas the thieves can only operate in A or B, since we will assume they cannot reach T in order to steal the television sets.

The detectives have been able to calculate certain probabilities for the capture of a thief, and estimate from experience that if a thief is in A and a detective in T, the probability of an arrest is 0.3. If the detective is in A, it is 0.4, and so on, for all the possible arrangements which are shown in Table 10.1.

TABLE 10.1

One detective	One thief: A	B
T	0.3	0.5
A	0.4	0.2
B	0.1	0.7

But the two detectives may operate separately or together in A, B, or T. It is easy to calculate the total probabilities of an arrest for cases TT, where both detectives are in T, AA (both detectives in A), TA (one detective in T, and the other in A), and so on. Indeed, in accordance with the principle of total probability,

$$p_{TT} = p_T + p_T - p_T \cdot p_T = 2p_T - p_T{}^2,$$
$$p_{TA} = p_T + p_A - p_T \cdot p_A \text{, etc.}$$

Thus,

$$p_{TT} = 0.3 + 0.3 - 0.3 \times 0.3 = 0.51,$$
$$p_{TA} = 0.3 + 0.4 - 0.3 \times 0.4 = 0.58\text{, etc.}$$

In this way, we obtain Table 10.2, where the twelve possible situations have all been allocated the appropriate probabilities of an arrest.

The problem to be solved is: what periods (frequencies of presence) should the detectives choose for each of the three areas? Suppose, for instance, the following *strategy* were adopted: 25% of the time in situation AA, 20% in BB, 15% in TB, and 40% in AB, then the probability of arresting a thief who is in A would be

$$0.64 \times 0.25 + 0.19 \times 0.20 + 0.37 \times 0.15 + 0.46 \times 0.40 = 0.4375;$$

and if he is in B,

$$0.36 \times 0.25 + 0.91 \times 0.20 + 0.85 \times 0.15 + 0.76 \times 0.40 = 0.7035.$$

TABLE 10.2

Two detectives	One thief A	One thief B	
TT	0.51	0.75	x_1
AA	0.64	0.36	x_2
BB	0.19	0.91	x_3
TA	0.58	0.60	x_4
TB	0.37	0.85	x_5
AB	0.46	0.76	x_6
	y_1	y_2	

As we can see, there are any number of possible strategies for the detectives, and we shall express a strategy as a set of frequencies

$$x_1, \quad x_2, \quad x_3, \quad x_4, \quad x_5, \quad x_6,$$

that is, six positive or zero numbers with a sum equal to 1, representing the distribution of time to the combined surveillance in *TT*, *AA*, *TB*, *AB*, and so on.

We will imagine that the thieves are concerned over the plans being devised by the detectives, and themselves decide to adopt a strategy y_1, y_2, composed of two positive or zero numbers with a sum equal to 1, representing the allocation of time to their operative visits to *A* or *B*.

It is clear that the two sets of frequencies must remain the secret of the side which is adopting them. Further, it is necessary that the successive *decisions* taken by both sides should be random ones made by some kind of draw which preserves the chosen frequencies; otherwise what a windfall it would be for the thieves to be able to discover the successive positions of the detectives, or what a disaster to them if the detectives were to discover their strategy!

We shall assume, therefore, that the detectives and thieves are both equally *intelligent* and *prudent*. The detectives will follow a strategy which will assure them *at least* a probability g of making an arrest, whatever the behavior of the thieves may be. Similarly, the thieves will follow a strategy (y_1, y_2) which will assure them *at most* a probability g of being arrested, in whatever manner the detectives operate. As a result, an equilibrium will be established between men of intelligence and prudence, which is what usually occurs.

How are we to obtain the two sets of frequencies giving the optimal strategies? It can be seen that these frequencies and their common limit of g must satisfy the relations shown in the tabulation.

Relations for the detectives	Relations for the thieves	
$x_1 + x_2 + x_3 + x_4 + x_5 + x_6 = 1$ (the frequencies total 1)	$y_1 + y_2 = 1$	
	$0.51y_1 + 0.75y_2 \leqslant g$ detectives in	TT
$0.51x_1 + 0.64x_2 + 0.19x_3 + 0.58x_4 + 0.37x_5 + 0.46x_6 \geqslant g$ (the detectives wish to ensure at least g if the thieves only enter A)	$0.64y_1 + 0.36y_2 \leqslant g$	AA
	$0.19y_1 + 0.91y_2 \leqslant g$	BB
$0.75x_1 + 0.36x_2 + 0.91x_3 + 0.60x_4 + 0.85x_5 + 0.76x_6 \geqslant g$ (the detectives wish to ensure at least g if the thieves only enter B)	$0.58y_1 + 0.60y_2 \leqslant g$	TA
	$0.37y_1 + 0.85y_2 \leqslant g$	TB
	$0.46y_1 + 0.76y_2 \leqslant g$	AB

All the variables are between the inclusive bounds of 0 and 1.

Because of the number of variables, the equations and inequalities for the detectives are difficult to solve; on the other hand, those for the thieves, which only include two independent variables, are easily solved graphically (Fig. 10.2). If we substitute $y_2 = 1 - y_1$ in all the nonstrict inequalities for the thieves, treated as equations, we find

$$\begin{aligned} g &= 0.75 - 0.24y_1 && \text{line (1)} \\ g &= 0.36 + 0.28y_1 && \text{line (2)} \\ g &= 0.91 - 0.72y_1 && \text{line (3)} \\ g &= 0.60 - 0.02y_1 && \text{line (4)} \\ g &= 0.85 - 0.48y_1 && \text{line (5)} \\ g &= 0.76 - 0.30y_1 && \text{line (6)} \end{aligned} \qquad (0 \leqslant y_1 \leqslant 1)$$

Let us now draw these six straight lines in the system of coordinates gOy_1 shown on Fig. 10.2. Any point in the hachured area will constitute a possible solution, since it will satisfy all the inequalities considered by the thieves. It will be seen that the smallest value of g is found at the intersection of straight lines (2) and (4), since (4) has a negative slope.

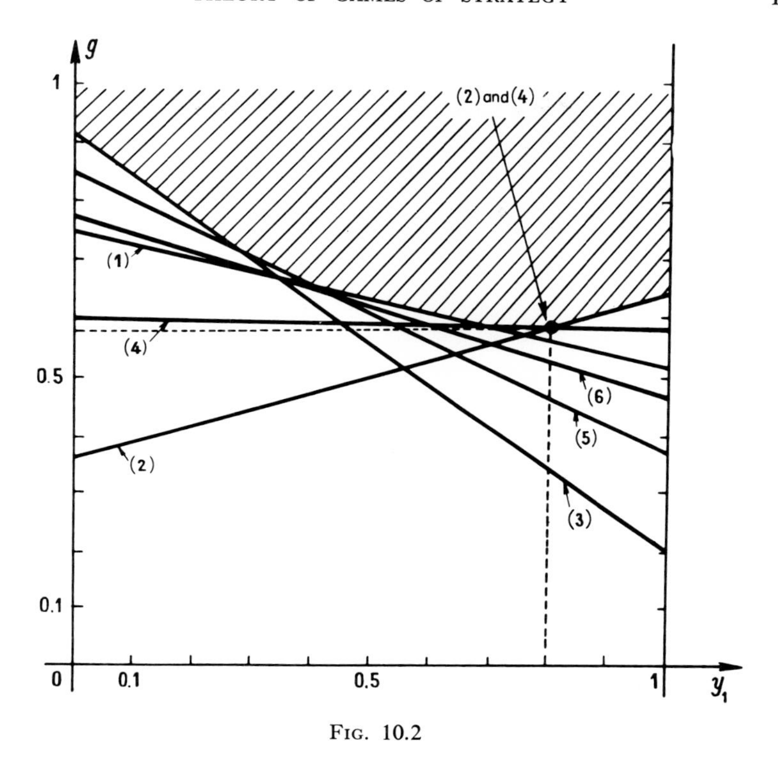

FIG. 10.2

We have

$$0.36 + 0.28y_1 = 0.60 - 0.02y_1 ,$$

that is,

$$y_1 = 0.8 \quad \text{and} \quad y_2 = 0.2 ,$$

whence

$$g = 0.584.$$

Thus, by choosing the strategy $y_1 = 0.8$, $y_2 = 0.2$, the thieves will have a minimal probability of arrest equal to 0.584.

To learn the optimal strategy for the detectives, we must assume, without proving,[1] the two fundamental properties of the theory of games of strategy with two players:

(1) There is a single number g which is both an upper bound for the thieves and a lower bound for the detectives.

[1] The full proof can be found in any work on the theory of games of strategy.

(2) For every nonstrict inequality for one player which in the optimal solution is shown as a strict inequality, there is a corresponding zero variable for the other player. [In our example, inequality (3) for the thieves becomes a strict inequality so that x_3 must be zero.]

Here, the optimum corresponds to the intersection of straight lines (2) and (4); the inequalities of these lines become the equations for this optimum, a condition which is not true for the other four lines. We conclude, therefore, that x_1, x_3, x_5, and x_6 must be nil and find

$$0.64x_2 + 0.58x_4 = g = 0.584;$$
$$0.36x_2 + 0.60x_4 = g = 0.584;$$

whence,

$$x_2 = 1/15 \qquad \text{and} \qquad x_4 = 14/15.$$

Finally, by spending 1/15 of their time together in A and 14/15 with one situated in T and the other in A, the detectives will ensure a probability of an arrest which will always be equal to 0.584, whatever strategy is chosen by the thieves. If the thieves adopt a strategy of stealing 4 out of 5 times in A and once out of 5 times in B, they will ensure that the probability of their arrest will not exceed 0.584, whatever strategy is chosen by the detectives.

This result seems less favorable to the detectives than to the thieves, and is due to the nature of the problem, since the former can choose from six strategies and the latter only from two. In reality the result is not unfavorable to the detectives: it is only that they can evaluate their chances more exactly, since they have more choices open to them. In other problems, we find situations where the optimal strategies are such that one side can affirm that its *gain* will be greater than or equal to g, whereas the other side can affirm that its *loss* will be less than or equal to g.

Fortunately for thieves and unluckily for honest people, circumstances are not always so favorable for the capture of pickpockets. Moreover, an incontrovertible law states that the larger the theft, the smaller the chance of detection. Therefore, as these remarks are intended to show, the number of thieves and crooks does not rapidly tend towards zero, either in Mexico City or in Paris.

One of our friends, to whom we showed this problem, was unkind enough to state that if the detectives and thieves were intelligent, the Manager of *Pronto* certainly wasn't. To support this statement, he pointed out that this personage evidently had not examined the efficiency of his system of surveillance.

	A	B	
AA	0.64	0.36	x_1
BB	0.19	0.91	x_2
AB	0.46	0.76	x_3
	y_1	y_2	

FIG. 10.3

"Suppose," he said, "we were to eliminate the television as a part of the system, the table for the game will be reduced to that of Fig. 10.3. It is easy to discover, in Fig. 10.2, that the solution of the game is then given by the intersection of straight lines (2) and (6), so that

$$y_1 = 0.69, \quad y_2 = 0.31; \quad x_2 = 0.53, \quad x_6 = 0.47, \quad \text{and} \quad g = 0.55.$$

As a result, the television set only increases the probability of an arrest by 0.034, which must surely raise the question whether the use of this expensive equipment is justified by such a wretched return."

To which we replied:

(1) That it was not contrary to the nature of a detective to prefer to be seated for some half of the time he was on duty.

(2) That the mere presence of television cameras might act as a powerful psychological deterrent for apprentice thieves who had not yet definitely decided on adopting the profession.

(3) It was scarcely credible that the management had not been informed of the poor return from the use of television.

(4) It was not beyond the bounds of possibility that the management, after taking stock of the situation, had decided to retain it because of its modern character and psychological effect.

Introduction to the Theory of Games

The theory relating to games with n players is a difficult one, but where the game is limited to two players or two groups of players, as in the example treated earlier, the theory is quite simple, and we propose to give a short resume of it.

The table which sums up the rule of the game is termed the *matrix* of the game; it expresses the gains of player *A*, known as the *maximizing* player (or the losses of player *B*, termed the *minimizing* player), if the game has a *zero sum*, in other words, if the gains of one player are equal to the losses of the other (Fig. 10.4).

		Player B		
		I	II	III
Player A	1	2	—1	1
	2	—2	1	—1
	3	—2	1	—2
	4	2	—2	3

FIG. 10.4

Assuming that in every *round* of the game player *A* and player *B* must each *simultaneously* choose a pure strategy, that is, one line for *A* and one column for *B*:

if *A* chooses 2 and *B* chooses II, *A* will receive one token;

if *A* chooses 3 and *B* chooses III, *A* will receive —2 tokens, which means he will hand over two tokens to *B*; and so on.

If the game is limited to *one round*, the reasoning of *A* and *B* might be as follows, in accordance with the elementary theorem of Von Neumann.

PLAYER *A*: My minimal gain for each of the pure strategies 1, 2, 3, and 4 amounts to —1, —2, —2, —2. Hence, I shall choose the maximum of these minimal gains and shall select pure strategy 1 which, whatever my opponent's strategy may be, will ensure me a *maximum* of —1. Given the sign, this could read, "will not make me lose more than 1," while at the same time offering me possibilities of gain.

PLAYER *B*: My maximal loss for each of the pure strategies I, II, and III would be 2, 1, 3; I shall choose the minimum from these maximal losses and adopt pure strategy II; which, whatever the strategy of my opponent, will ensure the *minimax* 1, that is, while still offering possibilities of gain, it will limit my loss to 1.

Indeed, in accordance with this reasoning, in a game of one round, player A would lose 1 and player B would gain 1, with the limited risks which they have selected.

Such would be the behavior of intelligent and prudent players. But assuming that the players were only intelligent, and not prudent. A might reason: "B is going to choose II, and under these conditions I shall select strategy 2 or 3, either of which will ensure me a gain of 1." Equally, B might reason: "A will undoubtedly play 2 or 3, and I shall therefore play I, so as to be certain of gaining 2." And so on.

It will be seen that to adopt strategies other than those defined by the theorem of Von Neumann only has the effect of increasing the risk for each player.

Let us now assume that the two players decide to play a *game*, that is, a number of successive rounds. In certain cases, such as that of the matrix of Fig. 10.5, the search for the maximin induces player A to

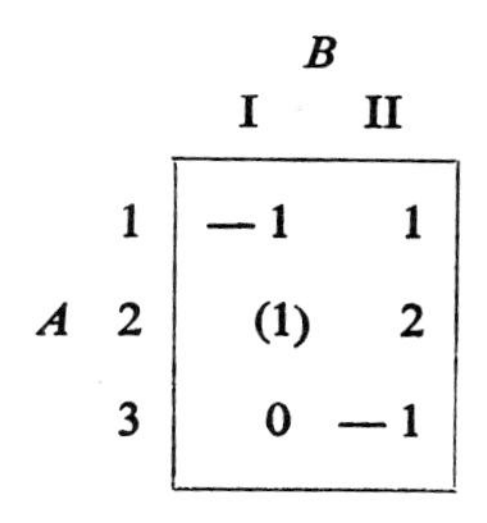

FIG. 10.5

adopt pure strategy 2, which will ensure a minimal gain of 1, while the search for the minimax leads player B to choose pure strategy I, which will ensure a minimal loss of 1. Here, the maximin and minimax coincide: they have as their value a solitary element of the matrix, which is called the *saddle point*, and has the property of being the smallest element in its line and the largest one in its column. Then, whatever the number of rounds, the optimal strategies chosen will remain invariable. A will always play line 2, and B column I, with the result that each round will end with a gain of 1 for A and a loss of 1 for B. Here, we are not considering a game with equilibrium; the value of the game $g = 1$ represents a gain for A and a loss for B with each round.

On the contrary, if we turn back to Fig. 10.4, we can see that there is no saddle point so that in a game of *several rounds*, the players might reason:

PLAYER *A*. If my opponent plays columns I, II, and III with frequencies of y_1, y_2, and y_3, and I, myself, play lines 1, 2, 3, and 4 with frequencies of x_1, x_2, x_3, and x_4, the expected value of my gain will be

$$(2x_1 - 2x_2 - 2x_3 + 2x_4)y_1 + (-x_1 + x_2 + x_3 - 2x_4)y_2 + (x_1 - x_2 - 2x_3 + 3x_4)y_3,$$

my aim being to maximize this expected value.

PLAYER *B*. Contrary to my opponent, my aim is to minimize the expected value of my loss.

For *B*, this is represented by the expression

$$(2y_1 - y_2 + y_3)x_1 + (-2y_1 + y_2 - y_3)x_2 + (-2y_1 + y_2 - 2y_3)x_3 + (2y_1 - 2y_2 + 3y_3)x_4 .$$

By assuming that there is only one value for the game, namely g, which is true, as we shall see in connection with the duality of linear programs, it becomes clear (since the expected value for each player must be maximized) that, whatever strategy is adopted by the opponent—especially if it is any pure strategy—we finally arrive at two series of inequalities and equations.

	Series 1 (player *A*)	Series 2 (player *B*)	
(*a*)	$2x_1 - 2x_2 - 2x_3 + 2x_4 \geqslant g$	$2y_1 - y_2 + y_3 \leqslant g$	(*a*′)
(*b*)	$-x_1 + x_2 + x_3 - 2x_4 \geqslant g$	$-2y_1 + y_2 - y_3 \leqslant g$	(*b*′)
(*c*)	$x_1 - x_2 - 2x_3 + 3x_4 \geqslant g$	$-2y_1 + y_2 - 2y_3 \leqslant g$	(*c*′)
(*d*)	$x_1, x_2, x_3, x_4 \geqslant 0$	$2y_1 - 2y_2 + 3y_3 \leqslant g$	(*d*′)
(*e*)	$x_1 + x_2 + x_3 + x_4 = 1$	$y_1, y_2, y_3 \geqslant 0$	(*e*′)
		$y_1 + y_2 + y_3 = 1.$	(*f*′)

We discover a linear program *prime* to the left and *dual* to the right (or inversely). Fortunately, a close examination will provide an easy solution. Indeed, we can at once see that, by adding (*a*′) and (*b*′), the value of the game can only be positive or nil: $g \geqslant 0$.

Next, by adding (a) and 2(b), we have

$$\begin{array}{r} 2x_1 - 2x_2 - 2x_3 + 2x_4 \geqslant 0 \\ -2x_1 + 2x_2 + 2x_3 - 4x_4 \geqslant 0 \\ \hline -2x_4 \geqslant 0 \end{array}$$

and, as $x_4 \geqslant 0$, we must take $x_4 = 0$.

Consequently (b) and (c) become

$$-x_1 + x_2 + x_3 \geqslant 0,$$
$$x_1 - x_2 - 2x_3 \geqslant 0,$$

whence, by addition, $-x_3 \geqslant 0$ which, with $x_3 \geqslant 0$, ensures $x_3 = 0$.

Finally, we have

$$-x_1 + x_2 \geqslant 0,$$
$$x_1 - x_2 \geqslant 0,$$

whence $x_1 = x_2 = \frac{1}{2}$, and $g = 0$.

The mixed optimal strategy chosen by player B will therefore be

$$x_1 = \tfrac{1}{2}, \qquad x_2 = \tfrac{1}{2}, \qquad x_3 = 0, \qquad x_4 = 0, \qquad \text{with} \qquad g = 0.$$

System II is then reduced to

$$2y_1 - y_2 + y_3 = 0,$$
$$2y_1 - 2y_2 + 3y_3 \leqslant 0,$$
$$y_1,\ y_2,\ y_3 \geqslant 0,$$
$$y_1 + y_2 + y_3 = 1,$$

the solutions for which are

$$y_1 = \tfrac{1}{7} + 2\lambda, \qquad y_2 = \tfrac{4}{7} + \lambda, \qquad y_3 = \tfrac{2}{7} - 3\lambda,$$

with $0 \leqslant \lambda \leqslant \frac{2}{21}$. For the limiting values of λ, we have

$$(\lambda = 0) \qquad y_1^1 = \tfrac{1}{7}, \qquad y_2^1 = \tfrac{4}{7}, \qquad y_3^1 = \tfrac{2}{7},$$

and

$$(\lambda = \tfrac{2}{21}) \qquad y_1^2 = \tfrac{1}{3}, \qquad y_2^2 = \tfrac{2}{3}, \qquad y_3^2 = 0.$$

This is another case where a choice seems easier for player B, but this is only so in appearance. His expected value of gain is of the form

$$E(B) = (-\tfrac{2}{7} + 3\lambda)x_3 - 7\lambda x_4;$$

hence it becomes nil from the moment when A ceases to use frequencies of x_3 and x_4. Thus,

$$E(A) = E(B) = g = 0.$$

To operate the mixed optimal strategies, each player should use tables of random numbers or a lottery wheel[2] which will allow him to respect the frequencies he has chosen, while keeping his opponent in ignorance of the succession of plays which he has planned.

Observation I. System II can be reduced to two equivalent equations (a') and (b') and two strict inequalities (c') and (d'); hence it conforms to the rule given earlier, that $x_3 = x_4 = 0$. System I can be reduced to three equations, and we find that y_1, y_2, and y_3 differ from 0.

Observation II. The existence of an optimal mixed strategy is merely an extension of Von Neumann's theorem. We discover in it the concepts of *equilibrium* (solitary value for the game) and of *stability* and *security*, revealed by the impossibility for either player to deviate from the optimal strategies without increasing his risk.

[2] For example, if $x_1 = x_2 = \frac{1}{2}$ for player A, he could use a wheel with 100 numbers from 00 to 99, and would play strategy 1 each time he draws a number between 00 and 49, and strategy 2 for any draw between 50 and 99 (inclusive bounds).

CHAPTER 11

ONE AND ONE MAKE ONE—A PROPAGANDA HIT IN TWO ACTS

(Use of Boolean Algebra)

Act I

SCENE I

(*Peter and John have just met in the street.*)

Peter. I have a wonderful idea for the fair.

John. What is your brain wave?

Peter. That we should manufacture small radio sets and sell them from our own stand. All the fellows are keen on radio, and if we all work at it there will be no labor costs, and all we need do is to buy the parts and assemble them.

John. A bright idea; but have you got diagrams for the wiring?

Peter. Several. I'll show them to you tomorrow.

SCENE II

(*Next day, at John's home.*)

Peter. Here are three types of assembly; I have found out the price for the tubes, the parts, and the cases. Any of them can be used, subject to certain conditions:

(1) As you see, we can use any of the three series of tubes T_1, T_2, or T_3, but they must be kept separate and not combined in the same set.

(2) We could make a wooden case E or we could buy a plastic case P but we can't use T_2 with the latter, and as there is not space enough in P for a transformer, we shall have to fit a special feed, A.

(3) If we choose the T_1 tubes we must use the transformer F.

(4) T_2 and T_3 require the special feed A.

The prices of the tubes and other parts are:

Set of tubes T_1 costs	28 F,	Special feed A costs	23 F,
T_2	30 F,	Wooden case E	9 F,
T_3	31 F,	Plastic case P	6 F.
Transformer F	25 F,		

The other parts which will be needed (resistances, coils, condensers, mechanical parts, switches, potentiometers, dials) will only differ slightly with the three series of tubes: with T_1 they will cost 27 F, with T_2, 28 F, with T_3, 25 F.

I have studied the prices in the shops, and have calculated that we can afford to sell our sets for 30% less than they are asking. With a wooden case our radios will sell at 110 F, and with a plastic case for 105 F.

Unfortunately, the choice of the model to assemble is almost as complicated as the wiring. What is your opinion? We could decide on the T_2 tubes, but which case shall we use? Perhaps the T_3 series would be preferable, after all.

John. I suggest we use the tubes and cases which will show the largest profit.

Peter. You're perfectly right, and I'll go home now and work out the calculations.

Act II

Scene I

(*Peter's home, the following day.*)

Peter. I have tried to work out the cost prices, as we agreed, but unfortunately I wasn't able to reconcile all those contradictory conditions I mentioned to you.

John. Then we'll go and consult my brother, Louis. He's a confounded mathematician, and no problem seems too difficult for him.

SCENE II

(*John's house, ten minutes later.*)

Louis. My friends, you have an interesting problem here! Have you ever heard of George Boole?

Both. Who is he?

Louis. The story of his life would make interesting telling. He was an English mathematician who lived over a hundred years ago, and who had the idea of expressing logical propositions in the form of algebra. Under these conditions, finding whether or not a set of propositions is true becomes a sequence of quite simple operations. It's very interesting, as you will see.

Both. We are listening.

(*At this point a lengthy monologue begins, conforming to the tradition of propaganda plays.*)

Louis. Let us assume two elements *a* and *b* of a proposition, connected by the linking conjunction *and*, which we express as $a \cdot b$. Let us further assume that these elements are connected in such a manner that the word *and* in reality means "one or other or the two together," representing, in fact, the Latin *vel*, which can be translated "and/or." We now express this as $a \dot{+} b$, and must be careful not to confuse this dual significance of *and* with the exclusive *or* used in such a phrase as: "your money *or* your life!"

Let us now examine the proposition: "in order to write, one requires a pen or a pencil and a sheet of paper." We shall use this notation:

To possess a pen:	a	Not to have a pen:	$\bar{a}$
a pencil:	b	a pencil:	$\bar{b}$
paper:	c	paper:	$\bar{c}$
To be able to write:	1	Not to be able to write:	0

With this notation, the previous sentence would be accurately expressed as $(a \dot{+} b) \cdot c = 1$. How simple this is! It is, in fact, more precise than words, for the English language does not differentiate between the exclusive and nonexclusive *or*, which is a great pity.

Let us now slightly alter our proposition, so that it reads: "in order to write, one must have a pen *or* a pencil in one's hand and a sheet of paper in front of one." Here, the *or* is exclusive (try to write with a pen and a pencil at the same time!), and the proposition will be expressed as

$$(a \cdot \bar{b} \dotplus \bar{a} \cdot b) \cdot c = 1.$$

Thus, the exclusive *or* is shown as $a \cdot \bar{b} \dotplus \bar{a} \cdot b$, signifying a pen and no pencil or no pen and a pencil.

In this manner we can construct a system of elementary algebra very similar to the algebra taught in school and to which the usual rules can be applied, with the proviso that

$$a \cdot a = a \tag{1}$$

and

$$a \dotplus a = a. \tag{2}$$

Let us consider certain notations and properties:

if a is true, we state $a = 1$;
if a is false, we write $a = 0$.

Consequently, we use a variable which can only possess two values, 0 or 1. Given two variables of this type, or *binary* variables, a and b:

$$\begin{array}{llll} \text{If:} & a = 0,\quad b = 0, & \text{then:} & a \cdot b = 0,\quad a \dotplus b = 0, \\ & a = 0,\quad b = 1, & & a \cdot b = 0,\quad a \dotplus b = 1, \\ & a = 1,\quad b = 0, & & a \cdot b = 0,\quad a \dotplus b = 1, \\ & a = 1,\quad b = 1, & & a \cdot b = 1,\quad a \dotplus b = 1, \end{array}$$

whence we obtain the table of the logical product and sum

$$\begin{array}{cccc} 0 \cdot 0 = 0, & 0 \cdot 1 = 0, & 1 \cdot 0 = 0, & 1 \cdot 1 = 1, \\ 0 \dotplus 0 = 0, & 0 \dotplus 1 = 1, & 1 \dotplus 0 = 1, & 1 \dotplus 1 = 1. \end{array}$$

Here the dot does not represent "multiplied by," but "and," while the Boolean plus sign does not mean "added to," but replaces "and/or." We could also employ the signs $\cap$ and $\cup$, used in the theory of sets, but this is not of much advantage in binary algebra.

Let us now return to your problem and try to discover the type of set which would yield the most profit. You stated four conditions which we will call C_1, C_2, C_3, and C_4.

C_1. We shall use one and only one series of tubes, a decision which, in Boolean algebra, is expressed as

$$T_1 \cdot \bar{T}_2 \cdot \bar{T}_3 \dotplus \bar{T}_1 \cdot T_2 \cdot \bar{T}_3 \dotplus \bar{T}_1 \cdot \bar{T}_2 \cdot T_3 = 1,$$

where T_1 means: "we shall use series T_1," and $\bar{T}_1$: "we shall not use series T_1," and so on for the other T_i symbols.

Before we discuss the other conditions, let me point out that there is no need to retain seven variables. Five are sufficient, since E and P are mutually exclusive, and the same is true of A and F. Hence we can state

$$E = \bar{P} \quad \text{or} \quad \bar{E} = P, \qquad \text{and} \qquad A = \bar{F} \quad \text{or} \quad \bar{A} = F.$$

C_2. If we use a case P, this implies that we cannot include a T_2 series and a transformer F. How is this *implication* to be expressed? If a implies b, we should have $a \cdot \bar{b} = 0$, which means that it is false to have a and not to have b. But this relation is equivalent to $\bar{a} \dotplus b = 1$, which is the complementary proposition.[1]

Condition C_2 can therefore be expressed as

$$P \cdot (T_2 \dotplus F) = 0$$

or

$$\bar{P} \dotplus \bar{T}_2 \cdot \bar{F} = 1.$$

C_3. Using the T_1 series implies the use of transformer F; another implication:

$$T_1 \cdot \bar{F} = 0$$

or

$$\bar{T}_1 \dotplus F = 1.$$

[1] It is easy to show that

$$\overline{a \dotplus b} = \bar{a} \cdot \bar{b}, \qquad \overline{a \cdot b} = \bar{a} \dotplus \bar{b},$$

$$\overline{a \dotplus \bar{b}} = \bar{a} \cdot b, \qquad \overline{a \cdot \bar{b}} = \bar{a} \dotplus b,$$

which can, moreover, be expressed in a general form.

C_4. Using T_2 or T_3 implies a feed A, expressed as

$$(T_2 \dotplus T_3) \cdot \bar{A} = 0$$

or else

$$\bar{T}_2 \cdot \bar{T}_3 \dotplus A = 1;$$

but $A = \bar{F}$, so that the condition can be shown as

$$\bar{T}_2 \cdot \bar{T}_3 \dotplus \bar{F} = 1.$$

If these four conditions are to be verified, it must be true that

$$C_1 \cdot C_2 \cdot C_3 \cdot C_4 = 1,$$

that is

$$T_1 \cdot \bar{T}_2 \cdot \bar{T}_3 \dotplus \bar{T}_1 \cdot T_2 \cdot \bar{T}_3 \dotplus (\bar{T}_1 \cdot \bar{T}_2 \cdot T_3) \cdot (\bar{P} \dotplus \bar{T}_2 \cdot \bar{F}) \cdot (\bar{T}_1 \dotplus F) \cdot (\bar{T}_2 \cdot \bar{T}_3 \dotplus \bar{F}) = 1. \tag{3}$$

This expression can be greatly simplified if we use Eqs. (1) and (2) and also

$$a \dotplus \bar{a} = 1, \quad a \cdot \bar{a} = 0, \quad a \dotplus 1 = 1, \quad a \cdot 1 = a,$$
$$a \dotplus 0 = a, \quad a \cdot 0 = 0,$$

which should be obvious to you.

The products (in the sense used by Boole) in Eq. (3) can be worked out in any order; let us take the last one:

$$(\bar{T}_1 \dotplus F) \cdot (\bar{T}_2 \cdot \bar{T}_3 \dotplus \bar{F}) = \bar{T}_1 \cdot \bar{T}_2 \cdot \bar{T}_3 \dotplus \bar{T}_1 \cdot \bar{F} \dotplus \bar{T}_2 \cdot \bar{T}_3 \cdot F;$$

then let us use Boolean multiplication to find the product of this result and C_2.

$$(\bar{P} \dotplus \bar{T}_2\bar{F}) \cdot (\bar{T}_1 \cdot \bar{T}_2 \cdot \bar{T}_3 \dotplus \bar{T}_1 \cdot \bar{F} \dotplus \bar{T}_2 \cdot \bar{T}_3 \cdot F)$$
$$= \bar{T}_1 \cdot \bar{T}_2 \cdot \bar{T}_3 \cdot \bar{P} \dotplus \bar{T}_1 \cdot \bar{F} \cdot \bar{P} \dotplus \bar{T}_2 \cdot \bar{T}_3 \cdot F \cdot \bar{P} \dotplus \bar{T}_1 \cdot \bar{T}_2 \cdot \bar{F}.$$

It will be seen that, of the six terms in the product, one is zero:

$$\bar{T}_2 \cdot \bar{F} \cdot \bar{T}_2 \cdot \bar{T}_3 \cdot F = 0,$$

and another is included in $\bar{T}_1 \cdot \bar{T}_2 \cdot \bar{F}$; we have:

$$(\bar{T}_2 \cdot \bar{F}) \cdot (\bar{T}_1 \cdot \bar{T}_2 \cdot \bar{T}_3) = \bar{T}_1 \cdot \bar{T}_2 \cdot \bar{T}_3 \cdot \bar{F}$$

and $\bar{T}_1 \cdot \bar{T}_2 \cdot \bar{T}_3 \cdot \bar{F}$ is only part of $\bar{T}_1 \cdot \bar{T}_2 \cdot \bar{F}$, since

$$(\bar{T}_1 \cdot \bar{T}_2 \cdot \bar{F}) \cdot 1 = (\bar{T}_1 \cdot \bar{T}_2 \cdot \bar{F}) \cdot (T_3 \dot{+} \bar{T}_3) = \bar{T}_1 \cdot \bar{T}_2 \cdot T_3 \cdot \bar{F} \dot{+} \bar{T}_1 \cdot \bar{T}_2 \cdot \bar{T}_3 \cdot \bar{F}$$

We have now to find the Boolean product of the last result and C_1.

$$\begin{aligned}(T_1 \cdot \bar{T}_2 \cdot \bar{T}_3 \dot{+} \bar{T}_1 \cdot T_2 \cdot \bar{T}_3 \dot{+} \bar{T}_1 \cdot \bar{T}_2 \cdot T_3)& \\ \cdot (\bar{T}_1 \cdot \bar{T}_2 \cdot \bar{T}_3 \cdot \bar{P} \dot{+} \bar{T}_1 \cdot \bar{F} \cdot \bar{P} \dot{+} \bar{T}_2 \cdot \bar{T}_3 \cdot F \cdot \bar{P} \dot{+} \bar{T}_1 \cdot \bar{T}_2 \cdot \bar{F})& \\ = T_1 \cdot \bar{T}_2 \cdot \bar{T}_3 \cdot F \cdot \bar{P} \dot{+} \bar{T}_1 \cdot T_2 \cdot \bar{T}_3 \cdot \bar{F} \cdot \bar{P} \dot{+} \bar{T}_1 \cdot \bar{T}_2 \cdot T_3 \cdot \bar{F}.&\end{aligned}$$

If the final result is to be equal to 1, at least one of the terms of the sum must also be 1:

$$T_1 \cdot \bar{T}_2 \cdot \bar{T}_3 \cdot F \cdot \bar{P} = 1$$

means a possible solution, that is, one compatible with the conditions is an assembly T_1FE;

$$\bar{T}_1 \cdot T_2 \cdot \bar{T}_3 \cdot \bar{F} \cdot \bar{P} = 1$$

means T_2AE is a possible solution;

$$\bar{T}_1 \cdot \bar{T}_2 \cdot T_3 \cdot \bar{F} = 1$$

means a possible assembly is T_3A, and as either E or P may be used, we must consider both T_3AE and T_3AP.

We will now calculate the profits corresponding to these solutions:

$$\begin{aligned} T_1FE&: \quad 110 - (28 + 25 + 9 + 27) = 21 \text{ F},\\ T_2AE&: \quad 110 - (30 + 23 + 9 + 28) = 20 \text{ F},\\ T_3AE&: \quad 110 - (31 + 23 + 9 + 25) = 22 \text{ F},\\ T_3AP&: \quad 105 - (31 + 23 + 6 + 25) = 20 \text{ F}.\end{aligned}$$

Accordingly, it is the model with a wooden case equipped with T_3 tubes and feed A which will give you the largest profit, namely 22 F.

(*His listeners can, at last, put in a word.*)

Peter. Why did you have to go into all those calculations? Wouldn't it have been simpler to enumerate all the possible combinations and eliminate those which were incompatible with the conditions?

Louis. In this particular case you are quite right. From the diagram I am sketching [Fig. 11.1], you will see that there are twelve combinations, of which only four are possible. The truth is I wanted to take advantage of your little problem to tell you something about Boole's algebra and the type of problem in which it can be useful. Of course,

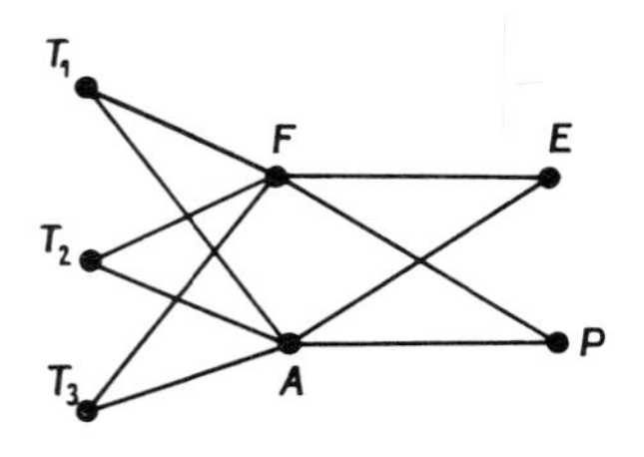

FIG. 11.1

industrial problems are much more complex than yours, and the parts to be considered are often very varied as well as numerous. In these cases an astronomical number of solutions would need examining, whereas Boole's algebra greatly restricts the number. Sometimes, too, it is almost impossible to analyze the final assembly from the specifications of the parts, and Boole's algebra is then virtually indispensable.

CURTAIN

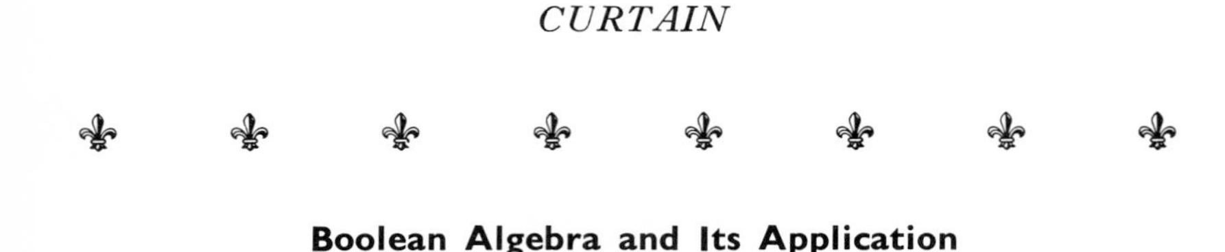

Boolean Algebra and Its Application

A. PROPERTIES OF UNION AND INTERSECTION

In our brief survey of Boole's algebra[2] we shall begin by justifying the rules used in the last problem. Let us start by considering a set of objects, such as a collection of different-currency bills. This set will constitute the *referential* within whose limits our reasoning will be confined. Let us now separate the hundred bills into several groups,

[2] For a more complete study, the reader should consult *Cours de calcul booléien appliqué* by Denis-Papin, A. Kaufmann, and R. Faure, Albin Michel, Paris.

placing the 36 bills of large denomination in the first of two receptacles A and B, and the smaller bills in the second receptacle (Figs. 11.2 and 11.3).

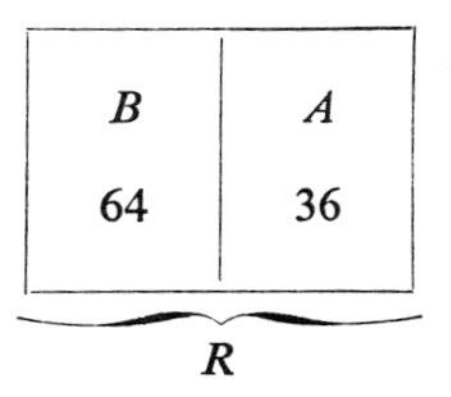

FIG. 11.2

B	A	
11	6	r
8	3	y
17	9	g
14	12	b
14	6	v
64	36	

$\underbrace{\hspace{2em}}_{B}$ $\underbrace{\hspace{2em}}_{A}$

FIG. 11.3

But the bills are of different colors—red, yellow, green, blue, and violet, and we shall divide each of the receptables into five compartments. The number of bills of various colors placed in these compartments is shown in Fig. 11.3.

CONCEPT OF UNION. If we effect the *union* of the bills in A and B we obtain the set of bills of the referential R,

$$A \cup B = R.$$

We may also group the bills according to color in each of the classes A and B:

$$A_r \cup A_y \cup A_g \cup A_b \cup A_v = A,$$
$$B_r \cup B_y \cup B_g \cup B_b \cup B_v = B,$$

referring to A_r, B_r, A_y, B_y, etc. as the respective *subsets* of A and B, which contain only red bills, yellow bills, and so on.

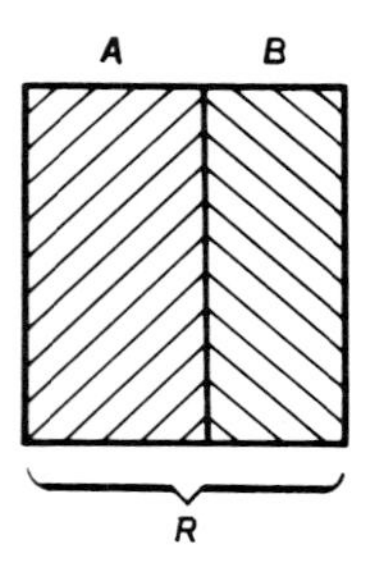

FIG. 11.4. The union is shown by the hatching of both zones.

Naturally, we can invert the order in which union is carried out:

$$A \cup B = B \cup A = R;$$

the operation known as union is, then, *commutative*.

We can also carry out partial unions; for example,

$$\{[(A_r \cup A_y) \cup A_g] \cup A_b\} \cup A_v = A,$$

$$A_r \cup \{[(A_y \cup A_g) \cup A_b] \cup A_v\} = A.$$

This shows that union is *associative*.

CONCEPT OF INTERSECTION. Let us now consider the set of red bills containing 11 ordinary and 6 large notes. If we call this set E_r, we have

$$E_r = A_r \cup B_r .$$

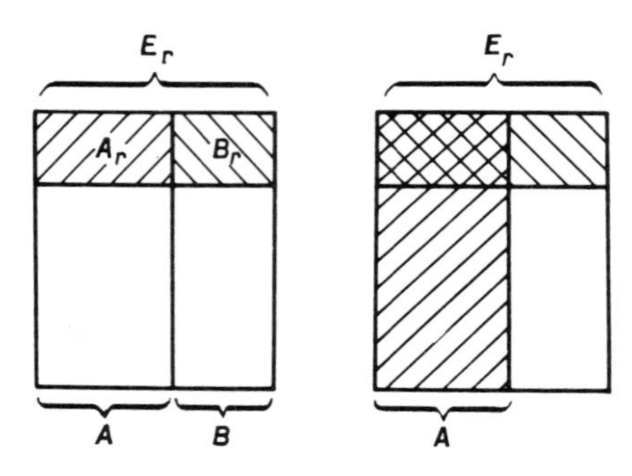

FIG. 11.5. Intersection A_r is formed by the crosshatching.

	T	P		T
	32	32	21	15
r	5	6	3	3
y	4	4	2	1
g	9	8	4	5
b	6	8	9	3
v	8	6	3	3
	64		36	
	B		A	

FIG. 11.6

Sets E_r and A have a common part which is the subset A_r ; this is expressed as

$$E_r \cap A = A_r ,$$

and is called an *intersection*. Similarly,

$$E_r \cap B = B_r .$$

It can easily be seen that intersection is *commutative*.

Let us now assume that some of the bills are made of terra cotta and some of plastic, and to sort these we make further subdivisions of the compartments. We can state, for instance, that

$$E_g = A_g \cup B_g = A_{gT} \cup A_{gP} \cup B_{gP} \cup B_{gT} ,$$

using A_{gT} and A_{gP} to represent the subdivisions of compartment A_g which contain bills made respectively of terra cotta and plastic.

Let us now consider the operation

$$(A \cap P) \cap E_g .$$

This consists in first taking the intersection of set A by set P, that is [Fig. 11.7 (left)], all the bills contained in the space $\alpha\beta\gamma\delta$, then the intersection of the resulting set by E_g , that is, the bills contained in the space *abcd*. It would amount to the same thing if we were to use Fig. 11.7 (right) and first take the intersection of P by E_g , that is $a\beta'\gamma'd$,

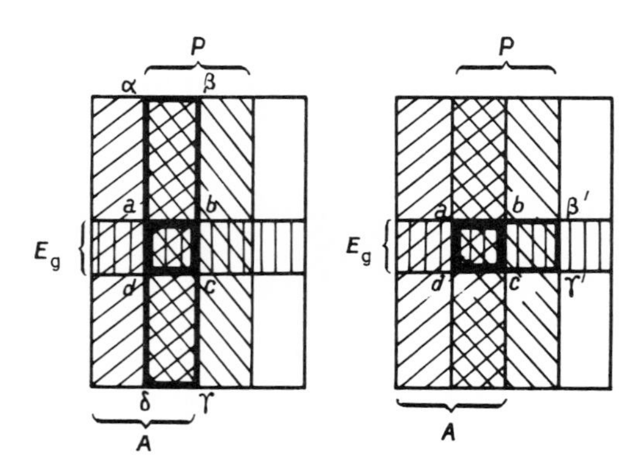

FIG. 11.7. Left: $(A \cap P) \cap E_g$; right: $A \cap (P \cap E_g)$. Only square *abcd* has three kinds of hatching.

then the intersection of this space by A, namely *abcd*. In either case we obtain A_{gP}.

Thus,

$$A \cap (P \cap E_g) = (A \cap P) \cap E_g\,,$$

which shows that intersection is *associative*.

Let us calculate

$$A \cup (P \cap E_g).$$

We show that

$$A \cup (P \cap E_g) = (A \cup P) \cap (A \cup E_g).$$

Figures 11.8(a) and (b) show that *union is distributive in relation to intersection*, which constitutes a remarkable property: for instance, addition is not distributive in relation to multiplication, since we do not find

$$7 + (3 \times 5) = (7 + 3) \times (7 + 5).$$

Let us now show that intersection is distributive in relation *to union*: in other words, that if L, M, and N are three sets, then

$$L \cap (M \cup N) = (L \cap M) \cup (L \cap N).$$

For the sake of an example, let us show that

$$A \cap (P \cup E_g) = (A \cap P) \cup (A \cap E_g).$$

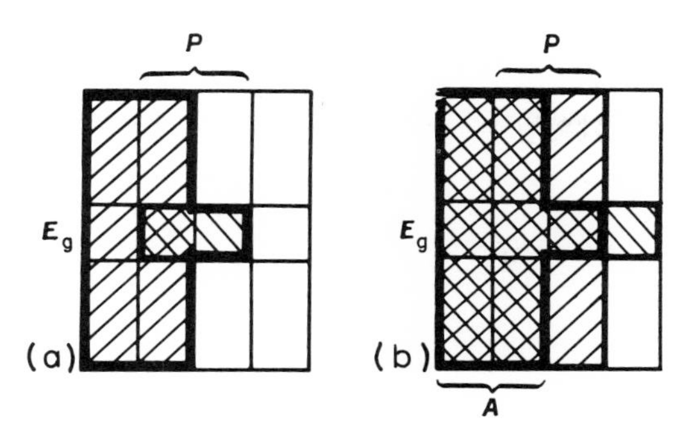

FIG. 11.8(a). The complete figure (union) is hatched: $A \cup (\bar{P} \cap E_g)$.

FIG. 11.8(b). The common area (intersection) has two types of hatching: $(A \cup P) \cap (A \cup E_g)$.

Figure 11.9(a) represents the results of the operations corresponding to the left member of this equality; Fig. 11.9(b) shows the development of the right member. It can easily be seen that we arrive at the same result.

MORGAN'S THEOREM. Let us begin by introducing class $\bar{M}$ of a class M: it can be defined as including all the elements which belong to the referential but which do not belong to M. For instance, in Fig. 11.10 we have hatched everything which is included in the referential and which is external to E_g and by so doing have obtained $\bar{E}_g$. If we now consider $\bar{E}_g \cup \bar{P}$ (Fig. 11.11), it is easy to see that this is identical to

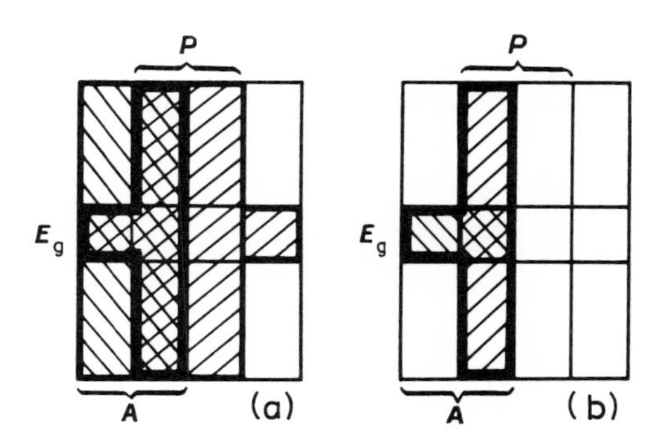

FIG. 11.9(a). The area in common (intersection) is doubly hatched: $A \cap (P \cup E_g)$.

FIG. 11.9(b). The resulting figure (union) is entirely hatched: $(A \cap P) \cup (A \cap E_g)$.

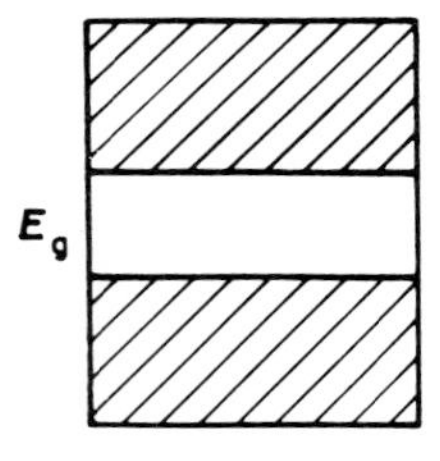

FIG. 11.10

$\overline{E_g \cap P}$ (Figs. 11.12 and 11.13). In the same way, we see from Figs. 11.14 and 11.15 that

$$\overline{E_g \cup P} = \bar{E}_g \cap \bar{P}.$$

If we place the two identities

$$\overline{E_g \cap P} = \bar{E}_g \cup \bar{P} \qquad \text{and} \qquad \overline{E_g \cup P} = \bar{E}_g \cap \bar{P}$$

together, we observe the symmetry or, as it is termed, the *duality* between these two relations which constitute Morgan's theorem.

In more general terms, given two sets L and M,

$$\overline{L \cap M} = \bar{L} \cup \bar{M}, \qquad \overline{\bar{L} \cap \bar{M}} = L \cup M,$$

$$\overline{L \cup M} = \bar{L} \cap \bar{M}, \qquad \overline{\bar{L} \cup \bar{M}} = L \cap M.$$

B. INTRODUCTION OF THE UNIVERSAL ELEMENTS

By convention the set of the referential is designated as 1, that is $R = 1$. Any objects outside the referential which are considered form an empty set represented by 0, so that $\bar{R} = 0$. Let us therefore take the referential 1 and two sets A and B which form parts of it in such a way that B is included in A, the latter condition being shown as

$$B \subset A.$$

We notice that

$$B \cap A = B$$

and

$$B \cup A = A.$$

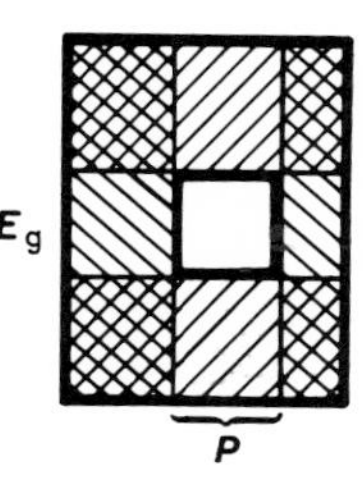

FIG. 11.11. $\bar{E}_g \cup \bar{P}$ (it is the hatched zone).

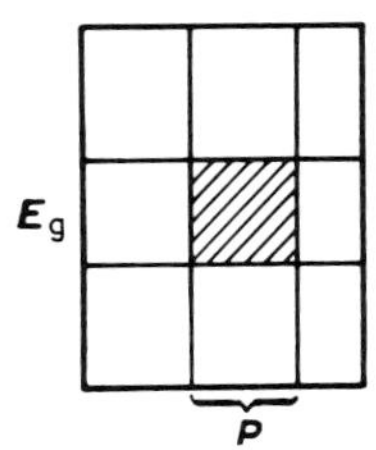

FIG. 11.12. $E_g \cap P$.

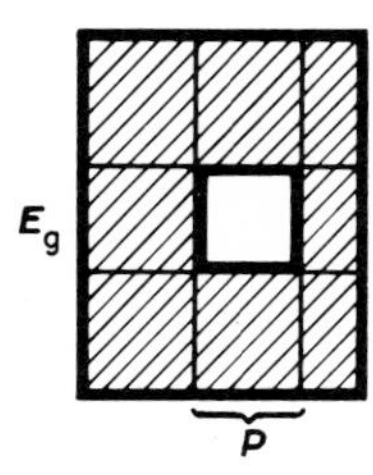

FIG. 11.13. $\overline{E_g \cap P}$ (it is the hatched zone).

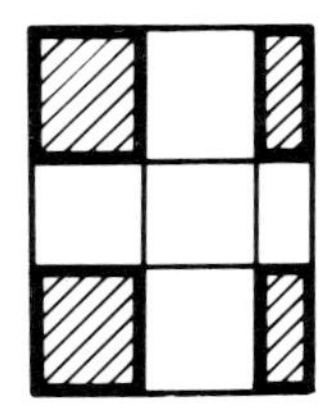

FIG. 11.14. $\overline{E_g \cup P}$.

FIG. 11.15. $\bar{E}_g \cap \bar{P}$ (it is the zone with the two kinds of hatching).

Figures 11.16 and 11.17 show two ways of expressing $B \subset A$.

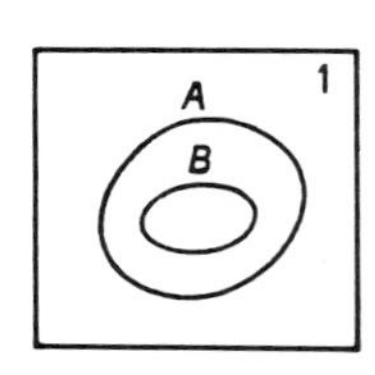

FIG. 11.16

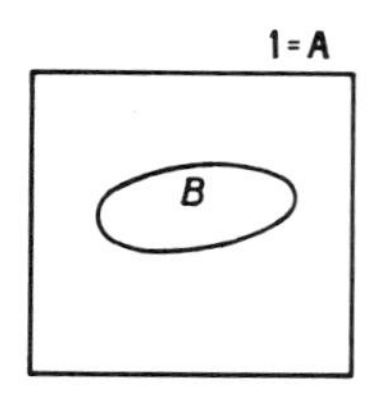

FIG. 11.17

If we now assume that A coincides with the referential (Fig. 11.17), we obtain

$$B \cap A = B \cap 1 = B,$$
$$B \cup A = B \cup 1 = 1.$$

Let us again replace A by the empty class

$$B \cap A = B \cap 0 = 0,$$
$$B \cup A = B \cup 0 = B.$$

It is easy to see that

$$1 \supset B \supset 0, \qquad B \cup \bar{B} = 1, \qquad \text{and} \qquad B \cap \bar{B} = 0,$$

Similarly, it is clear that

$$B \cup B = B,$$

and

$$B \cap B = B.$$

Finally, let us observe a new way of representing the inclusion:

$$A \cup \bar{B} = 1 \qquad \text{and} \qquad \bar{A} \cap B = 0.$$

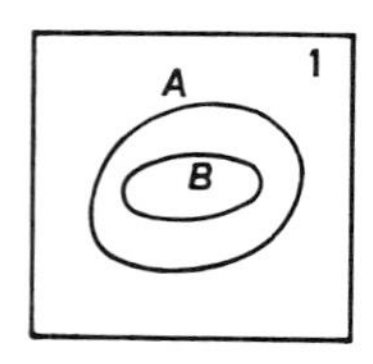

FIG. 11.18

These two expressions are also duals in the sense given to them by Morgan.

C. Boole's Binary Algebra

In a certain referential R, let us consider a set A, and let us decide to allocate to every element x of R a characteristic function, which will take the value 1 if x is an element of A, and 0 if it is not.

In Fig. 11.19, we have $f(x) = 1$. Let us now take two sets A and B

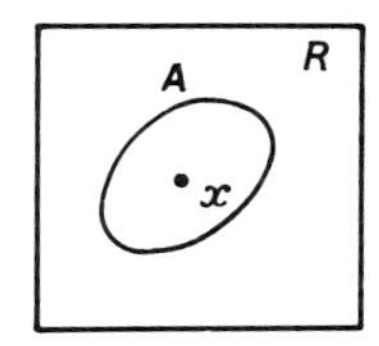

Fig. 11.19

with a nonvoid intersection in the referential R; diagram 1 of Fig. 11.20 is such that

$$f_A(x) = 1, \qquad f_B(x) = 1,$$

and also that

$$F_{A \cap B}(x) = 1.$$

Diagram 2 gives

$$f_A(x) = 1, \qquad f_B(x) = 0, \qquad \text{and} \qquad F_{A \cap B}(x) = 0.$$

From diagram 3 we can say

$$f_A(x) = 0, \qquad f_B(x) = 1, \qquad \text{and} \qquad F_{A \cap B}(x) = 0.$$

Finally, from diagram 4

$$f_A(x) = 0, \qquad f_B(x) = 0, \qquad \text{and} \qquad F_{A \cap B}(x) = 0.$$

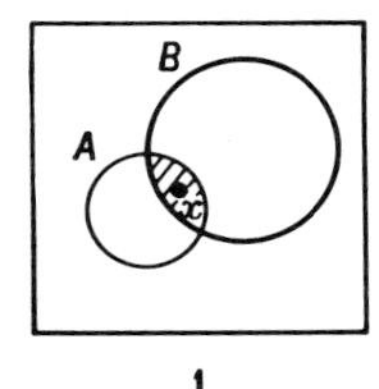

1

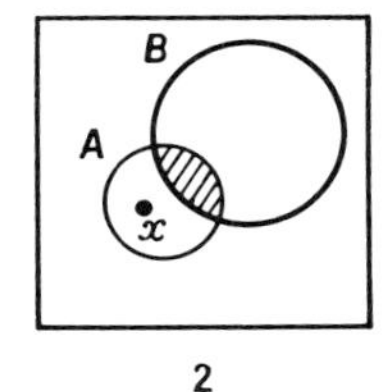

2

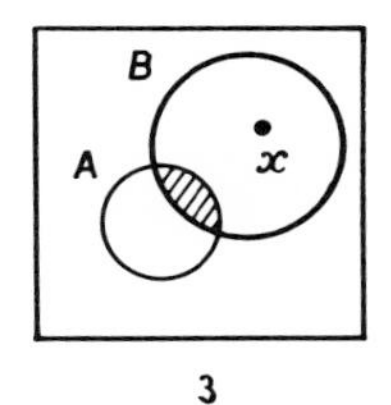

3

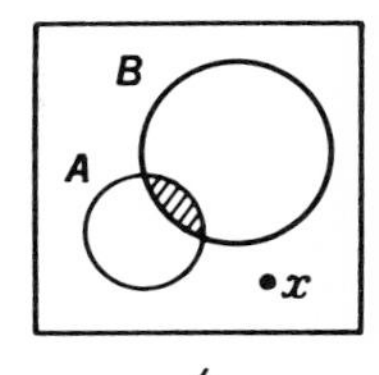

4

Fig. 11.20

We find that

$$F_{A\cap B}(x) = f_A(x) \cdot f_B(x)$$

with the usual table of products,

$$1 \cdot 1 = 1, \qquad 0 \cdot 1 = 0,$$
$$1 \cdot 0 = 0, \qquad 0 \cdot 0 = 0.$$

But we are dealing with the *logical product*, which we explained earlier: indeed, the elements of the intersection belong to *A and B*, in other words, they possess both the distinctive properties of A, which we will call p, and those of B, which we will call q; hence they possess *p and q*.

Let us now examine the case of union (Fig. 11.21). With the same

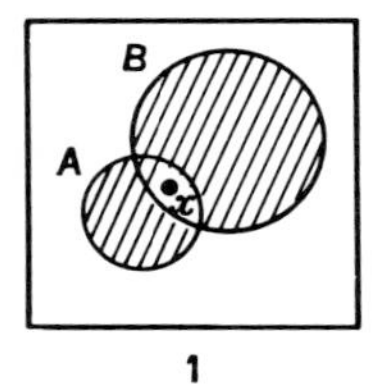

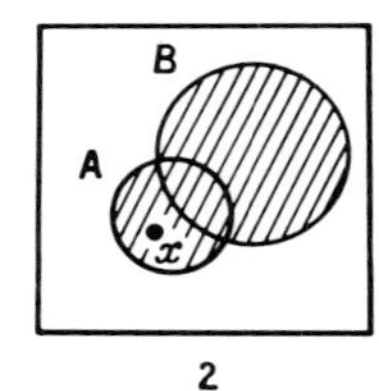

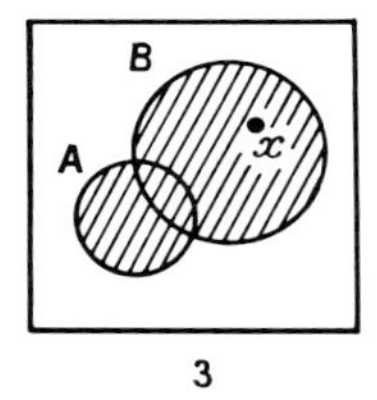

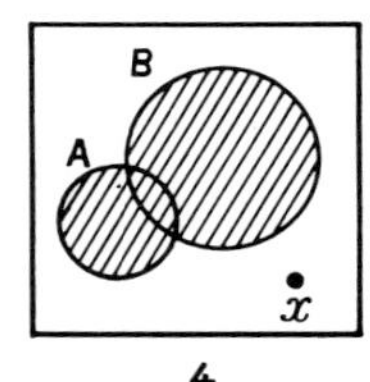

Fig. 11.21

conditions for the values of $f_A(x)$ and $f_B(x)$ as those given above, we obviously obtain

$$\begin{array}{llll} (1) & f_A(x) = 1, & f_B(x) = 1, & F_{A\cup B}(x) = 1, \\ (2) & f_A(x) = 1, & f_B(x) = 0, & F_{A\cup B}(x) = 1, \\ (3) & f_A(x) = 0, & f_B(x) = 1, & F_{A\cup B}(x) = 1, \\ (4) & f_A(x) = 0, & f_B(x) = 0, & F_{A\cup B}(x) = 0. \end{array}$$

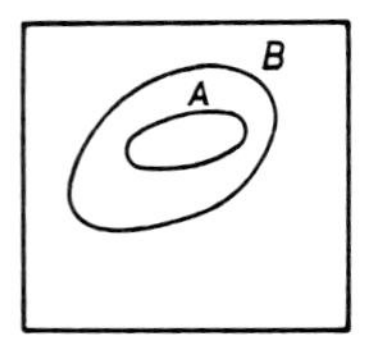

Fig. 11.22

We conclude from this that the characteristic function of a union is not the sum of the characteristic functions of the sets of which it is composed. We must therefore formulate a new table of the *logical sum*

$$1 \dotplus 1 = 1, \qquad 0 \dotplus 1 = 1,$$
$$1 \dotplus 0 = 1, \qquad 0 \dotplus 0 = 0.$$

Let us recollect that the Boolean sum of the elements of two sets A and B is composed of the elements of A and/or B; in other words, it possesses either property p (the characteristic of A), or property q (the characteristic of B), or the two properties p and q together (p or q or p and $q = p$ and/or q).

We believe it is not necessary to dwell on the other properties, which are now obvious

$$A \cdot A = A, \qquad A \dotplus A = A,$$
$$A \dotplus \bar{A} = 1, \qquad A \cdot \bar{A} = 0,$$
$$A \dotplus 1 = 1, \qquad A \cdot 1 = A,$$
$$A \dotplus 0 = A, \qquad A \cdot 0 = 0,$$

nor on the expressions of the inclusion $A \subset B$ (which in logic is sometimes termed *implication*):

$$\bar{A} \dotplus B = 1,$$
$$A \cdot \bar{B} = 0,$$

these two relations being, moreover, connected by Morgan's theorem.

Naturally, the commutative, associative, and distributive properties apply to Boole's binary algebra.

We hope that these few reflections will have served to introduce Boole's binary or logical algebra to our readers in a ... logical manner.

D. Application of Boole's Algebra

As we have seen, Boole's algebra can be used as an instrument of symbolic binary logic, where the principles of noncontradiction ($A \cdot \bar{A} = 0$) and of the excluded third ($A \dotplus \bar{A} = 1$) are allowed.

But it has an even more important use in the analysis and synthesis of chains of contact which constitute the organs of industrial automotisms and numerical calculators. For a number of years it has been used when relay or sequential circuits were worked out in detail. Its value is equally recognized when the logical organs are tubes, semiconductors, toruses, parametrons, etc.

And this is not all. Suitable as it is for representing combinatorial phenomena, it is frequently used in operations research, in which it is often coupled with the theory of grids.

CHAPTER 12

INTERPRETERS FOR TEOTIHUACAN

(Problem of Personnel Management)

The authentic monuments which form the Pyramids of the Sun and of the Moon at Teotihuacan are of earlier date than that of Columbus, and throughout the year crowds of tourists, especially from the United States, visit this archaeological mecca. For years, the company called *Las Tres Estrellas* has been organizing daily tours from Mexico City, the main attraction of which is always the ruins of Teotihuacan.

This company rents chauffeur-driven cars (hired from another firm) and provides interpreter-guides for tourists. Some of the interpreters are *permanents* working on a monthly basis at a daily guaranteed salary, with expenses, of 41 pesos. Since they are employed for a five and a half-day week, this amounts to a salary of 52 pesos per day for the actual period of work. Sometimes, it is true, they manage to augment their salary by private arrangements with the sellers of *caritas*[1] (at least this is what some tourists claim, but perhaps they are no more to be believed than the guides).

The number of permanent interpreters employed by the company is such that S of them are available daily; when the demand for their services exceeds S, supplementary interpreter-guides or *extras* are taken on at a daily salary of 70 pesos. Sometimes the shortage of extras will necessitate canceling a tour, and when this happens, the loss is reckoned at 400 pesos. How many permanent interpreters should the company employ so that their overall costs will be minimal, if there is no limitation on the number of chauffeur-driven cars?

[1] These are stone statuettes guaranteed as authentic, but actually contemporary products copied from the few originals still in existence. But the workmanship is so good that the new statuettes are just as artistic as the old ones.

The study of this type of problem requires a certain number of statistics; in this case it is

the daily demand for interpreters;

the daily offers of work by extras.

It was found that separate statistics were needed for weekdays and Sundays as far as the offers, but not the demand, was concerned. By taking into account the seasonal character of the demand and of extras available, and by choosing the four months when tourist activity is greatest, it was possible to obtain the following tables, in which the frequencies will be treated as probabilities.

TABLE 12.1

DAILY DEMAND FOR INTERPRETER-GUIDES

Demand	4	5	6	7	8	9	10	11	12	13	14	15	16
Frequency[a]	2	4	4	8	10	12	12	12	10	10	8	6	2
Probability	0.02	0.04	0.04	0.08	0.10	0.12	0.12	0.12	0.10	0.10	0.08	0.06	0.02
Cumulative probability	0.02	0.06	0.10	0.18	0.28	0.40	0.52	0.64	0.74	0.84	0.92	0.98	1

[a] Frequencies obtained by considering 100 days during the tourist season, from which the probabilities shown on the third and fourth lines are derived. The average demand is 10.32.

TABLE 12.2

SUPPLY OF EXTRAS (WEEKDAYS)

Supply (weekday)	0	1	2	3	4	5	6	7
Frequency[a]	3	9	15	20	22	14	10	7
Probability	0.03	0.09	0.15	0.20	0.22	0.14	0.10	0.07
Cumulative probability	0.03	0.12	0.27	0.47	0.69	0.83	0.93	1

[a] Frequencies obtained by considering 100 weekdays during the tourist season, from which the probabilities shown on the third and fourth lines are derived. The average weekday availability by extras is 3.66.

TABLE 12.3

SUPPLY OF EXTRAS (SUNDAYS)

Supply (Sundays)	0	1	2	3	4	5	6	7
Frequency[a]	7	13	14	9	4	2	1	0
Probability	0.14	0.26	0.28	0.18	0.08	0.04	0.02	0
Cumulative probability	0.14	0.40	0.68	0.86	0.94	0.98	1	1

[a] Frequencies obtained by considering 50 Sundays during the year (the Sunday availability of extras is not seasonal). The average offer to work on Sunday is 1.96.

Further on, we shall show how to find the optimal number S^* of permanent employees by an analytical method, which is really preferable in this case, but we shall first use a method of simulation, in order to explain this procedure.

For the purpose of simulation, we shall proceed to reconstitute *artificial histories*, each of which will represent one week's management. With this purpose, we must first obtain a list of equiprobable numbers, that is, numbers obtained by some kind of draw in which those drawn have the same probability as any others. With this object, we can use a lottery wheel divided into ten equal sectors numbered from 0 to 9 (Fig. 12.1); this wheel is assumed to revolve perfectly, so that each

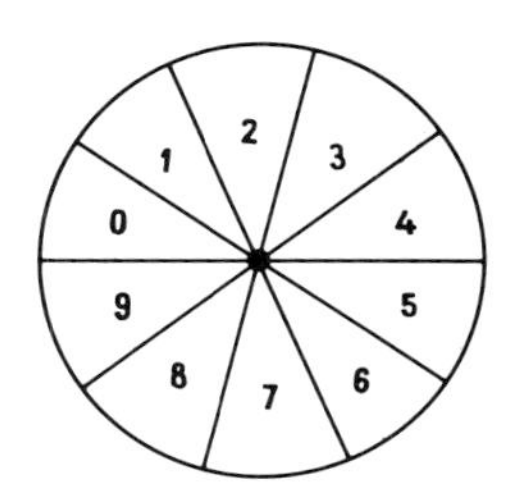

FIG. 12.1

draw is completely divorced from the previous one. By revolving it, we might, for instance, obtain the sequence of numbers

$$5\ 6\ 6\ 3\ 8\ 7\ 0\ 0\ 5\ 4\ 1\ 9\ 4\ 2\ 7\ 2\ 4\ 8\ 1\ 1\ 3\ 7\ \cdots.$$

If we make a thousand draws of numbers with one digit we shall find that each of the numbers appears roughly 100 times; from this we shall obtain observed frequencies which will approximate more closely to the theoretical frequencies the larger the draw.

In practice, such sequences are obtained much more quickly by arithmetical means, by the use of a computer, or by some physical method. There are, in fact, tables giving hundreds of thousands of equiprobable numbers, of which the following is a sample:

4 7 1 7 2 2 9 4 6 7 0 3 3 9 7 2 7 1 6 7 5 3 4 3 9 7 3 0 9 8 6 0 2 7 1 7
7 3 9 7 8 1 3 1 0 0 3 9 2 5 4 5 7 2 8 7 1 6 0 3 9 5 4 1 9 3 0 1 0 9 8 5
6 8 7 0 2 0 8 3 3 1 0 8 9 2 3 8 3 1 7 3 6 7 0 8 8 1 8 7 4 2 4 7 9 8 0 0
0 3 7 2 3 2 5 5 5 1 0 3 8 1 6 9 7 6 1 2 9 9 8 3 3 0 6 7 7 9 4 7 6 1 9 1
6 2 3 6 1 5 9 1 0 5 3 9 3 3 8 5 9 3 5 8 6 3 1 9 3 1 5 5 8 6 5 7 6 9 5 8
6 8 4 9 9 4 2 3 0 8 3 8 3 8 7 5 2 1 6 3 6 4 5 6 3 0 2 8 4 3 4 5 5 7 7 9

It is clear that by taking the numbers in pairs, we obtain numbers with a probability of $\frac{1}{00}$; by taking them three at a time, we obtain a probability of $\frac{1}{1000}$, etc.

Starting with a sequence of random numbers with equiprobability, we can form samples of random values, of which the arbitrary laws of probability are given; all we need do is employ the observed laws of cumulative probability, as we shall now show in the problem of the Teotihuacan interpreter-guides.

To produce artificial sequences for a demand with a law of probability equal to the one in Table 12.1, we shall make it correspond to the law of cumulative probability given in the fourth line. For example, a demand of 4 will correspond to any number 00 or 01 taken from the sample of equiprobable numbers given above, grouping them in pairs; a demand of 5 to any number between 02 and 05 inclusive; a demand of 6 to any number between 06 and 09 inclusive. In this manner, we obtain Table 12.4 which is drawn up so as to respect the frequencies given in Table 12.1. We shall proceed in the same manner for the laws of probability for the supply of extras, both on weekdays and Sundays. Thus, starting with Tables 12.2 and 12.3, we shall obtain Tables 12.5 and 12.6.

We are now in the process of creating artificial samples of the laws of demand and supply. For instance, if we take a sequence of seven equiprobable numbers with two digits from the first line of the table

47–17–22–94–67–03–39,

TABLE 12.4

Draw for the Demand

Equiprobable random number	Demand
00 or 01	4
02–05	5
06–09	6
10–17	7
18–27	8
28–39	9
40–51	10
52–63	11
64–73	12
74–83	13
84–91	14
92–97	15
98 or 99	16

TABLE 12.5

Draw for Supply (Weekdays)

Equiprobable random number	Supply
00–02	0
03–11	1
12–26	2
27–46	3
47–68	4
69–82	5
83–92	6
93–99	7

TABLE 12.6

Draw for Supply (Sundays)

Equiprobable random number	Supply
00–13	0
14–39	1
40–67	2
68–85	3
86–93	4
94–97	5
98 or 99	6

we find, from Table 12.4, that it corresponds to the following numbers for the demand:

10–7–8–15–12–5–9.

If we use the same procedure for the supply of extras, and take the second line of the table of equiprobable numbers,

73–97–81–31–00–39–25,

we find, from Table 12.5, that the first six numbers correspond to a weekday supply of extras equal to

5–7–5–3–0–3.

For the seventh number we must refer to Table 12.6, where we obtain 1, and we have now created *an artificial week*. By taking a large number of such weeks, obtained in the same way, and by making a statistical study of the numbers which they provide, we shall obtain

TABLE 12.7

WEEK 1: $S = 10$

Day	Availability	N	Demand	Excess	N	Supply	Number of extras	Shortage	Cost of Permanents	Cost of extras	Cost of shortage	Total cost
Mon	10	47	10	0	73	5	0	0	520	0	0	520
Tues	10	17	7	0	97	7	0	0	520	0	0	520
Wed	10	22	8	0	81	5	0	0	520	0	0	520
Thurs	10	94	15	5	31	3	3	2	520	210	800	1520
Fri	10	67	12	2	00	0	0	2	520	0	800	1320
Sat	10	03	5	0	29	3	0	0	520	0	0	520
Sun	10	39	9	0	25	1	0	0	520	0	0	520
												5450

TABLE 12.8

WEEK 1: $S = 9$

Day	Availability	N	Demand	Excess	N	Supply	Number of extras	Shortage	Cost of Permanents	Cost of extras	Cost of shortage	Total cost
Mon	9	47	10	1	73	5	1	0	468	70	0	538
Tues	9	17	7	0	97	7	0	0	468	0	0	468
Wed	9	22	8	0	81	5	0	0	468	0	0	468
Thurs	9	94	15	6	31	3	3	3	468	210	1200	1878
Fri	9	67	12	3	00	0	0	3	468	0	1200	1668
Sat	9	03	5	0	39	3	0	0	468	0	0	468
Sun	9	39	9	0	25	1	0	0	468	0	0	468
											Total:	5956

TABLE 12.9

WEEK 1: $S = 11$

Day	Availability	N	Demand	Excess	N	Supply	Number of extras	Shortage	Cost of Permanents	Cost of extras	Cost of shortage	Total cost
Mon	11	47	10	0	73	5	0	0	572	0	0	572
Tues	11	17	7	0	97	7	0	0	572	0	0	572
Wed	11	22	8	0	81	5	0	0	572	0	0	572
Thurs	11	94	15	4	31	3	3	1	572	210	400	1182
Fri	11	67	12	1	00	0	0	1	572	0	400	972
Sat	11	03	5	0	39	3	0	0	572	0	0	572
Sun	11	39	9	0	25	1	0	0	572	0	0	572
											Total:	5014

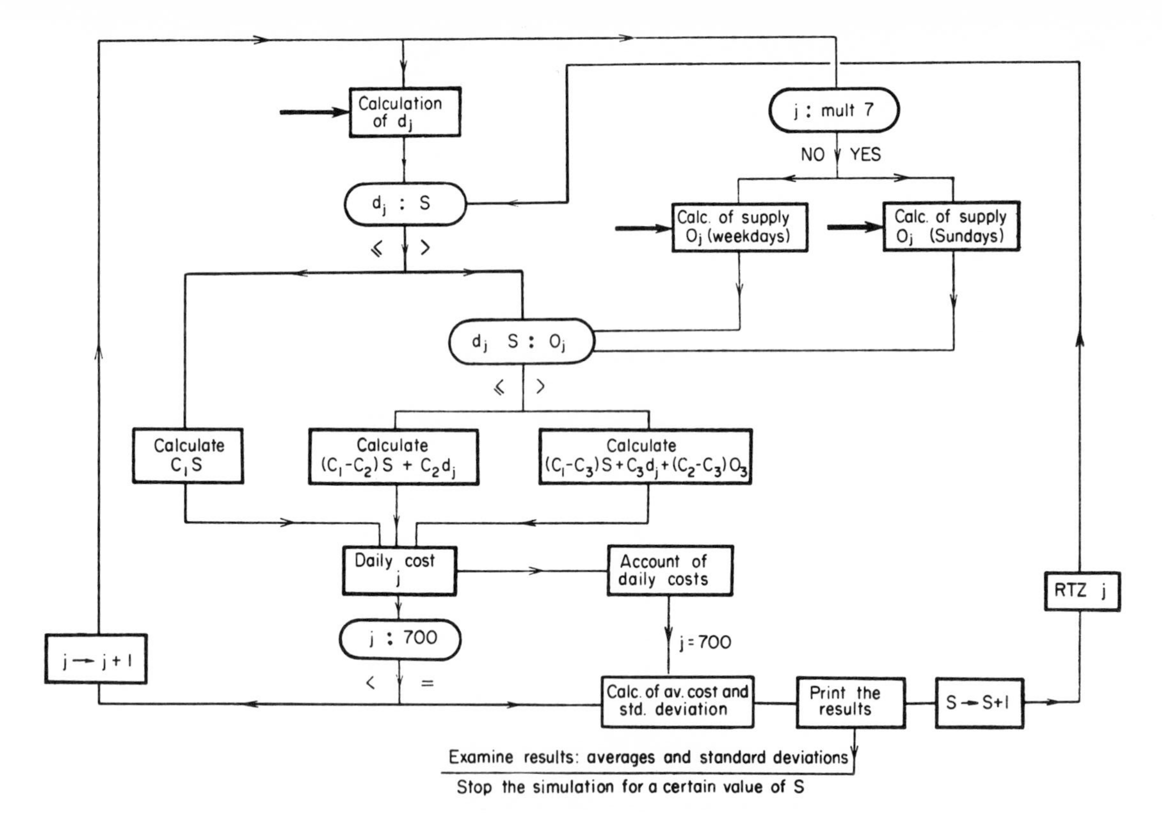

FIG. 12.2. Organigram of simulation (700-day period). *Symbols*: C_1, daily cost of permanent; C_2, daily cost of extra; C_3, cost of shortage; S, permanents available daily; d_j, daily demand; O_j, supply for the day; : means *compare with*; → represents ntroduction of random equiprobable sequences; RTZ, means *return to zero*.

relative frequencies which approximate very closely to the given probabilities.

After an artificial week has been created, we shall calculate the corresponding balance sheet. If we assume that the company has decided to have 10 permanents available daily,[2] we shall obtain Table 12.7.

With perhaps 100 artificial weeks available, we shall find the average cost and will then calculate the standard deviation from this cost. A similar table will then be calculated and simulated 100 times for other values of S: 8, 9, 11, 12, 13, etc.

Tables 12.8 and 12.9 give examples of simulation for the same week based on Table 12.4, but with $S = 9$ in one case and $S = 11$ in the other.

A complete simulation for this problem could be effected in a few minutes with an average electronic computer, and in a few hours with a small office machine. Generally speaking, simulation should be reserved for much more complex problems which may be difficult, if not impossible, to solve by an analytical method. That we used simulation here was because the simplicity of the problem made the method easy to explain.

We shall now apply the method of anlysis to this problem.

Simulation and Analysis

Let us take X for the random variable representing the daily demand, and $p(x)$ for the probability of a demand x, where $x = 4, 5, 6, \ldots, 16$, as given in Table 12.1, and the probability is nil for other values of x. Let Y be the random variable representing the daily supply of extras, $q_1(y)$ being the probability of a supply y (weekday), where $y = 0, 1, 2, \ldots, 7$ and $q_2(y)$ being the probability of a supply y (Sunday), where $y = 0, 1, 2, \ldots, 6$. Laws $q_1(y)$ and $q_2(y)$ are given respectively by Tables 12.2 and 12.3; outside these values, the probabilities are zero.

[2] Since a permanent employee is available for work on $5\frac{1}{2}$ out of 7 days, it would have amounted to the same thing if we had calculated the total number of permanents to be engaged.

For a certain value x of X and y of Y, assuming the number of permanents available daily is S, the cost for a day will amount to

$$
\begin{aligned}
\Gamma(S) &= C_1 S && \text{if } 0 \leqslant x \leqslant S && \text{(no extras)} \\
&= C_1 S + C_2(x - S) && \text{if } 0 < x - S \leqslant y && \text{(extras needed, but no shortage)} \\
&= C_1 S + C_2 y + C_3(x - S - y) && \text{if } y < x - S && \text{(extras needed, and there is still a shortage).}
\end{aligned}
$$

Accordingly, the set of possible values for X and Y can be divided into three regions (Fig. 12.3) in which all the values are represented

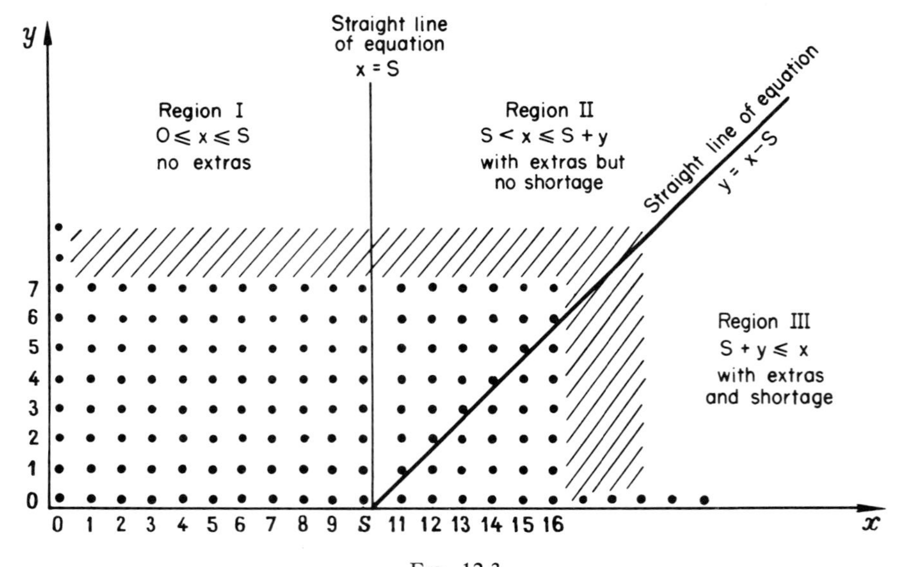

FIG. 12.3

by points. To find the average total value, or expected value of $\Gamma(S)$, that is $\overline{\Gamma(S)}$, we should have to calculate the cost for each of these points, multiply it by the corresponding probability

$$p(x) \cdot q_1(y) \qquad \text{or} \qquad p(x) \cdot q_2(y),$$

depending on whether we are considering a weekday or a Sunday, and finally find the sum of all these products. For instance, the cost for point $x = 12$, $y = 4$, if $S = 10$ (Fig. 12.3) is

$$\Gamma(10)\,\Big|_{\substack{x=12\\y=4}} = 10C_1 + 2C_2\,,$$

with a probability

$$p(12)\cdot q_1(4) = (0.10)\cdot(0.22) = 0.022,$$

whence

$$(0.022)(10C_1 + 2C_2).$$

The average cost $\overline{\Gamma(S)}$ is obtained by finding the sum of such quantities, calculated for every point. This summation, however, can be carried out by means of a formula which, at first sight, may appear complicated, but ceases to be if we interpret it with the help of Fig. 12.3.

$$\bar{\Gamma}_1(S) = C_1 S + C_2 \sum_{y=1}^{\infty}\ \sum_{x=S+1}^{x=S+y} (x - S)\, p(x)\, q_1(y)$$

$$+ \sum_{x=S+1}^{\infty}\ \sum_{y=0}^{y=x-S-1} [C_2 y + C_3(x - S - y)]\, p(x)\, q_1(y) \qquad (1)$$

for a weekday and $\bar{\Gamma}_2(S)$ for a Sunday by using $q_2(y)$ instead of $q_1(y)$.

For the benefit of readers who are not fanatical about mathematics, we shall explain the details of the formula. $C_1 S$ is a cost, with a probability of 1, corresponding to S permanents;

$$C_2 \sum_{y=1}^{\infty}\ \sum_{x=S+1}^{y=S+y} (x - S)\, p(x)\, q_1(y)$$

represents the sum of the costs for all the points in region II, with their respective probabilities allocated to them: it is the cost of the extras.

$$\sum_{x=S+1}^{\infty}\ \sum_{y=0}^{y=x-S-1} [C_2 y + C_3(x - S - y)]\, p(x)\, q_1(y)$$

represents the corresponding sum for region III: it is the cost of the extras and the shortage.

Finally, the average weekly cost will be

$$\bar{\Gamma}^*(S) = 6\bar{\Gamma}_1(S) + \bar{\Gamma}_2(S).$$

The calculation of a formula such as (1) should be made clear to some of our readers. Let us suppose that we take $S = 12$, with the data

$$C_1 = 52, \qquad C_2 = 70, \qquad C_3 = 400;$$

in addition $1 \leqslant y \leqslant 7$, $x \leqslant 16$:

$$\bar{\Gamma}_1(12) = 624 + 70 \sum_{y=1}^{7} \sum_{x=13}^{x=12+y} (x - 12)\, p(x)\, q_1(y)$$

$$- 330 \sum_{x=13}^{16} \sum_{y=0}^{y=x-13} y p(x)\, q_1(y) + 400 \sum_{x=13}^{16} \sum_{y=0}^{y=x-13} (x - 12)\, p(x)\, q_1(y).$$

Let us calculate

$$\sum_{y=1}^{7} \sum_{x=13}^{x=12+y} (x - 12)\, p(x)\, q_1(y),$$

taking into account that $p(>16) = 0$. We have

$$\begin{aligned}
(1) \cdot p(13) \cdot q_1(1) &+ [(1) \cdot p(13) + (2) \cdot p(14)] \cdot q_1(2) \\
&+ [(1) \cdot p(13) + (2) \cdot p(14) + (3) \cdot p(15)] \cdot q_1(3) \\
&+ [(1) \cdot p(13) + (2) \cdot p(14) + (3) \cdot p(15) + (4) \cdot p(16)] \\
&\quad \cdot [q_1(4) + q_1(5) + q_1(6) + q_1(7)] \\
= 1 \times 0.10 \times 0.09 & \\
&+ [1 \times 0.10 + 2 \times 0.08] \times 0.15 \\
&+ [1 \times 0.10 + 2 \times 0.08 + 3 \times 0.06] \times 0.20 \\
&+ [1 \times 0.10 + 2 \times 0.08 + 3 \times 0.06 + 4 \times 0.02] \\
&\quad \times [0.22 + 0.14 + 0.10 + 0.07] = 0.4116.
\end{aligned}$$

Let us go on to:

$$\begin{aligned}
\sum_{x=13}^{16} \sum_{y=0}^{y=x-13} & y \cdot p(x) \cdot q_1(y) \\
&= (1) \cdot q_1(1) \cdot p(14) + [(1) \cdot q_1(1) + (2) \cdot q_1(2)] \cdot p(15) \\
&\quad + [(1) \cdot q_1(1) + (2) \cdot q_1(2) + (3) \cdot q_1(3)] \cdot p(16) \\
&= 1 \times 0.09 \times 0.08 + [1 \times 0.09 + 2 \times 0.15] \times 0.06 \\
&\quad + [1 \times 0.09 + 2 \times 0.15 + 3 \times 0.20] \times 0.02 = 0.0504.
\end{aligned}$$

Finally,

$$\sum_{x=13}^{16} \sum_{y=0}^{y=x-13} (x - 12)\, p(x)\, q_1(y)$$
$$= (1) \cdot p(13) \cdot q_1(0) + (2) \cdot p(14) \cdot [q_1(0) + q_1(1)]$$
$$+ (3) \cdot p(15) \cdot [q_1(0) + q_1(1) + q_1(2)]$$
$$+ (4) \cdot p(16) \cdot [q_1(0) + q_1(1) + q_1(2) + q_1(3)]$$
$$= 1 \times 0.10 \times 0.03 + 2 \times 0.08 \times 0.12 + 3 \times 0.06 \times 0.27$$
$$+ 4 \times 0.02 \times 0.47 = 0.1084.$$

Thus,

$$\bar{\Gamma}_1(12) = 624 + 70 \times 0.4116 - 330 \times 0.0504 + 400 \times 0.1084 = 679.540.$$

A similar calculation, taking $q_2(y)$ instead of $q_1(y)$, gives

$$\bar{\Gamma}_2(12) = 784.512 \text{ pesos},$$

and thence

$$\bar{\Gamma}^*(12) = 6\bar{\Gamma}_1(12) + \bar{\Gamma}_2(12) = 4861.752 \text{ pesos}.$$

To find the optimum for $\bar{\Gamma}^*(S)$, we shall evaluate this quantity for $S = 8, 9, 10, \ldots, 14, 15$, and will discover that it corresponds to $S = 12$.

As the reader will have observed, the analytical method entails a considerable amount of calculation, and we shall show how the optimum can be found by another procedure which may not be as exact, but is considerably neater, that of *marginal analysis*, already used in the problem of the newsvendor (Chapter 1).

Let us assume that the company has S permanents available daily; each day it will be confronted by one of three situations.

(a) There are enough permanents to satisfy the demand: The probability is $1 = P(S + 1)$, whence

$$P(S + 1) = \sum_{r=S+1}^{\infty} p(r);$$

(b) There are not enough permanents, but sufficient extras can be engaged to meet the demand. The probability is

$$\sum_{u=1}^{\infty} p(u + S) \cdot Q_1(u),$$

where

$$Q_1(u) = \sum_{r=u}^{\infty} q_1(r)$$

and u is the number of extras required.

(c) There are not enough permanents, and the supply of extras is not sufficient, with the result that there is a shortage of at least one interpreter: the probability is

$$\sum_{u=1}^{\infty} p(u + S) \cdot [1 - Q_1(u)] = P(S + 1) - \sum_{u=1}^{\infty} p(u + S) \cdot Q_1(u).$$

If we now increase the number of permanents by 1, these now become $S + 1$, and the variation in the costs will be

(1) $+C_1$, whichever the situation;

(2) $-C_2$ if, and only if, we are in situation (b), since one less extra is then needed.

(3) $-C_3$ if, and only if, we are in situation (c), for the total number of permanents and extras has been increased by unity, with the result that the shortage is also diminished by unity.

Hence, the probable variation of cost is

$$\Delta\bar{\Gamma}_1(S) = C_1 - C_2 \sum_{u=1}^{\infty} p(u + S) Q_1(u)$$
$$- C_3 \left[P(S + 1) - \sum_{u=1}^{\infty} p(u + S) \cdot Q_1(u)\right].$$

To find the optimum, it will be observed that $P(S + 1)$ is a decreasing function of S; and

$$\sum_{u=1}^{\infty} p(u + S) \cdot Q_1(u)$$

is a function whose variation depends on the form of $p(x)$ and $q_1(y)$. As a result, $\bar{\Gamma}_1(S)$ is not necessarily convex.[3] A quick calculation results in Table 12.10.

[3] This is sometimes a complication in marginal optimization, but it is not the case here.

TABLE 12.10

S	7	8	9	10	11	12	13	14	15	16
$P(S+1)$	0.82	0.72	0.60	0.48	0.36	0.26	0.16	0.08	0.02	0
$\sum_{u=1}^{\infty} p(u+S)\cdot Q_1(u)$	0.4074	0.4114	0.3844	0.3418	0.2778	0.2218	0.1500	···	···	···
$\Delta(\bar{\Gamma}_1 S)$	−141.5	−100.2	−61	−27.2	−0.4	+21.1	+37.5	···	···	···

For $S = 11$,

$$\Delta\bar{\Gamma}_1 < 0, \quad \text{hence} \quad \bar{\Gamma}_1(12) < \bar{\Gamma}_1(11).$$

For $S = 12$,

$$\Delta\bar{\Gamma}_1 > 0, \quad \text{hence} \quad \bar{\Gamma}_1(12) < \bar{\Gamma}_1(13).$$

The optimum is therefore $S = 12$ for weekdays, and a similar calculation shows that for Sundays,

$$\Delta\bar{\Gamma}_2(11) = -32.2, \qquad \Delta\bar{\Gamma}_2(12) = -0.5, \qquad \Delta\bar{\Gamma}_2(13) = 24.7,$$

whence we obtain the optimum for $S = 13$. We can also calculate

$$\Delta\bar{\Gamma}^*(S) = 6\,\Delta\bar{\Gamma}_1(S) + \Delta\bar{\Gamma}_2(S),$$

it follows:

$$\Delta\bar{\Gamma}^*(11) = 6 \times (-0.4) + (-32.2) = -34.6,$$
$$\Delta\bar{\Gamma}^*(12) = 6 \times 21.1 + (-0.5) = 126.1,$$
$$\Delta\bar{\Gamma}^*(13) = 6 \times 37.5 + 24.7 = 249.7,$$

and we deduce that, taking Sundays into account, the optimum is still true for $S = 12$.

As it will have been observed, the method of marginal analysis, though simpler, still requires a considerable amount of calculation.

Actual problems are generally more complex, so that recourse is often had to simulation. It is nevertheless our advice to those undertaking this type of question to carry their analytical study as far as possible, even if it finally becomes necessary to have recourse to simulation. Indeed, a careful mathematical analysis will avoid their falling into the numerous pitfalls which are nearly always concealed in problems with concepts of probability and statistics.

And now, when you visit Mexico, go and see the majestic relics of Teotihuacan, but do not expect to find the automobiles of the *Las Tres Estrallas* company, which have been created purely for the purpose of the present chapter. Fortunately there are actual tourist companies with equally picturesque names!

CHAPTER 13

THE TRIUMPH OF DENIS-PAPIN

(Introduction to Linear Programming)

As a source of energy the atom may soon be triumphant; the rocket will perhaps become the accepted method of travel; where movement in cities is concerned, we are rapidly becoming dependent on the shoemaker. But there is one success which no one will question: that of Denis-Papin with the housewives of France. Truly, the pressure cooker and the pressurized coffee pot have become indispensable items in every household, so that every family is now, as it were, under pressure. In the kitchen, pressure means steam. Despite the reproofs of Dr. Edward de Pomiane, the high priest of hygienic cookery, we therefore feel obliged to record the vogue of the renowned pressure cooker.[1]

The Denis-Papin company manufactures pressure cookers A and pressurized coffee pots B, and in each case the principal operations of production, stamping, trimming, and assembly, are subject to certain unfortunate limitations. The available productive capacity for *either* of the two articles for the following week are given in Table 13.1.

Demand is virtually unlimited: the order books are filled up or, as we ought to say, under pressure. The profit[2] for a pressure cooker is 15 F and for a coffee pot 12.5 F, and we shall use x_1 and x_2 for the respective numbers of these articles to be produced the following week. The percentages[3] of total productive capacity for each manufactured unit are shown in Table 13.2, and can easily be calculated from Table 13.1.

[1] We must in fairness explain that Dr. de Pomiane excepted cabbage soup and salted beef from his diatribes against pressure cookers.

[2] We are obviously ignoring the actual profits; the values shown are merely being used for the numerical treatment of the problem.

[3] Percentages of available time for manufacture.

TABLE 13.1

PRODUCTIVE CAPACITY (IN UNITS)

Operation	*A* (Pressure cookers)	*B* (Pressure coffee pots)
Stamping	25,000	35,000
Trimming	33,333	16,667
Assembly of *A*	22,500	—
Assembly of *B*	—	15,000

Our problem is to find the number of each article to be produced in order to obtain a maximal profit.

The equations expressing the limitations on productive capacity can easily be given from Table 13.2.

$$\begin{aligned}\text{Stamping:}\quad & 0.004x_1 + 0.00286x_2 \leqslant 100\\ \text{Trimming:}\quad & 0.003x_1 + 0.006x_2 \leqslant 100\\ \text{Assembly } A\text{:}\quad & 0.00444x_1 \leqslant 100\\ \text{Assembly } B\text{:}\quad & 0.00667x_2 \leqslant 100\end{aligned}$$

TABLE 13.2

Operation	*A* (Pressure cookers)	*B* (Pressure coffee pots)
Stamping	0.004	0.00286
Trimming	0.003	0.006
Assembly of *A*	0.00444	0
Assembly of *B*	0	0.00667

We are therefore required to satisfy these relations and to maximize the function of profit

$$F = 15x_1 + 12.5x_2 .$$

To begin (Fig. 13.1), we shall employ orthogonal axes Ox_1 and Ox_2 to draw the straight lines

$$\begin{aligned}(1)\quad & 0.004x_1 + 0.00286x_2 = 100;\\ (2)\quad & 0.003x_1 + 0.006x_2 = 100;\\ (3)\quad & 0.00444x_1 = 100;\\ (4)\quad & 0.00667x_2 = 100.\end{aligned}$$

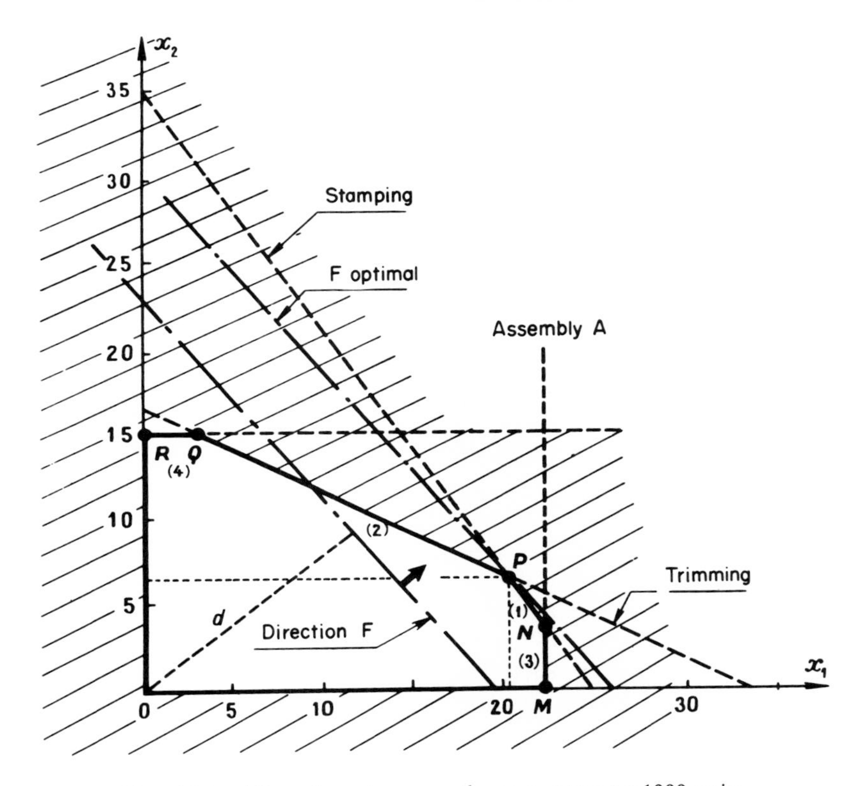

FIG. 13.1. The values shown on the axes represent 1000 units.

It is clear that the value of the variables must always lie below lines (1), (2), and (4) and to the left of (3). Further, these variables cannot be negative, since this would be nonsensical from an economic point of view. Hence, every point giving a solution must lie inside or on the boundary line of the nonhatched zone of Fig. 13.1.

Let us now consider the group of straight lines

$$F = 15x_1 + 12.5x_2 .$$

It is an elementary property of analytical geometry that F is proportionate to the distance d of the straight line from its point of origin. Let us therefore move the straight line F parallel to itself to a limit P, at which F ceases to have any point in common with the area $OMNPQR$; it is there that the values of x_1 and x_2 which maximize F are to be found. Hence,

$$\max F = 386{,}562.5 \text{ F}$$

for $x_1 = 20{,}370$ and $x_2 = 6481$.

These values of x_1 and x_2 correspond to the intersection of the straight lines relating to stamping and trimming and are such that the limits on the capacity for assembling A and B are not reached. We have

$$\begin{aligned}
0.004 \times 20{,}370 + 0.00286 \times 6481 &= 100 && \text{(saturation)}\\
0.003 \times 20{,}370 + 0.006 \times 6481 &= 100 && \text{(saturation)}\\
0.00444 \times 20{,}370 &= 90.45 && \text{(nonsaturation)}\\
0.00667 \times 6481 &= 43.23 && \text{(nonsaturation)}
\end{aligned}$$

Thus, by producing 20,370 pressure cookers and 6481 coffee pots the following week, an optimal profit will be made. The capacity for stamping and trimming will be saturated, but not that for assembly. Indeed, the assembly capacity for coffee pots is markedly below 100%, and it will be advisable to diminish it, thereby reducing the cost price and increasing the profit. It will be observed in Fig. 13.1 that as long as line F has a steeper gradient than the line corresponding to trimming (the slope of F can vary according to the profit per unit for each of the items), we can appreciably reduce the capacity for the assembly of coffee pots until it reaches 6481 instead of 15,000.

An interesting dialogue from an economic standpoint can accordingly begin with Fig. 13.1 as a starting point, as the reader should be able to imagine.

TABLE 13.3

AVAILABLE CAPACITY (IN UNITS)

Operation	Pressure cookers	Pressure coffee pots	Samovars
Stamping and shaping	20,000	30,000	12,000
Trimming	30,000	10,000	10,000
Assembling:			
pressure cookers	20,000		
coffee pots		12,000	
samovars			8000

But at the period at which we are writing, the cold war has shown a distinct tendency to slow down and fashion has turned to articles and clothing of Russian origin—fur hats, boots, and samovars. It is to take advantage of this trend that the Denis-Papin company has decided to extend its manufacturing to samovars. The available capacity for producing these or either of the other two items only, should the need arise, is shown in Table 13.3.

The respective weekly outputs x_1, x_2, and x_3 must therefore satisfy the following inequalities:

$$(\Delta_1) \qquad \frac{x_1}{200} + \frac{x_2}{300} + \frac{x_3}{120} \leqslant 100;$$

$$(\Delta_2) \qquad \frac{x_1}{300} + \frac{x_2}{100} + \frac{x_3}{100} \leqslant 100;$$

$$(\Delta_3) \qquad \frac{x_1}{200} \leqslant 100;$$

$$(\Delta_4) \qquad \frac{x_2}{120} \leqslant 100;$$

$$(\Delta_5) \qquad \frac{x_3}{80} \leqslant 100.$$

If the new function of profit is expressed as

$$F = 15x_1 + 12x_2 + 14x_3 ,$$

what values for the three unknowns will maximize the profit?

The graphic method produces the three-dimensional representation of Fig. 13.2, in which it is not convenient to find the vertex, corresponding to the maximum for F, of the convex polyhedron which represents the constraints (Δ). Under these conditions, we shall employ the *simplex method* introduced by the American mathematician, George Dantzig.

To begin, constraints Δ_3 and Δ_4 which are implicitly satisfied by Δ_1 and Δ_2, can be eliminated; for instance, if

$$\frac{x_1}{200} + \frac{x_2}{300} + \frac{x_3}{120} \leqslant 100,$$

a fortiori $x_1/200 \leqslant 100$ is satisfied.

Hence, the problem is reduced to

$$F = 15x_1 + 12x_2 + 14x_3 ,$$

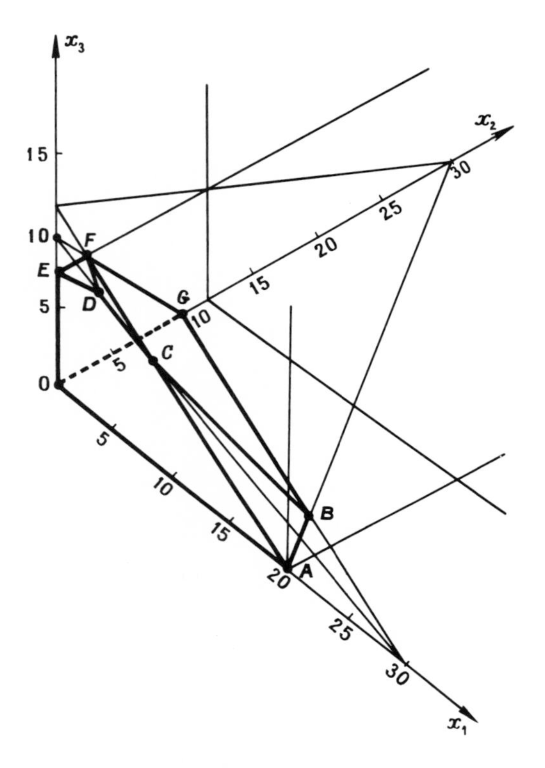

FIG. 13.2

taking into account the strictest of the *constraints*

$$\frac{x_1}{200} + \frac{x_2}{300} + \frac{x_3}{120} \leqslant 100;$$

$$\frac{x_1}{300} + \frac{x_2}{100} + \frac{x_3}{100} \leqslant 100;$$

$$\frac{x_3}{80} \leqslant 100.$$

Let us take x_4, x_5, and x_6 for the deviations between the values of the first and second members of our three inequations.

The latter can then be replaced by the equations

$$\begin{aligned}
\rightarrow \frac{x_1}{200} + \frac{x_2}{300} + \frac{x_3}{120} + x_4 \qquad\qquad &= 100 \\
\frac{x_1}{300} + \frac{x_2}{100} + \frac{x_3}{100} \qquad + x_5 \qquad &= 100 \\
\frac{x_3}{80} \qquad\qquad + x_6 &= 100 \\
&\vdots \\
15x_1 + 12x_2 + 14x_3 &= F \\
\uparrow \qquad\qquad\qquad &
\end{aligned}$$

An obvious, but valueless, solution is to take

$$x_1 = x_2 = x_3 = 0,$$

that is to say,

$$x_4 = 100, \qquad x_5 = 100, \qquad x_6 = 100, \qquad \text{and} \qquad F = 0,$$

which results in not producing anything (a valid solution only in the case of the annual closure for holidays!). However, if we compare Fig. 13.2 with Fig. 13.1, we discover that any optimal solution must correspond to one of the vertices of the convex polyhedron $OABCDEFG$. One of these vertices, in fact, must constitute a solution for which three of the six variables are nil. The solution which we rejected gives us the vertex O, and we shall proceed to a neighboring vertex, at the same time, if possible, increasing the value of F.

Let us select the variable with the largest positive coefficient in F, x_1. By means of line by line substitution, we shall ensure that only a single nonzero coefficient is left in the x_1 column and that the coefficient of x_1 disappears in F. But where is this solitary coefficient to be placed? Dantzig has shown that it is advisable to examine the relations such as

$$\frac{100}{\frac{1}{200}} = 20{,}000, \qquad \frac{100}{\frac{1}{300}} = 30{,}000, \qquad \frac{100}{0} = \infty$$

and to choose the line which has the smallest positive relation; in the present example it is 20,000, corresponding to line 1. This condition enables the solution to be changed without any of the variables becoming negative.

Let us, therefore, multiply the first line by 200 in order to obtain x_1 instead of $x_1/200$:

$$x_1 + \frac{2}{3}x_2 + \frac{2}{1.2}x_3 + 200x_4 = 20{,}000;$$

then let us add this line, previously multiplied by $-\frac{1}{300}$, to the second line and, after multiplying it by -15, to the line of F. We obtain

$$\begin{array}{lcl} x_1 + \frac{2}{3}x_2 + \frac{2}{1.2}x_3 + 200x_4 & & = 20{,}000 \\ \rightarrow \frac{7}{900}x_2 + \frac{4}{900}x_3 - \frac{2}{3}x_4 + x_5 & & = \frac{100}{3} \\ \qquad\qquad \frac{x_3}{80} & + x_6 & = 100 \\ & & \vdots \\ 2x_2 - 11x_3 - 3000x_4 & & = F - 300{,}000 \\ \uparrow & & \end{array}$$

We thereby find a more favorable solution

$$x_2 = x_3 = x_4 = 0, \qquad x_1 = 20{,}000, \qquad x_5 = \frac{100}{3}, \qquad x_6 = 100,$$

with $F = 300{,}000$. We are at vertex A of Fig. 13.2.

Continuing, we find there is still a coefficient of a variable which is positive, that of x_2 (if there had been several, we should have chosen the largest). In the column for x_2 let us form the relations

$$\frac{20{,}000}{2/3} = 30{,}000, \qquad \frac{100/3}{7/900} = \frac{30{,}000}{7}, \qquad \frac{100}{0} = \infty;$$

hence we choose line 2, for which we have the smallest positive relation, 30,000/7. This line will be multiplied by 900/7, and then added to all those which contain x_2, after the required multiplication by numbers which produce nil coefficients in the x_2 column, except in line 2 which has a coefficient of unity. We now find

$$\begin{array}{lcl} x_1 + \frac{9}{7}x_3 + \frac{1800}{7}x_4 - \frac{600}{7}x_5 & & = \frac{120{,}000}{7} \\ x_2 + \frac{4}{7}x_3 - \frac{600}{7}x_4 + \frac{900}{7}x_5 & & = \frac{30{,}000}{7} \\ \qquad \frac{x_3}{80} & + x_6 & = 100 \\ & & \vdots \\ -\frac{85}{7}x_3 - \frac{19{,}800}{7}x_4 - \frac{1800}{7}x_5 & & = F - 308{,}571 \end{array}$$

The corresponding solution is

$$x_3 = x_4 = x_5 = 0, \qquad x_1 = \frac{120{,}000}{7} = 17{,}142, \qquad x_2 = \frac{30{,}000}{7} = 4285,$$

and $F = 308{,}571$ F; we are at vertex B in Fig. 13.2.

We can state that this solution constitutes the maximum; indeed, all the coefficients of F are negative, and the passage from B to all the adjacent points G, C, or A would diminish the value of F. This is a general statement, since every polyhedron such as the one which we constructed, starting with inequalities and positive or nil values for x_1, x_2, and x_3, is *convex*. This property would still be true if we were to consider (in a suitable space) a greater number of variables.

Thus, after calculating the capacities and profits, we conclude that samovars should not be produced, since the required reorganization would reduce the profits from 386,562.5 F to 308,571 F, and we can only express the hope that abandoning the project will not have an adverse effect on East–West relations.

In considering the above problem, it appears that a different allocation of productive capacity, or the manufacture of a different type of samovar, might possibly increase the profits; in any case, this possibility could easily be explored at the opportune time by the method of linear programming which we have just explained.

A Practical Rule for the Simplex

It would not be within the scope of this short work to undertake the proofs of the different algorithms connected with linear programming. We believe also that the reader has been sufficiently instructed in the principles: progress from vertex to vertex of the convex polyhedron of the constraints, with the economic function being optimized at each stage. We shall therefore limit ourselves to giving the *practical rule* which can be employed for solving problems of lesser importance, with the proviso that the treatment of any problem with more than twelve variables will certainly require the use of an electronic computer.

Let us take as an example the program

$$\begin{aligned} 2x_1 \quad\quad + 3x_2 &\leqslant 8, \\ 2x_2 + 5x_3 &\leqslant 10, \\ 3x_1 + 2x_2 + 4x_3 &\leqslant 15, \end{aligned}$$

where we have to maximize

$$F = 3x_1 + 5x_2 + 4x_3 ,$$

the x_1 , x_2 , and x_3 terms being, of course, either positive or zero.

To start the program, we must first avail ourselves of *deviation variables* to express it as a system of equations

$$\begin{aligned} 2x_1 + 3x_2 \quad\quad + x_4 \quad\quad\quad &= 8, \\ 2x_2 + 5x_3 \quad\quad + x_5 \quad\quad &= 10, \\ 3x_1 + 2x_2 + 4x_3 \quad\quad\quad\quad + x_6 &= 15, \end{aligned}$$

while retaining the economic function F and the nonnegative constraints in their original form.

Any vector of the appropriate space can be represented as a function of a certain number of unitary vectors, called the *bases*, the first vectors which come to mind being those of the axes x_4 , x_5 , and x_6 . We can then give the proposed program an initial symbolic form:

Cost $C_{(i)}$	Base column $P_{(i)}$	P_1	P_2	P_3	P_4	P_5	P_6	P_0
0	P_4	2	3	0	1	0	0	8
0	P_5	0	2	5	0	1	0	10
0	P_6	3	2	4	0	0	1	15
	C_j	3	5	4	0	0	0	
	Solution	0	0	0	8	10	15	
	Δ_j	3	5 ↑	4	—	—	—	
	$\frac{P_{0(i)}}{x_{ie}}$	—	—	—	8/3	10/2	15/2	
			e		s			

(1) At each iteration, we evaluate, for the j columns, which are not a part of the base, the quantities

$$\Delta_j = C_j - \sum_i x_{ij} C_{(i)} ,$$

where x_{ij} represents the elements of the central table.

Example

$$\begin{aligned} \Delta_1 &= 3 - \sum_4^6 x_{i1} C_{(i)} \\ &= 3 - x_{41} C_{(4)} - x_{51} C_{(5)} - x_{61} C_{(6)} \\ &= 3 - (2 \times 0) - (0 \times 0) - (3 \times 0) = 3; \\ \Delta_2 &= 5; \\ \Delta_3 &= 4. \end{aligned}$$

We then take the largest positive value of Δ_j (one at least of the x_{ij} terms of column P_j must be positive), and decide to make the P_j column with the same index *enter the new base*. If we take e for the index of the entering column it is clear that if there are no positive or zero values of Δ_j, the optimal solution has then been found; if such values exist, there are equivalent solutions. Here, $e = 2$.

(2) Taking $P_{0(i)}$ for the elements of P_0, we calculate the quotients $P_{0(i)}/x_{ie}$, the divisor consisting of the elements of the *entering* column. We select the smallest such quotient which is positive, and use s for the index i corresponding to it, in order to define the column *leaving* the base.

Example

$$\frac{P_{0(i)}}{x_{ie}}: \quad \frac{P_{0(4)}}{x_{42}} = \frac{8}{3}; \qquad \frac{P_{0(5)}}{x_{52}} = \frac{10}{2}; \qquad \frac{P_{0(6)}}{x_{62}} = \frac{15}{0}.$$

(3) The column leaving the base contains zeros and one 1; we use the term *distinguished element* for the element of the entering column which is on the same line as the 1 of the leaving column.

(a) We divide all the elements of the line thus defined by the distinguished element.

(b) We calculate the algebraical multipliers which will produce zeros in the entering column in place of the other elements of the leaving column.

Example. Here, the distinguished element of P_2, corresponding to the 1 in column P_4, is 3. As a result, the first line of the table becomes

$$\frac{2}{3} \quad 1 \quad 0 \quad \frac{1}{3} \quad 0 \quad 0 \quad \cdots \quad \frac{8}{3}$$

We must next subtract the element 1 twice from the 2 in the second line, and twice from the 2 in the third line of column P_2, in order to obtain 0. We then find the second and third lines by subtracting from their original elements the products of -2 and their corresponding elements, column by column, of the new first line.

$C_{(i)}$	$P_{(i)}$	P_1	P_2	P_3	P_4	P_5	P_6	P_0
5	P_2	2/3	1	0	1/3	0	0	8/3
0	P_5	— 4/3	0	5	— 2/3	1	0	14/3
0	P_6	5/3	0	4	— 2/3	0	1	29/3
	C_j	3	5	4	0	0	0	
	Solution	0	8/3	0	0	14/3	29/3	$F = 40/3$
	Δ_j	— 1/3	.	4 ↑	— 5/3	.	.	
	$\frac{P_{0(i)}}{x_{ie}}$	.	∞	.	.	14/15	29/12	
				e		s		

In this manner, we obtain P_1 to P_6 and P_0. We then modify the left-hand table of $P_{(i)}$ and $C_{(i)}$, taking account of the replacement of column which has been carried out. We also inscribe the new solution under the costs C_j, and calculate the new value of the economic function, $F = 40/3$.

(4) We resume the iterations.

Example. (1) $\Delta_1 = -\frac{1}{3}$, $\Delta_3 = 4$, etc. We have $e = 3$. It should be noted that we can obtain the new Δ_j elements by subtracting, from the old ones in the preceding table, the products of Δ_e and the elements of the new line s.

(5) Calculation of the

$$\frac{P_{0(i)}}{x_{ie}} = \frac{P_{0(i)}}{x_{i3}},$$

the least positive one of which is 14/15, whence $s = 5$.

The reader may complete the calculation, which will comprise two further iterations, so as to arrive at the new tabulation.

$C_{(i)}$	$P_{(i)}$	P_1	P_2	P_3	P_4	P_5	P_6	P_0
5	P_2	0	1	0	15/41	8/41	— 10/41	50/41
4	P_3	0	0	1	— 6/41	5/41	4/41	62/41
3	P_1	1	0	0	— 2/41	— 12/41	15/41	89/41
	C_j	3	5	4	0	0	0	
	Solution	89/41	50/41	62/41	0	0	0	$F = 765/41$
	Δ_j	.	.	.	— 45/41	— 24/41	— 11/41	

Note. To minimize F is the same as maximizing $-F$, and the constraints

$$\sum x_{ij}x_j \geqslant b_j\,,$$

then become

$$\sum (-x_{ij})x_j \leqslant -b_j\,.$$

Concept of Dualism

Let us consider the following initial linear program

$$x_1 \geqslant 2,$$
$$x_1 + x_2 \geqslant 3,$$
$$3x_2 \geqslant 2,$$

where it is required to minimize

$$F = 20x_1 + 40x_2$$

and where the constraints of the variables are understood as being nonnegative.

If we summarize the program in the form of a table, we discover that this single or *primal* program has a corresponding *dual* which is expressed as

$$y_1 + y_2 \leqslant 20,$$
$$y_2 + 3y_3 \leqslant 40,$$

for which we have to *maximize*

$$\Phi = 2y_1 + 3y_2 + 2y_3 .$$

	x_1	x_2	$\geqslant$
y_1	1	0	2
y_2	1	1	3
y_3	0	3	2
$\leqslant$	20	40	*OP*

Each of these programs can be solved graphically. We discover from Fig. 13.3(a,b) that the solution of the former gives to the economic function a value

$$F = 20 \times (7/3) + 40 \times (2/3) = 220/3,$$

whereas the solution of the latter is such that

$$\Phi = 2 \times 0 + 3 \times 20 + 2 \times (10/3) = 220/3.$$

These programs accordingly possess the property of giving the same optimal value to the economic function. Moreover, if we had given the complete programs, with their deviation variables,

$$\begin{array}{l} x_1 \quad - x_3 \quad = 2 \\ x_1 + x_2 \quad - x_4 \quad = 3 \\ \quad 3x_2 \quad - x_5 = 2 \end{array} \quad \vdots \quad \begin{array}{l} y_1 + y_2 \quad + y_4 \quad = 20 \\ y_2 + 3y_3 \quad + y_5 = 40 \\ \end{array}$$

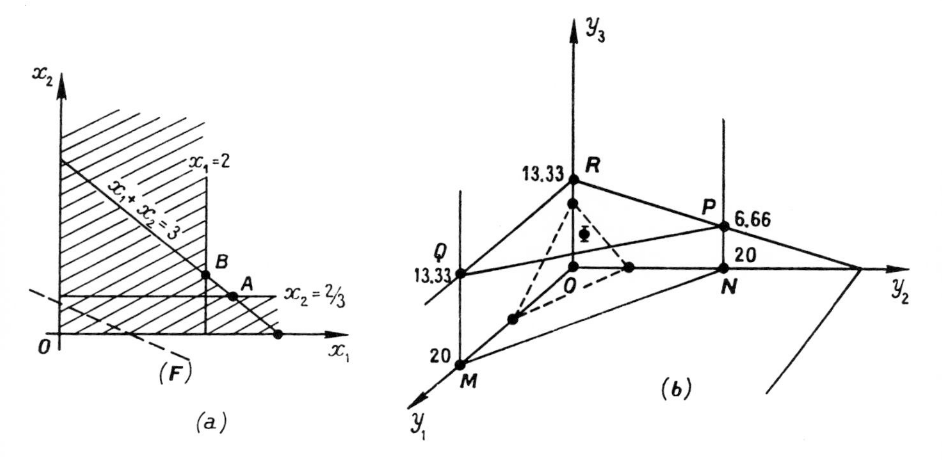

FIG. 13.3. (a) *Primal program*: solution must be provided by the coordinates of A or B; direction of the economic function shows that it is given by A, for which $x_1 = \frac{7}{3}$ and $x_2 = \frac{2}{3}$. (b) *Dual program*: direction of plane D shows that point P provides the solution $y_1 = 0$, $y_2 = 20$, and $y_3 = \frac{20}{3}$.

the first would provide—

$$\text{values of the variables:} \quad x_1 = \frac{7}{3}, \quad x_2 = \tfrac{2}{3}, \quad x_3 = \tfrac{1}{3}, \quad x_4 = 0, \quad x_5 = 0$$

$$\text{marginal costs:} \quad \Delta_1 = 0, \quad \Delta_2 = 0, \quad \Delta_3 = 0, \quad \Delta_4 = 20, \quad \Delta_5 = \frac{20}{3}$$

and the second would give—

$$\text{values of the variables:} \quad y_1 = 0, \quad y_2 = 20, \quad y_3 = \frac{20}{3}, \quad y_4 = 0, \quad y_5 = 0$$

$$\text{marginal costs:} \quad \Delta_1' = \tfrac{1}{3}, \quad \Delta_2' = 0, \quad \Delta_3' = 0, \quad \Delta_4' = \tfrac{7}{3}, \quad \Delta_5' = \tfrac{2}{3}$$

which shows that the variables of one program have the same values as the marginal costs of the other, and reciprocally.

The economic interpretation of the dual of a program is not always clear, which is why we have not developed the subject any further.

CHAPTER 14

LIBRE O COMPLETO

(Choice of a Criterion in the Face of Uncertainty)

On the main motoring routes of Mexico there now exist motels similar to those in the United States, and a tourist approaching Mexico City finds himself observing the signs *Libre* or *Completo* displayed on the front of the buildings. Though few in number, these motels enjoy great success, both with gringos and Mexicans, and it is not surprising that our friend, Salvador Arnoldo, should decide to invest his savings in building a motel on the outskirts of the city.

Salvador's capital amounts to several million pesos, of which he has spent 250,000 pesos on a fine site bordering a main road. Here his motel will be built, but he has yet to decide whether it should contain 20, 30, 40, or 50 rooms. The estimate of expenses is now given.

(1) ANNUAL EXPENSES WHICH ARE INDEPENDENT OF THE NUMBER OF ROOMS S TO BE BUILT

IMPROVEMENT OF THE SITE: 100,000 pesos. On the assumption that the building and improvements will last ten years, the fixed expenses will be spread over the same period, making an annual cost of . . . . . 10,000 pesos

REPAIRS AND MAINTENANCE. It is agreed that these will consist partly of a fixed sum, independent of the number of rooms, and partly of a sum proportional to the size of the establishment. The fixed annual part will be . . . . 1500 pesos

ONE NIGHT WATCHMAN at 15 pesos a day, that is, with various allowances . . . . 6000 pesos

ONE MAINTENANCE MAN at 20 pesos a day and extras	8000 pesos

The purchase price of the land is not taken into account, since its value is assumed to increase to approximately the same extent as the capital it represents, if invested at normal rates of interest.

The total of these fixed annual expenses amounts to 25,500 pesos

(2) ANNUAL EXPENSES PROPORTIONAL TO THE NUMBER OF ROOMS BUILT

	$S=20$	30	40	50
CONSTRUCTION, DECORATING, AND FURNISHING ROOMS. Each room costs 40,000 pesos and, with the expenditure spread over 10 years, the annual cost is	80,000	120,000	160,000	200,000
DOMESTIC HELP. One is reckoned for ten rooms; at a salary of 6000 pesos, this is	12,000	18,000	24,000	30,000
PROPORTIONATE MAINTENANCE AND REPAIRS	3000	4500	6000	7500
FIRE INSURANCE at 25 pesos per room	500	750	1000	1250
TOTAL	95,500	143,250	191,000	238,750

(3) ANNUAL EXPENSES PROPORTIONATE TO THE AVERAGE NUMBER OF ROOMS RENTED, R[1]

	$R=0$	10	20	30	40	50
LAUNDRY AND CLEANING at 5 pesos a day per room	0	18,000	36,000	54,000	72,000	90,000
UTILITIES at 5 pesos a day	0	18,000	36,000	54,000	72,000	90,000
TOTAL	0	36,000	72,000	108,000	144,000	180,000

[1] For simplification, we shall only consider values of 0, 10, 20, 30, 40, and 50 for R.

RENT FOR A ROOM. TAKINGS

The Mexican Tourist Department has fixed a daily rent of 60 pesos per room, and for the different values of R, the takings will be:

	$R = 0$	10	20	30	40	50
takings:	0	219,000	438,000	657,000	876,000	1,095,000

By combining all the above figures, it has been possible to produce Table 14.1 which gives the annual profit for the different values of R and S.

TABLE 14.1

PROFIT IN THOUSANDS OF PESOS

	R					
S	0	10	20	30	40	50
20	−121	62	245	245	245	245
30	−168.75	14.25	197.25	380.25	380.25	380.25
40	−216.5	−33.5	149.5	332.5	515.5	515.5
50	−264.25	−81.25	101.75	284.75	467.75	650.75

It has to be admitted that, without valid information as to the probable value of R, the return on a motel is very difficult to assess, and Salvador realizes that the first year will be crucial. Thereafter, it will be soon enough to plan enlargements when the situation warrants it, though it will, of course, require upwards of a year to carry them out, once the decision has been taken.

Salvador is extremely perplexed over this question of size. Should he decide to begin with 20 rooms, his profit will be limited to 245,000 pesos and his possible loss to 121,000 pesos; if he builds more, his possible profit and loss will both be increased. What criterion should he choose to help him in this predicament ? As chance has it, he possesses a work, Milnor's *Games Against Nature*, which analyzes the different criteria which can be used in the face of uncertainty.

LAPLACE'S CRITERION. The great mathematician Laplace reasoned that, since we do not know anything as to future states of nature, we can treat them as having equiprobability. According to this criterion, Salvador would allot a probability of $\frac{1}{6}$ to every value of R, with the result that, for the different values of S, his probable profit would be:

	Probable profit
$S = 20$	153.5
$S = 30$	197.25
$S = 40$	210.5 ←
$S = 50$	193.5

If he followed this criterion Salvador would decide to build 40 rooms; but this solution does not satisfy him, and he feels that the number of rooms which he can let must depend on quite other factors than equiprobability.

WALD'S CRITERION. The statistician and economist Wald reasoned that where the states of nature are unknown one should adopt the most prudent policy. "In each line of the table take the smallest value of a_{ij} and then choose the largest of these quantities." This is Von Neumann's criterion for a game with two players and a zero sum, where nature is the second player. If we follow this criterion we must choose the line for which we have

$$\max_i [\min_j a_{ij}]$$

and, in the present case, this gives

	$\min_j a_{ij}$
$S = 20$	−121 ←
$S = 30$	−168.75
$S = 40$	−216.5
$S = 50$	−264.25

By choosing $S = 20$, our friend cannot lose more than 121,000 pesos. But what a pessimistic criterion this is! Indeed, by carrying such reasoning a step further, Salvador would decide not to build a motel at all. He would then have to decide anew what to do with his capital, in the knowledge that nothing is certain in this world and every investment entails a risk.

HURWICZ'S CRITERION. According to Hurwicz, it is not reasonable to ignore the highest profit in favor of the smallest, and we should therefore subjectively introduce a certain coefficient of optimism α. If a is the smallest number in a line and A is the largest, we must evaluate

$$H = \alpha A + (1 - \alpha)a$$

for each line and choose the one with the greatest value for H. It should be observed that where $\alpha = 0$, we are back at Wald's criterion (that of the complete pessimist), whereas for $\alpha = 1$, the criterion becomes that of the complete optimist.

Here, the values of H for the different values of α are those shown in Table 14.2.

In this problem, a predominantly pessimistic outlook leads to the choice of $S = 20$, an optimistic outlook to that of $S = 50$.

TABLE 14.2

	α				
S	0.1	0.2	0.5	0.8	0.9
20	−84.40 ←	−47.80 ←	62	171.80	206.40
30	−113.85	−58.95	105.75	270.45	325.35
40	−143.30	−70.10	149.50	369.10	442.30
50	−172.75	−81.25	193.25 ←	467.75 ←	559.25 ←

SAVAGE'S CRITERION. This criterion is obtained by finding the highest element (representing the most favorable case) for each state, that is here for each value of R, and then subtracting it from every element in its column. Savage describes this calculation as representing "the regret between the choice made and the most favorable choice if the intentions of nature had been known to us." In our example, we should subtract −121 from the column of $R = 0$, 62 from the $R = 10$ column, and so on, obtaining Table 14.3.

For the different values of S, the minimal regrets are then

$S = 20$ −405.75
$S = 30$ −270.50
$S = 40$ −135.25 ←
$S = 50$ −143.25

TABLE 14.3

	R					
S	0	10	20	30	40	50
20	0	0	0	−135.25	−270.50	−405.75
30	−47.75	−47.75	−47.75	0	−135.25	−270.50
40	−95.50	−95.50	−95.50	−47.75	0	−135.25
50	−143.25	−143.25	−143.25	95.50	−47.75	0

By choosing $S = 40$, Salvador's regret could not be greater than 135.25 (or less than -135.25).

Superfluity of Choices. We see that Salvador can choose between these diverse solutions:

(a) Follow Laplace's criterion and build 40 rooms.

(b) Follow Wald and only build 20.

(c) Adopt Hurwicz's criterion and build 20 if he is pessimistic and 50 if he is optimistic.

(d) Build 40 if he accepts Savage's criterion.

Economists, moreover, have defined other criteria, so what is Salvador to decide?

We should like to observe at this point that the choice of a criterion embodies the highest form of liberty allowed to an industrialist. Any criterion chosen should suit the plans and conform to the character of the person who selects it. As we have seen, the choice of any criterion involves a decision very different from those which would have resulted from other criteria.

A cynic might maintain that the criterion of *minimal regret* is the one implicitly accepted by women, and that in the matter of their wives' purchases of dresses and hats, husbands may well regard it as that of *maximal regret*.

Nonetheless, this is the criterion which French economists accept as being the best, especially, as in this problem, in cases of fairly long term investment.

In point of fact, as we shall no longer conceal, our friend Salvador (who has provided the pretext for explaining various criteria useful in games against nature) would not have embarked on this scheme if he had not first obtained information about his prospects of success. To be precise, he had discovered that the existing motels had had the following demand over the last few years.

Demand:	0	10	20	30	40	50
Probability:	0.01	0.09	0.20	0.30	0.30	0.10

As a result of these statistics, he was in a far better position to make his choice: in fact, all he had to do was to find the expected value of the returns for each of the hypotheses:

$$S = 20, \qquad E(20) = -121 \times 0.01 + 62 \times 0.09 + 245 \times [0.2 + 0.3 + 0.3 + 0.1] = 224.87;$$

$$S = 30, \qquad E(30) = -168.75 \times 0.01 + 14.25 \times 0.09 + 197.25 \times 0.2 + 380.25 \times [0.3 + 0.3 + 0.1] = 305.22;$$

$$S = 40, \qquad E(40) = -216.5 \times 0.01 - 33.5 \times 0.09 + 149.5 \times 0 + 332.5 \times 0.3 + 515.5 \times [0.3 + 0.1] = 330.675;$$

$$S = 50, \qquad E(50) = -264.25 \times 0.01 - 81.25 \times 0.09 + 101.75 \times 0.2 + 284.75 \times 0.3 + 467.75 \times 0.3 + 650.75 \times 0.1 = 301.12,$$

and to compare these returns, from which he found that easily the most profitable decision was to build a motel with 40 rooms.

THE CHOICE OF A CRITERION. As we have seen, the choice of a criterion is one of the most difficult problems in operations research, but it is also one of the most exciting. Indeed, it transcends the province of the normal worker in this science, whose duties are restricted to using the criteria he is given, and who is not expected to impose his personal criterion on the public; such a choice, should therefore be made only at the highest level.

For ourselves, we believe that, without sufficiently precise information, a method of choice might lie in calculating one's chances both of failure and success. Supposing we take α for the subjective probability of an unfavorable result and γ for that of complete success. The intermediate situations will be allocated a probability β such that

$$\alpha + \beta + \gamma = 1.$$

Under these conditions, if $\sum P$ is the sum of the bad results, $\sum I$ the sum of the intermediate ones, and $\sum S$ that of the satisfactory ones, the weighted total

$$\alpha \cdot \frac{\sum P}{m} + \beta \cdot \frac{\sum I}{n} + \gamma \cdot \frac{\sum S}{p}$$

represents, for each hypothesis, a subjective estimate of the expected value, where m, n, and p are the respective number of results placed in each category.

The fundamental problem is to decide the category in which each result is to be placed. Let us, therefore, examine the list of proportionate expenses given previously [Section (2)].

A preliminary solution could be to class as bad results all those corresponding to a loss, that is, those with negative values in the table. To this it could be objected that, since we are taking the weighted average, $\sum P/m$ is equal (in the case where $S = 40$) to

$$-\frac{216.5 + 33.5}{2} = -125,$$

whereas, if $S = 30$,

$$\frac{\sum P}{m} = -168.75.$$

From this, we are left with a decided belief that the risk must increase, the greater the number of rooms.

It is because of this influence on our thinking that we prefer to consider as bad results only those in the first column, while a slight loss or profit will be treated as equivalent: for example, when $R = 10$, $14.25 \simeq -33.5$.

By symmetry, this solution leads us logically to take as satisfactory results those corresponding to the maximal demand, $R = 50$. We are thus led to the following allocation, which we shall explain by a concrete example by supposing that Salvador estimates his probability of ruin at 10% and his probability of success at 20%.

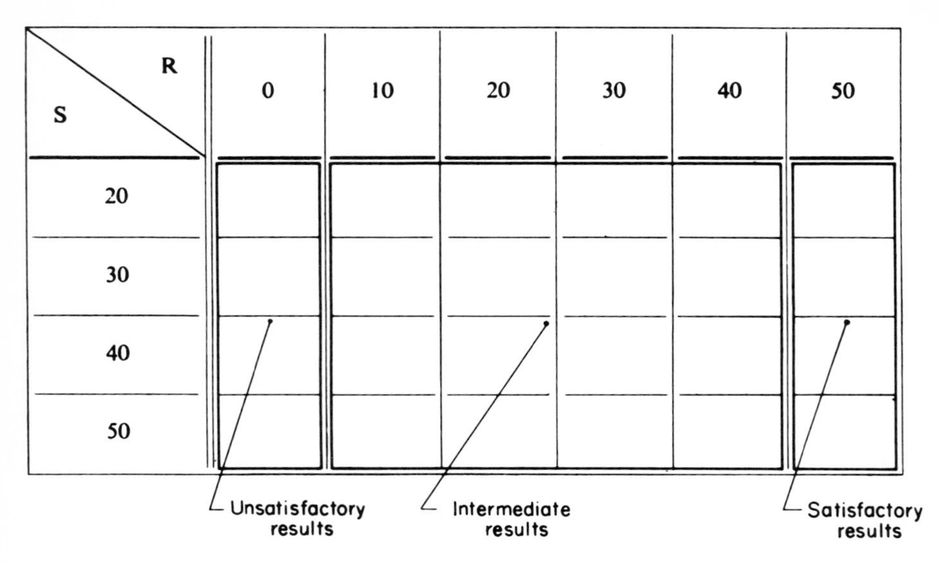

FIG. 14.1

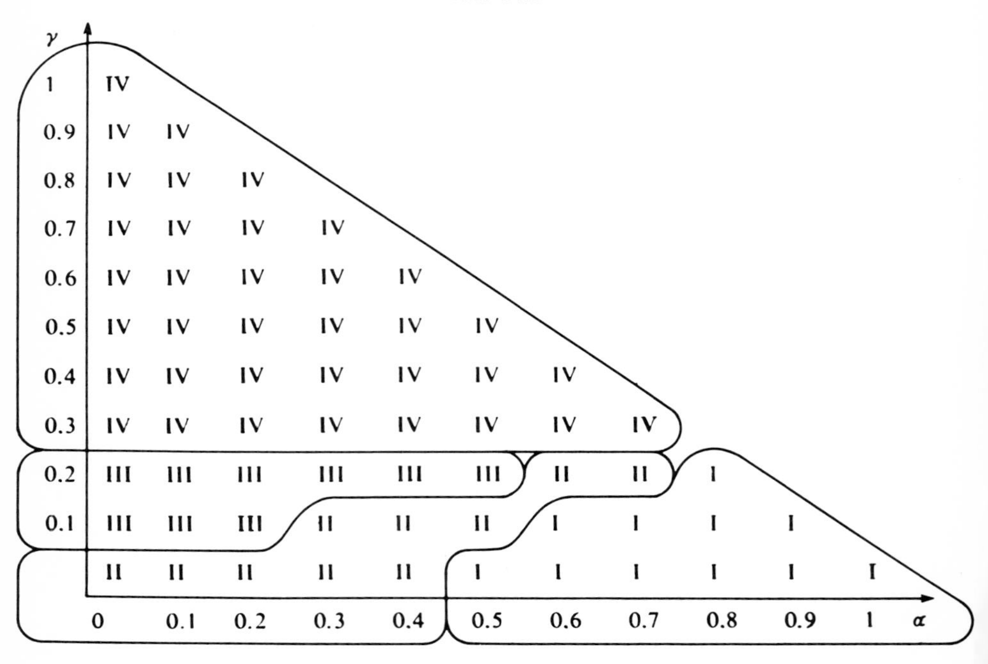

FIG. 14.2. Map of the most favorable decision. Every decision to build 20, 30, 40, 50 rooms is represented by I, II, III, IV. For each pair of estimates (α, γ), we can obtain the more advantageous decision.

We thus find $\alpha = 0.1$, $\gamma = 0.2$; hence, $\beta = 0.7$, and we can evaluate:

$$\begin{aligned}\mathscr{E}(20) &= -\frac{121}{1} \times 0.1 + \frac{62 + 3 \times 245}{4} \\ &\quad \times 0.7 + \frac{245}{1} \times 0.2 \\ &= 176.4;\end{aligned}$$

$$\begin{aligned}\mathscr{E}(30) &= -\frac{168.75}{1} \times 0.1 + \frac{14.25 + 197.5 + 2 \times 380.25}{4} \\ &\quad \times 0.7 + \frac{380.25}{1} \times 0.2 \\ &= 229.3;\end{aligned}$$

$$\begin{aligned}\mathscr{E}(40) &= -\frac{216.5}{1} \times 0.1 + \frac{-33.5 + 149.5 + 332.5 + 515.5}{4} \\ &\quad \times 0.7 + \frac{515.5}{1} \times 0.2 \\ &= 250.2;\end{aligned}$$

$$\begin{aligned}\mathscr{E}(50) &= -\frac{264.5}{1} \times 0.1 + \frac{-81.25 + 101.75 + 284.75 + 467.75}{4} \\ &\quad \times 0.7 + \frac{650.75}{1} \times 0.2 \\ &= 238.8.\end{aligned}$$

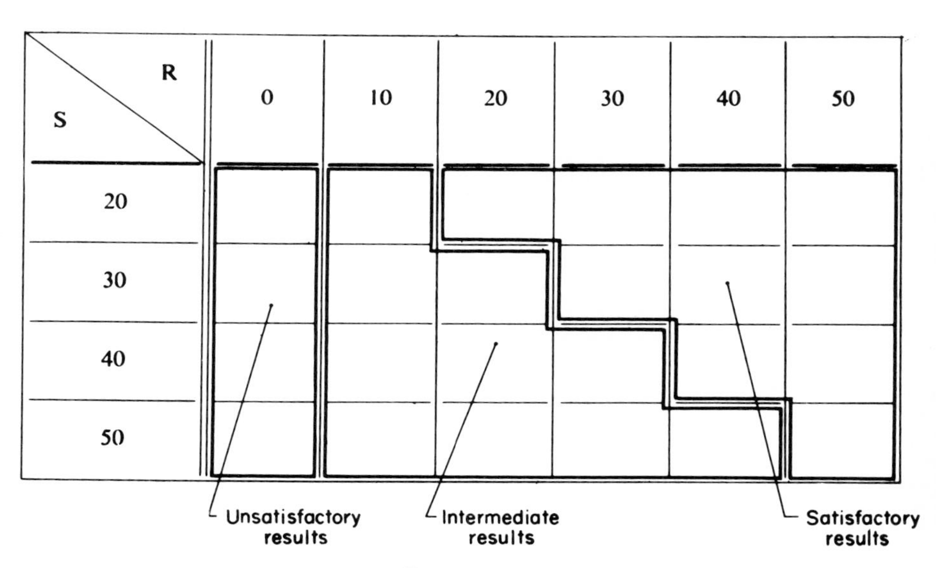

FIG. 14.3

To improve the method, it is possible to represent in the plan of the estimates for α and γ (for each value of these coefficients from 0 to 1, by intervals of 0, 1) the diagram of the most favorable decision. We can then envisage this map as having a plain of moderation which separates the heights of optimism from the swamps of pessimism.

In point of fact, while this second solution appears satisfactory as regards the unfavorable results, it is open to the objection that it places in two different categories (those of the intermediate and the favorable results) results which bring our friend an equal profit. In other words, we estimate that Salvador is more optimistic if he hopes to refuse 20 clients than if he expects to turn away 10. It would accordingly be more logical to accept a third solution in which we should choose as unfavorable events those where no client appears, whereas we should regard as favorable those which led to all the rooms being rented. The distribution in this case would be that shown in Fig. 14.3., and the reader might find it instructive to draw the plan corresponding to this new distribution.

CHAPTER 15

POVERTY AND RICHES

(Finding an Index of Poverty. Weighting the Values)

When it is a question of receiving a state grant for the communes[1] in his district, every councillor is inclined to represent them as all basically poor; while, if you were to question the electors, you would find difficulty in hearing of a single rich commune. Thus in 1961, the prefect of the department of Haute-Seine was greatly perplexed as to the manner in which the funds received from the government were to be allocated to the 475 communes in his area. A criterion of wealth and of poverty is undoubtedly hard to discover, and must be clearly arbitrary and lacking in universality. An inhabitant of Neuville, for instance, would certainly say that his commune was poor, since the population is thinly scattered, the yield from the local taxes is low, and public assistance reaches a high level. In his view, the people in Villeneuve are far better off with their high return from license fees and their communal property of all kinds, not to speak of the yield from their rich forests: in fact, as he understands it, the tax collector of Villeneuve actually hands out money instead of receiving taxes!

For a long time the prefecture of Haute-Seine had felt the need of a criterion for classifying the communes in order of poverty. The first attempt in this direction was to class as poor those communes in which an extra centime tax for each inhabitant yielded less than 60 F. This extra centime is, it should be recalled, a supplementary contribution which, in theory, is calculated as 1 % of the main payment, but which can be much more important, thanks to the theories of modern algebra on which tax assessment is now based. Such a method, however, failed to differentiate those who were very poor from the fairly rich, and even

[1] The French commune is roughly equivalent to the parish, and above it, in increasing size, are the cantons and départements, the latter administered by prefects. All these French subdivisions are smaller than the Province. [Translator's note.]

prominent statisticians found great difficulty in assessing the correlation between real riches and the tax paid on it.

In a second attempt to obtain a criterion, recourse was had to an index of poverty defined by the following formula:

$$i = 1000 + 1000 \frac{I}{V} - 300 \frac{c}{n} + (300 - n) \qquad \text{if} \quad n < 300$$

or

$$i = 1000 + 1000 \frac{I}{V} - 300 \frac{c}{n} \qquad \text{for} \quad n \geqslant 300,$$

where the symbols represent:

I, the annual yield from taxes in the commune;
I/V, a parameter of poverty;
c, the extra centime tax in the commune;
n, the number of inhabitants;
c/n, a parameter of wealth.

Where $i < 1200$ the commune was considered poor, and in the contrary case it was considered rich.

But this formula took no account of the true source of riches or of the real causes of poverty; its arbitrary character was realized by everyone, and the classification resulting from it was the source of constant objections.

After a study group had been formed, its first conclusion was that they must discover quantities which would be a true index of riches or of poverty. It was agreed that this index should not represent the total wealth of a commune but should be on a *per capita* basis. Which parameters should they introduce in order to obtain it? The number of automobiles used for pleasure belonging to the inhabitants? The value of the buildings? The number of tourists visiting the commune in the summer? The monthly expenditure of the women at their hair dressers? The total of takings in the cafes? After some serious discussion, it was agreed by a commission composed of councillors, officials, and the study group to include nine parameters or significant values out of some twenty originally proposed, and these were called *partial indices*.

The 475 communes of the department are each distinguished by a number (here generalized as j) which appears as an index of the various quantities relating to the particular commune: for instance, M_j stands for the number of its inhabitants. The nine partial indices which were retained included seven indices of wealth and two of poverty.

Of the seven partial indices of wealth, four are concerned with the value of the components of the additional centime, that is the parts of the taxes which are received by the commune through different channels:

A_j : tax from buildings/M_j ;
B_j : tax from land/M_j ;
C_j : tax on personal property/M_j ;
D_j : license fees/M_j .

The two following refer to actual resources:

E_j : yield from the local tax/M_j ;
F_j : yield from property of the commune/M_j .

A further partial index refers indirectly to wealth:

G_j : percentage of total population/M_j .

The two partial indices of poverty were established as:

H_j : mileage of main roads/M_j ;
I_j : public assistance/M_j .

When these criteria had been accepted, a statistical study was made of the frequencies of the partial indices between the different communes, that is histograms of each of the nine indices were produced, so that they could be examined for possible correlations. The distributions obtained were approximately normal except for the D_j and F_j indices, which were widely removed. After an examination of the correlations, the group decided to consider the partial indices as statistically independent, and no further thought was given to the abnormal character of the D_j and F_j indices. The following averages and standard deviations were drawn up.

The nine partial indices of a commune constitute its *rough outline*; for instance, the commune of Courtebrise possessed the outline

$$P_{378} = [A_{378}, B_{378}, \ldots, I_{378}]$$
$$= [212, 628, 233, 822, 1400, 0, 860, 418, 1833].$$

Index	Average	Standard deviation	Unit
A_j	$\bar{A} = 487$	$\sigma_A = 1049$	Hundredths of a centime
B_j	$\bar{B} = 501$	$\sigma_B = 314$	Hundredths of a centime
C_j	$\bar{C} = 231$	$\sigma_C = 94$	Hundredths of a centime
D_j	$\bar{D} = 1031$	$\sigma_D = 2948$	Hundredths of a centime
E_j	$\bar{E} = 2641$	$\sigma_E = 2928$	Centimes
F_j	$\bar{F} = 2365$	$\sigma_F = 10{,}419$	Centimes
G_j	$\bar{G} = 399$	$\sigma_G = 266$	‰
H_j	$\bar{H} = 337$	$\sigma_H = 327$	dm
I_j	$\bar{I} = 905$	$\sigma_I = 1209$	Centimes

But before attempting a comparison between these outlines they had first to normalize them, and the *related indices* were calculated

$$a_j = \frac{A_j - \bar{A}}{\sigma_A}, \qquad b_j = \frac{B_j - \bar{B}}{\sigma_B} \quad \cdots \quad i_j = \frac{I_j - \bar{I}}{\sigma_I}$$

and the term *related profile of the commune* was used for the expression

$$p_j = [a_j, b_j, c_j, d_j, e_j, f_j, g_j, h_j, i_j].$$

After this process, the commune of Courtebrise showed a *related outline*

$$p_{378} = [-0.262; +0.405; -0.021; -0.071; -0.425; -0.022; +1.733; +0.247; +0.767].$$

It is clear that the components of rough or related outlines must be specifically defined for every department. That of Provence Maritime, for instance, might have an outline with twelve components, among which tourist taxes might well intervene as parameters. Every department, too, is free to choose its own components, as long the same general procedure is followed.

The problem is now to compare two related outlines, a task which proves very difficult unless one outline dominates the other, in other words, when every component of the first is greater than the corresponding component of the second, an obviously exceptional condition. In order to compare two *vectors* which are not parallel, we must, mathematicians tell us, introduce a *metric* or universal method of measurement. To compare the related outlines, it was decided to adopt a *weighting*, that is, nine weights λ_a, λ_b,..., λ_i, the sum of whose absolute values should be equal to 1. From this, the overall index of wealth of a commune is expressed as

$$K_j = K_0 + \lambda_a a_j + \lambda_b b_j + \cdots + \lambda_i i_j\,,$$

with

$$|\lambda_a| + |\lambda_b| + \cdots + |\lambda_i| = 1.$$

The weights λ_a, λ_b,..., λ_g will be positive (partial indices of wealth) and λ_h and λ_i will be negative (partial indices of poverty); the quantity K_0 is merely to adjust the position of the average of the K_j terms. The set of nine weights is called the *department outline*

$$\lambda = [\lambda_a, \lambda_b, ..., \lambda_i];$$

it expresses the importance attributed to a partial index of wealth or of poverty. After the study of K_0, and its fixation, the communes with a positive K_j index are considered rich, and the remainder are poor.

When this system was first adopted every councillor allocated the weights which he considered appropriate to each canton. For instance, the representative for the canton of Valfleury might propose

$$\lambda = [0.10; 0.10; 0.05; 0.20; 0.05; 0; 0.15; -0.25; -0.10].$$

When the other councillors had given their weightings, the averages were calculated and, after discussion and simplification, the following optimal outline was voted on and adopted

$$\lambda = [0.06; 0.04; 0.05; 0.17; 0.13; 0.25; 0.06; -0.15; -0.09].$$

In this manner, the formula was finally expressed as

$$\begin{aligned} K_j = 0.05 &+ 0.06\,\frac{A_j - 487}{1049} + 0.04\,\frac{B_j - 501}{314} + 0.05\,\frac{C_j - 231}{94} \\ &+ 0.17\,\frac{D_j - 1031}{2948} + 0.13\,\frac{F_j - 2641}{2928} + 0.25\,\frac{F_j - 2365}{10{,}419} \\ &+ 0.06\,\frac{G_j - 399}{266} - 0.15\,\frac{H_j - 337}{327} - 0.09\,\frac{I_j - 905}{1209}, \end{aligned}$$

the corrective coefficient $K_0 = 0.05$ representing a division into 53% of communes regarded as rich ($K_j > 0$) and 47% regarded as poor

($K_j < 0$). Under this partition, the commune of Courtebrise has an index of wealth of — 0.0747, as shown by the following calculation

$$\begin{aligned} K_{378} &= 0.05 + 0.06 \times (-0.262) + 0.04 \times 0.404 + 0.05 \times 0.021 \\ &\quad + 0.17 \times (-0.071) + 0.13 \times (-0.424) + 0.25 \times (-0.227) \\ &\quad + 0.06 \times 1.733 - 0.15 \times 0.248 - 0.09 \times 0.768 \\ &= -0.0747. \end{aligned}$$

This commune is accordingly poor and is entitled to a grant.

Figure 15.1 shows the histogram of the 475 communes. This method, it may be said, has the advantage of availing itself of all the quantities

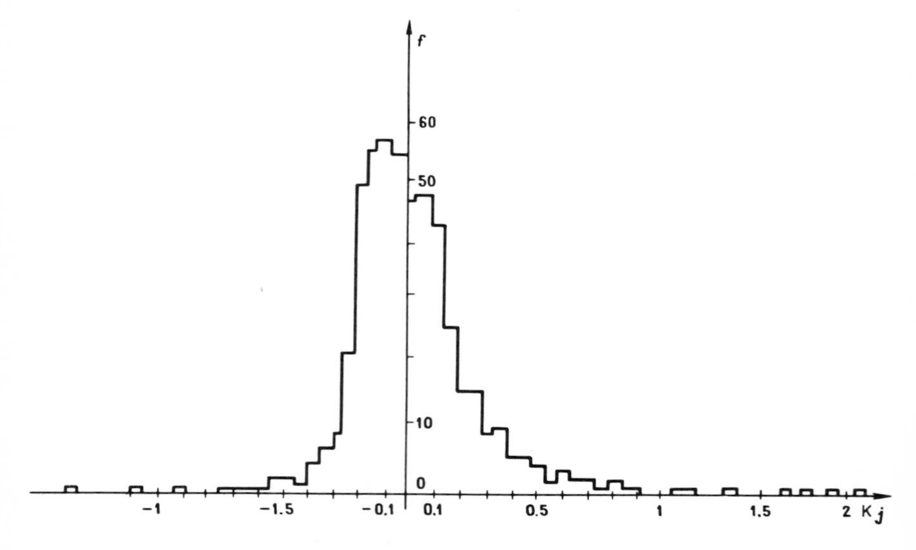

FIG. 15.1. Histogram of the communes of Haute-Seine: $K = 0$, $\sigma_K = 0.318$.

which appear significant factors in the wealth or poverty of an inhabitant. The weighting has the effect of reconciling the opposing opinions in a commission or council; while the outline of a commune or of a department enables local or regional aspects to be taken into account by the central administration.

The formulas which give the K_j values may seem complicated, but the entire calculation for 500 communes can be made with an average electronic computer in less than an hour.

A few observations and criticisms will not be out of place here. The real wealth of a commune would certainly seem to be proportionate to the number of its inhabitants. Even if they are individually wealthy, a small commune which is classed as rich will appear poor when confronted by some exceptional expenditure. Thus the classification is only valid for what may be termed ordinary grants.

Many variants of this method can be envisaged. For instance, the dynamic aspect of the problem might be taken into account. Communes evolve annually, and the partial indices could be based on several sets of figures. Perhaps their weighting should be on a temporal basis and allow for the relative changes in wealth and the number of inhabitants.

From the statistical angle it can be objected that certain distributions, particularly those of the D_j and F_j values, differ greatly from Laplace–Gauss's distributed variables; also, the correlations between the different factors, weak as they are, deserve to be further investigated.

Finally, it is possible that the voters who chose the weighting may have experienced regrets after the results were announced. In such circumstances it might be advisable to reopen the discussion and obtain a second vote. What is important is that the opinions expressed should not differ too widely and that the results should be unanimously accepted. This can often be achieved by facing the voters with the consequences of their vote, thus enabling them to revise it.

It was in this manner that the Council General of the Haute-Seine and the Central Administration came to an agreement, thanks to operations research and electronic calculation.

Weighting the Values

Whenever we desire to compare quantities we must obviously have at our disposal a unit for measuring and then classifying them.

One difficulty lies in the fact that the monetary unit undergoes temporal changes, thereby making it difficult to obtain a true comparison between data from different periods.

For the sake of an example, we propose finding the curve of variation for the turnover of a commercial company between 1954 and 1960. During this period, the company, which sells both domestic goods (class C) and imported articles (classes H, L, and M), has had the turnover shown in Table 15.1.

TABLE 15.1

TURNOVER (IN MILLIONS OF OLD FRANCS)

Year	Total sales	Percentage of foreign goods
1954	160.1	51.7
1955	152.1	54.8
1956	199.2	63.4
1957	206.7	60.0
1958	202.3	52.5
1959	211.2	59.0
1960	243.5	61.8

The average prices of each class of goods have been found and have then been scaled so that 1954 represents 100; from this, the relative evolution of the prices is shown in Table 15.2.

The ratio, in terms of price, of the different classes to the total turnover is then calculated, and is given in Table 15.3. Using α, β, γ, and δ for the coefficients of this table, it has been possible to calculate the average annual price

$$\pi = \frac{\alpha C + \beta H + \gamma L + \delta M}{100}.$$

The results of this evaluation are entered in Table 15.4. From this the turnover has been found, with 1954 again represented as 100 (Table 15.5).

With the above data it was an easy matter to draw the curve of variation for the turnover as a function of time (Fig. 15.2).

By drawing this graph, the causes of the variation in the turnover are brought into much greater relief. In 1955 the increases in price introduced by the management (policy II), resulted in a falling off in sales, which was fortunately compensated for in 1956–1957 by the general reduction in import duties that made it possible to sell a larger proportion of foreign goods. In 1958, import difficulties brought the turnover to much the same level as that of 1955. It fell even lower in 1959, and rose again in 1960, thanks to new measures favoring imports.

TABLE 15.2

Type →	C	H	L	M
1954	100	100	100	100
1955	103	105	102	108
1956	106	108	115	114
1957	118	113	141	124
1958	128	125	162	141
1959	134	152	214	167
1960	141	154	224	175
1961 (estimate)	148	163	246	188

TABLE 15.3

	(α)	(β)	(γ)	(δ)
Type →	C	H	L	M
1954	48.3	26.9	14.8	10
1955	45.2	24.3	23.4	7.1
1956	36.6	32	24.3	7.1
1957	40	30.3	23.7	6
1958	47.5	30.8	16.7	5
1959	41	26.2	20.8	12
1960	38.2	21	20.4	20.4
1961	43	20	18.5	18.5
(estimate)	38	21	20.5	20.5

TABLE 15.4

AVERAGE ANNUAL PRICE OF GOODS SOLD

1954	1955	1956	1957	1958	1959	1960	1961 (estimate)
100	103.6	109.4	122.3	133.4	159.3	167.6	{176.5 178.4

TABLE 15.5

TURNOVER REDUCED TO A PERCENTAGE OF 100 FOR 1954

Year	1954	1955	1956	1957	1958	1959	1960	1961
Actual sales	160.1	152.1	199.2	206.7	202.3	211.3	243.5	340(?)
Scaled sales	100	92.3	113.8	105.5	94.7	82.2	90.7	120(?)

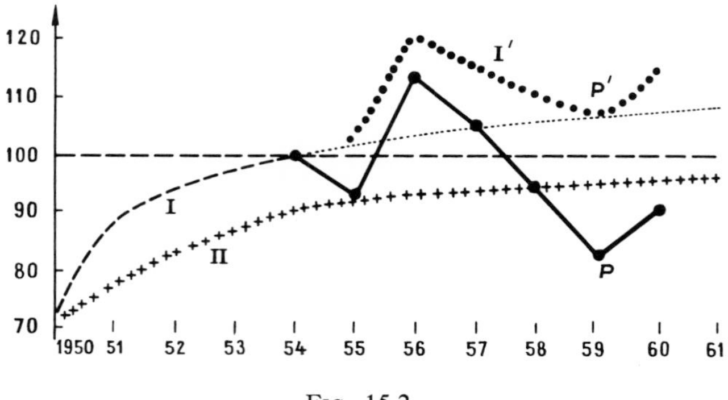

FIG. 15.2

Careful estimates make it possible to envisage that policy I, which was followed before 1954, could have ensured the development (I′) with P' as its lowest point (an economic situation similar to 1954). It still remains undecided whether the resulting turnover of 310 millions for 1960 would, in fact, have been preferable to the 243 millions actually obtained, taking into account the difference in prices between policies I and II.

CONCERNING "UTILITY"

In the above example, some simple calculations enabled us to compare the turnover for different years. We might also, with the requisite information, have compared the results of different policies of management. But, unfortunately, such is not always possible.

We can envisage another example involving a choice between different policies of management which would result in varying success according to a series of criteria: amount of dividends distributed, reserves set aside, improved wages, enlarged share of the market, increase in net profits, and so on. We prefer to confine our investigation to hypotheses of more immediate concern.

Let us assume that there exists a real lark pie (all lark, and not half lark, half horse) and a real blackbird pie.[2] We might ask several people to tell us their preferences. In reply, *A* might say that he prefers lark pie (not surprisingly, since he comes from Pithiviers), *B* that he prefers

[2] Small birds are not protected in France, and in rural districts it is (or used to be) possible to find a peasant in wait behind a large barricade for the arrival of a blackbird or sparrow. [Translator's note.]

the blackbird pie (he is a native of Ajaccio), *C* that he likes both equally, and so on. To give exactness to these different preferences, we shall now require those whom we question to evaluate their relative satisfaction in the event of not being able to obtain their preferred pie, with the understanding that the maximal satisfaction is limited to 1 in the contrary case. With this information available we shall draw up a table.

	Lark pie	Blackbird pie
A	1	0.7
B	0.6	1
C	0.5	0.5
⋮	⋮	⋮

After questioning a large number of persons, and after calculating the average of each column, we might find that there were 0.7 in favor of lark pie and 0.6 who preferred blackbird pie; from this we could conclude that the preferences amounted to:

$$\text{lark pie:}\quad 0.7/1.3 = 0.54; \qquad \text{blackbird pie:}\quad 0.6/1.3 = 0.46.$$

The problem becomes more complicated if we introduce another term of comparison, for instance thrush pie. After carrying out the same experiment as before, but this time offering a choice between the thrush pie and the blackbird pie, we might perhaps have obtained:

	Thrush pie	Blackbird pie
A	1	0.6
B	0.8	1
C	1	0.8
⋮	⋮	⋮

From this we should find an average of 0.8 for thrush pie and 0.6 for blackbird pie, which would give us the preferences:

$$\text{thrush pie:}\quad 0.8/1.4 = 0.57; \qquad \text{blackbird pie:}\quad 0.6/1.4 = 0.43.$$

Can we now assume that thrush pie is preferred to lark pie, since proportionate calculation gives us

thrush: 0.38; lark: 0.33; blackbird: 0.29?

A different procedure can be used with advantage. Let us first obtain figures for the relative satisfaction provided by the three dishes:

	Thrush pie	Lark pie	Blackbird pie
A	1	0.9	0.6
B	0.8	0.6	1
C	1	0.8	0.8
⋮	⋮	⋮	⋮

Let us next enquire the preferences between a carton containing thrush pie and two cartons, one containing lark and the other blackbird pie. If the first person questioned prefers thrush pie, the satisfaction which he obtains from it s_1 is greater than the sum of s_2 and s_3 which he would obtain from the others:

$$s_1 > s_2 + s_3 .$$

This would result in giving a value to s_1 greater than $0.9 + 0.6 = 1.5$, for instance 1.6, which gives the following figures for *A*'s preferences:

51.6, 29, and 19.3.

B might say that he prefers the carton with blackbird pie, whence

$$s_3 > s_1 + s_2 ,$$

and the respective preferences are

27.6, 20.7, and 51.7,

taking s_3 as 1.5. Finally, let us suppose *C* has no preference, in which case

$$s_1 = s_2 + s_3 ,$$

whence $s_1 = 1.6$, and the figures for *C* are

50, 25, and 25.

After the same calculations have been performed for all those questioned, we should find the average for each column, and by converting these results into percentages, we should obtain an expression for the different satisfactions, such as

$$48, \quad 28, \quad 24.$$

We must take note of the arbitrary nature of part of this procedure; to satisfy the condition $s_1 > s_2 + s_3$, for instance, we chose $s_1 = 1.6$, but might equally have chosen 1.7, 1.8, etc.

The classification of situations or results or objects of a greater number than two is therefore a possible undertaking, provided we accept the *hypothesis of additivity* with its arbitrary procedure.

Numerous works on this subject have appeared both in America and in France since Pareto first suggested an initial *preorder* for the comparison of objects, followed by an *order* under which they are placed in equivalence classes that are without any common element.

Given objects O_i between which a choice is to be made, the axioms generally accepted by American writers are as follows:

Axiom 1. Every object O_i possesses a correspondence with a non-negative number X_i.

Axiom 2. If O_i is preferable to O_j, then $X_i > X_j$; if O_i is equivalent to O_j, then $X_i = X_j$.

Axiom 3. If X_i and X_j possess correspondence with O_i and O_j, then $X_i + X_j$ corresponds to a choice which includes O_i and O_j. This axiom results in the following corollaries.

Corollary a. If we prefer O_i to O_j and O_j to O_k, then $(O_i + O_j)$ is preferred to O_k.

Corollary b. It is a matter of indifference whether we consider (O_j and O_k) or (O_k and O_j).

Corollary c. If it appears a matter of indifference whether we choose (O_j and O_k) or O_k only, it shows that $X_i = 0$.

Axiom 3 (the hypothesis of additivity) implies that O_i and O_j may be chosen *simultaneously*, that is, if we are dealing with situations, that each can be made to exist independently, a very important restriction.

French writers, for the most part, do not accept this axiom of independence, and Massé and Allais should be consulted on this subject. The argument, propounded by the advocates of a *subjective* theory of value, for passing from the scale of ordinal numbers for preferences to that of cardinal numbers for their values, is met by the counter arguments of those favoring an *objective* theory.

We must conclude that, even if we limit ourselves to defining a weighting of values, we are faced with a difficult problem, the solutions to which are far from universally accepted.[3]

[3] It will be noticed that writers have been at pains to set forth a mathematical interpretation of utility in connection with luxury articles. It is, in point of fact, very difficult to construct a scale of preference when we are considering articles of primary necessity: has bread, for instance, a greater utility than shoes? It will be said that, in our example of the pies, we were dealing with products of the same kind. But it is surely in such cases that men usually act contrary to their preferences, especially if they do not have a well-filled purse. In truth, the concept of preference only really applies to goods of equal value or those which we can give away. Otherwise our choice cannot fail to take account of the relative value of goods, having regard to our available funds. Hence it is somewhat paradoxical to try to construct a scale of monetary value based on a criterion which assumes that the goods being considered have the same monetary value or are valueless.

In any case, the method which we have set forth should rather be replaced by a sounding of consumer opinion in order to obtain better information about the overall demand. Such enquiries, frequently used in market research, could be applied on a vaster scale to determine the needs (of all kinds) of an entire people. These soundings, to make sense, should take account of the prices of the different goods and of the available funds of those requiring them: prices and present possibilities if we are making a short term survey, prices and provisional possibilities if we are producing a long term study.

CHAPTER 16

THE NEW FREGOLI

(Foulkes' Algorithm and Its Application)

A short time ago we were talking to our friend Fregoli about the secrets of the circus, of which he is such a popular figure in Mexico. It is, indeed, a well-known fact that Fregoli can change his costume in record time. "There is no secret in it," he told me, "but simply a logical method of dressing and undressing which I inherited from my ancestors." And being a well-educated man he added: "No doubt you will appreciate from your knowledge of mathematics how difficult it must have been for my great-grandfather to work out this problem."

The reader should not experience surprise at this statement. For whereas the mathematics of the past sufficed to enumerate the various possible combinations which could be used in dressing or undressing, our modern knowledge enables us to select the best of them. Let us assume, for simplification, that when he changes his costume Fregoli retains his undergarments and his shirt. To appear in his costume of a dandy, he still has pants, waistcoat, coat, tie, overcoat, socks, shoes, and gloves to put on, and his silver-knobbed cane to take in his hand. For these eight articles there are

$$8! = 8 \times 7 \times 6 \times 5 \times 4 \times 3 \times 2 \times 1 = 40{,}320 \text{ possibilities,}$$

a very large number of which can be eliminated owing to the impossibility of putting on his overcoat before his coat, the coat before the waistcoat, and so on.

To enable us to find our way in this labyrinth, let us establish classes between the different articles of clothing which, for purposes of brevity, we shall distinguish by letter: A, pants; B, waistcoat; C, coat; D, tie; E, overcoat; F, socks; G, shoes; H, gloves.

Knowing Fregoli as we do, we can rely on his putting his waistcoat on before his coat, and shall express this as $B < C$, which can be read as B prior to C. On the other hand, either the waistcoat or the tie can be put on first, which we shall express as $B \gtrless D$. Finally, we shall regard it as extremely unlikely that he will not put on his shoes immediately after his socks, this being represented as $F \,|\!< G$ (F is immediately prior to G).

Collecting the different types of relations which we have accepted for our problem, we have

$$A < B, D, G; \quad B < C; \quad B \gtrless D, F; \quad C < E;$$
$$D < C; \quad E \gtrless H; \quad F \,|\!< G; \quad G < C, H.$$

Such relations, as we have so often stressed, can be expressed in the form of a drawing or graph (Fig. 16.1). The graph itself can be

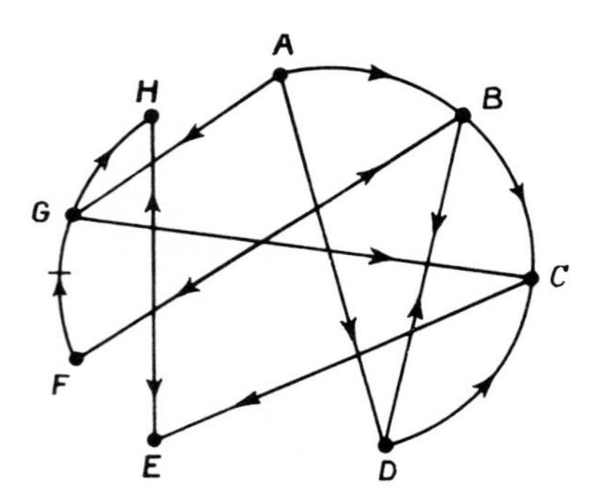

FIG. 16.1

	A	B	C	D	E	F	G	H
A	1	1	0	1	0	0	1	0
B	0	1	1	1	0	1	0	0
C	0	0	1	0	1	0	0	0
D	0	1	1	1	0	0	0	0
E	0	0	0	0	1	0	0	1
F	0	1	0	0	0	1	1	0
G	0	0	1	0	0	0	1	1
H	0	0	0	0	1	0	0	1

MATRIX 1

represented by a matrix possessing the condition that every connection between a letter in a line and a letter in a column will be shown by a 1 (matrix 1).

We now wish to discover whether there is a route, between any letter serving as a means of entry and any letter which can be used as an exit, such that Fregoli can complete his dressing without contravening any of the relations previously given. To solve this problem we shall perform an operation of a rather special kind, that is the product of matrix M (matrix 1) by itself, substituting, however, the Boolean sum of the factors for the usual arithmetical sum. The Boolean sum was fully discussed in Chapter 11 and we shall only recall it by means of the table now given.

$\dot{+}$	A	B	$A \dot{+} B$
	0	0	0
	0	1	1
	1	0	1
	1	1	1

Thus the term in the product, situated in the third square of the first line, is the product of line A by column C if we consider the Boolean sum of the factors:

$$[1\ 1\ 0\ 1\ 0\ 0\ 1\ 0] \odot \begin{bmatrix} 0 \\ 1 \\ 1 \\ 1 \\ 0 \\ 0 \\ 1 \\ 0 \end{bmatrix} = 1 \cdot 0 \dot{+} 1 \cdot 1 \dot{+} 0 \cdot 1 \dot{+} 1 \cdot 1 \dot{+} 0 \cdot 0 \dot{+} 0 \cdot 0 \dot{+} 1 \cdot 1 \dot{+} 0 \cdot 0;$$

hence it is equal to 1.

It will be found that the matrix obtained, which we shall call $M^{[2]}$, contains only zeros and ones. The same will be true of $M^{[4]}$. It should be observed that the (1) elements did not occur in M and are a part of $M^{[2]}$.

$M^{[2]} =$

	A	B	C	D	E	F	G	H
A	1	1	(1)	1		(1)	1	(1)
B		1	1	1	(1)	1	(1)	
C			1		1			(1)
D		1	1	1	(1)	(1)		
E					1			1
F		1	(1)	(1)		1	1	(1)
G			1		(1)		1	1
H					1			1

$M^{[4]} =$

	A	B	C	D	E	F	G	H
A	1	1	1	1	$\boxed{1}$	1	1	1
B		1	1	1	1	1	1	$\boxed{1}$
C			1		1			1
D		1	1	1	1	1	$\boxed{1}$	$\boxed{1}$
E					1			1
F		1	1	1	$\boxed{1}$	1	1	1
G			1		1		1	1
H					1			1

In matrix $M^{[4]}$ it will be seen that A is an element which can be followed by any other (directly or indirectly), but which cannot be preceded by any other.

It is not useful to retain either line or column A in $M^{[4]}$, in order to calculate $M^{[8]}$; hence we obtain $M'^{[8]}$, which we observe is exactly the same as the corresponding part of $M^{[4]}$.

$M'^{[8]} =$

	B	C	D	E	F	G	H
B	1	1	1	1	1	1	1
C		1		1			1
D	1	1	1	1	1	1	1
E				1			1
F	1	1	1	1	1	1	1
G		1		1		1	1
H				1			1

Under these conditions, we should, according to Foulkes' algorithm,[1] conclude our operations. By an exchange of lines and columns, matrix $M^{[4]}$ can be put in the form $\mathscr{M}^{[4]}$, which means that the problem produces five ordinate subgraphs.

$\mathscr{M}^{[4]} =$

	A	B	D	F	G	C	E	H
A	1	1	1	1	1	1	1	1
B	0	1	1	1	1	1	1	1
D	0	1	1	1	1	1	1	1
F	0	1	1	1	1	1	1	1
G	0	0	0	0	1	1	1	1
C	0	0	0	0	0	1	1	1
E	0	0	0	0	0	0	1	1
H	0	0	0	0	0	0	1	1

This set only possesses one Hamiltonian path[2] *ADBFGCEH*, which means (Figs. 16.2 and 16.3) that our friend Fregoli has one method and one only for dressing up as a dandy, and must put on his clothes in this order: pants, tie, waistcoat, socks, shoes, coat, overcoat, gloves.

[1] The algorithm is given on p. 258 of this chapter.

[2] A path which passes once and once only through all the vertices of a given graph.

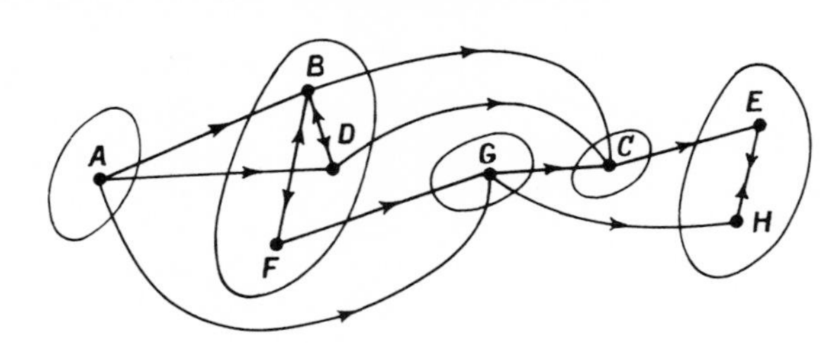

FIG. 16.2

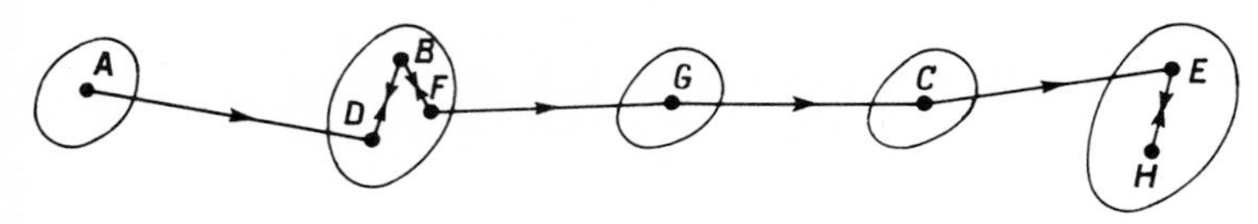

FIG. 16.3

Problems of this type sometimes produce several solutions, and in the present one, if we had been given the relation $D \gtrless F$, there would have been a second solution *ABDFGCEH*.

Although the example which we chose was of a frivolous kind it is obvious that Foulkes' algorithm could be used for more serious problems. Scheduling for industrial production shows the same combinatorial character, for a certain number of operations have to be performed on different machines, the order of these operations being governed by such relations as $<$, $\gtrless$ or $|<$. Where the number of machines and the number of operations are both large, a single solution is rarely obtained. Under these conditions, a criterion of cost or duration has to be used to decide the best solution from those available.

Foulkes' Algorithm

Let us consider the six operations A, B, C, D, E, F, between which the following relations exist:

$A < B$	$B \mid< C$	$C < D$	$E < D$	$F < D$
$A < D$	$B < D$			$F < E$
$A \gtrless F$	$B \gtrless E$			
	$B \gtrless F$			

The object of the problem is to find the paths (if any exist) which pass once and once only through each of the vertices while preserving the above relations: these will be Hamiltonian paths.

	A	B	C	D	E	F
A	1	1	0	1	0	1
B	0	1	1	1	1	1
C	0	0	1	1	0	0
D	0	0	0	1	0	0
E	0	1	0	1	1	0
F	1	1	0	1	1	1

If we study the graph of Fig. 16.4 we see that vertex D is the extremity of any Hamiltonian path (if there is one), since no arc has this vertex as its origin, whereas an arc from each of the other vertices ends there. This property is shown by the presence of a 1 in the entire D column and of 0 in the entire D line (except, of course, at the intersection).

There can also be the inverse situation where 1 occurs throughout the line representing a vertex, and throughout the corresponding column, except at the intersection, zeros occur; and in this case the vertex is the origin of any Hamiltonian path which may exist.

The matrix of the graph is simplified by provisionally crossing out the pairs of rows corresponding either to the origin or the extremity of every Hamiltonian path. Thus, in the present case, line and column D

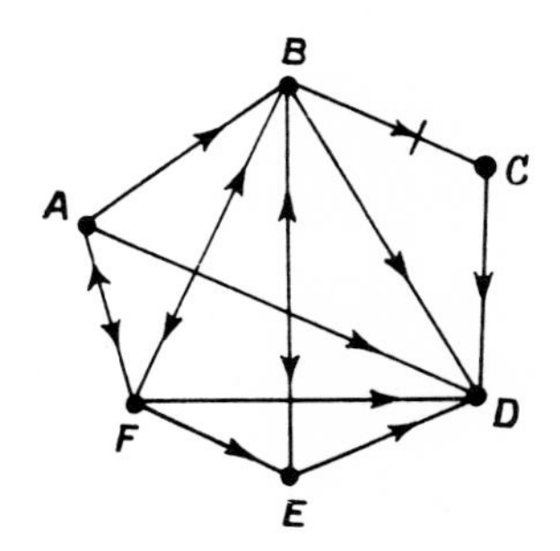

Fig. 16.4

can be provisionally omitted, and we thereby obtain matrix M'. We now form the products of the elements of any line, for instance A, and the elements of any column, for instance C, as if we were calculating $[M']^{[2]}$.

	A	B	C	E	F
A	1	1	0	0	1
B	0	1	1	1	1
C	0	0	1	0	0
E	0	1	0	1	0
F	1	1	0	1	1

The products of the elements, taken in order, are

(*a*) $1 \cdot 0 = 0$; (*b*) $1 \cdot 1 = 1$; (*c*) $0 \cdot 1 = 0$;

(*d*) $0 \cdot 0 = 0$; (*e*) $1 \cdot 0 = 0$.

These can be interpreted, if we are going from A towards C as:

(*a*) there is no direct route from A to C;

(*b*) there is a direct route from A to B and one from B to C, so that there is a route of length 2 from A to C;

(*c*) there is no direct route from A to C;

(*d*) there is no direct route from A to E nor from E to C;

(*e*) there is a direct route from A to F, but not from F to C.

In this way we have found all the routes from A to C of a length less than or equal to 2. Since we are looking for all the paths connecting the different vertices of the graph, instead of finding the arithmetical sum, as in an ordinary matricial product, we shall find the Boolean sum, thereby obtaining $[M']^{[2]}$. In this matrix every 1 reveals the existence of a route of length less than or equal to 2, and every 0 the inexistence of such a route.

In matrix $[M']^{[2]}$ it can be seen that vertex C must be the extremity of a Hamiltonian path, if one exists. We again provisionally cross out rows C, thus obtaining $[M'']^{[2]}$.

$[M']^{[2]} =$

	A	B	C	E	F
A	1	1	1	1	1
B	1	1	1	1	1
C	0	0	1	0	0
E	0	1	1	1	1
F	1	1	1	1	1

$[M'']^{[2]} =$

	A	B	E	F
A	1	1	1	1
B	1	1	1	1
E	0	1	1	1
F	1	1	1	1

$[M'']^{[3]} =$

A	B	E	F	
1	1	1	1	A
1	1	1	1	B
1	1	1	1	E
1	1	1	1	F

With the same procedure as we used to find the routes of length $\leqslant 2$ when calculating $[M'']^{[2]}$, we shall find those of length $\leqslant 3$ in calculating $[M'']^{[3]}$. This matrix contains only ones, which proves that there are paths of length $\geqslant 3$ between all the points A, B, E, F, taken in pairs. In particular, one can go from E to A through B and F. There is no purpose in calculating $[M'']^{[4]}$, which would obviously contain only ones.

In general, when we calculate successive symbolic powers of $[M]$, we can stop at n such that

$$[M]^{[n+1]} = [M]^{[n]},$$

since this signifies that there is no route in $[M]$ of length greater than n. Matrix $[M]^{[3]}$, obtained by the reintegration of rows C and D, can be regrouped in a form such that all the zeros are situated below the main diagonal and all the ones above it.

The square matrices formed by 1 resting on the main diagonal constitute *equivalence classes* in relation to the law: point X is joined to point Y, and reciprocally.

For example, A is joined to E through B or through F, and also through F and B; E is connected to A through B and F. We have

	A	B	E	F	C	D
A	1	1	1	1	1	1
B	1	1	1	1	1	1
E	1	1	1	1	1	1
F	1	1	1	1	1	1
C	0	0	0	0	1	1
D	0	0	0	0	0	1

simplified the initial graph by dividing it into classes, and the discovery of the only Hamiltonian path *AFEBCD* has become very easy (Fig. 16.5).

Returning to Fregoli's problem, we note that the calculation of $[M]^{[2]}$ gives us paths of length $\leqslant 2$; that of $[M]^{[4]}$, paths of length $\leqslant 4$. If we had calculated $[M]^{[7]}$, we would have had paths of length $\leqslant 7$; indeed, we calculated $[M]^{[8]}$, which gives all the paths, because every path of length >7 passes through a point twice. We established the identity of this matrix with $[M]^{[4]}$.

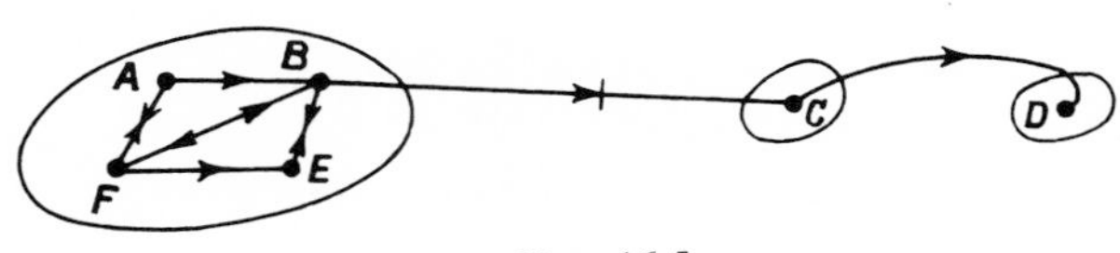

FIG. 16.5

Next we found the equivalence classes by putting $[M]^{[4]}$ in the form *ABDFGCEH*; in particular, (B, D, F) and (E, H) constitute equivalence classes.

Remark. It is evident that, when we write relations of *order* (for example, relations of priority) in a set, the Foulkes algorithm is one of the methods that permits us to find out whether they are *compatible* (since a circuit must not exist). It permits us, moreover, to find all the relations of order between two elements, which are deduced from hypotheses by virtue of the transitivity of a relation of order (given $A < B$ and $B < C$, we deduce $A < C$, although the latter relation may not have been explicitly given).

It is only then between points not connected by a relation that we are able validly to introduce a relation of indifference, $\gtrless$.

On the other hand, it often happens in practice that we have to deal with a relation of *preorder* (involving circuits), in which case the algorithm is the method adopted for treating the problem.

CHAPTER 17

ACTORS ON TOUR[1]

(A Scheduling Problem. Johnson's Algorithm)

Most Mexicans are avid theatregoers and a number of touring companies do a profitable business in the provincial towns. It is in consequence of such tours that the director of the *Alcazar Variety Company* is confronted each time a new town is visited by a problem he has been trying to solve for a long time.

The difficulty lies in the fact that the facilities for a variety troupe differ greatly in the various cities: in some theatres both the public and players are well catered to, but in others the stage arrangements are only suitable for a drama, and not for the series of acts in a variety show. The consequence of this is that if the various acts are to be given their usual time, the period required for dressing and make-up will vary by several minutes according to the facilities available. Since the director's aim is to produce the show in the shortest possible time, this means that he must minimize the intervals between the acts or (which amounts to the same thing) the total time spent on stage by the announcer.

To simplify the problem, we shall assume that the time required to change the rudimentary scenery is negligeable and will suppose that the initial moment for the show is the same for spectators, actors, and stage managers, that is, that the house and the stage are not available before this moment of origin.

In the town of Orizaba the time required to prepare each number has been evaluated as shown in Table 17.1.

It will be seen that the acts are to be presented in a particular order. Since there are eight acts, there are $8! = 40{,}320$ possible ways in which they can be presented, and our problem is to discover which is the best according to the criterion given above.

[1] We wish to thank Cullmann and Pertuiset for suggesting the theme for this anecdote.

TABLE 17.1

Act	Time (minutes)		Order of presentation
	Preparation	Presentation	
a	20	25	3
b	10	8	8
c	14	11	6
d	12	10	7
e	12	15	1
f	18	12	5
g	25	20	4
h	15	20	2

Let us first examine what happens by taking any arbitrary sequence *b*, *f*, *c*, *h*, *g*, *a*, *d*, *e*. Figure 17.1, which is a *Gantt diagram*, is a simple method of finding the time wasted or *dead time*. In it, the first line is composed of segments, placed end to end, the length of which is proportionate to the preparation time of the different acts taken in the chosen order.

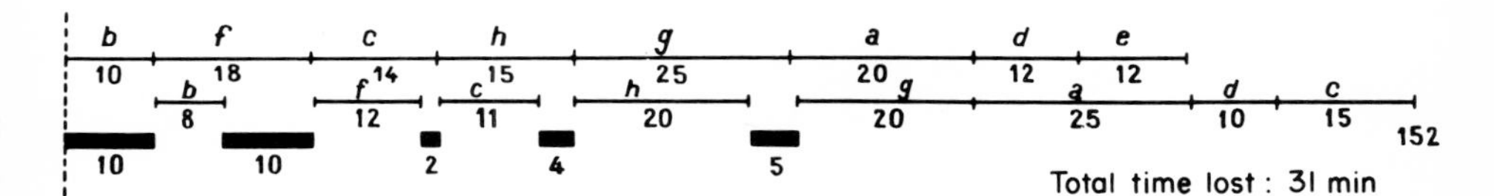

FIG. 17.1

The second line now makes it possible to determine the periods during which the stage will be occupied, on the simple principle that the preparation for a number must be completed before it can be presented, and that one act must end before the next can begin. The third line shows the lost time which can be deduced from the diagram, and in the example chosen this amounts to 31 minutes.

On the other hand, the lost time for the sequence *e*, *h*, *a*, *g*, *f*, *c*, *d*, *b* (Fig. 17.2) amounts to only 13 minutes, of which 12 occur before the performance begins. This saving is fairly considerable, and it will be useful to explain the procedure for Johnson's algorithm by which it has been obtained.

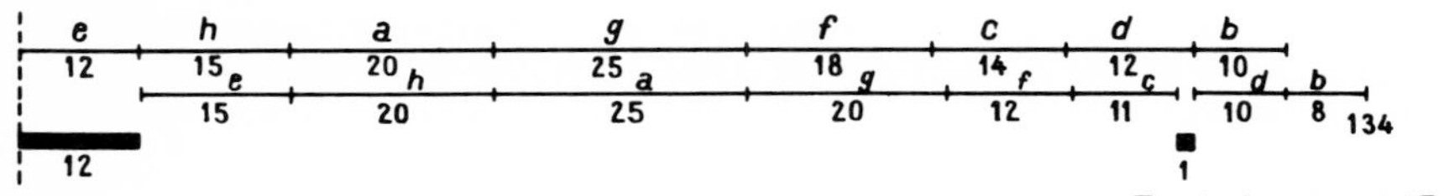

FIG. 17.2

(1) We examine the table of the periods required for the two operations (preparation and presentation of an act) and we retain the smaller of the two: here, in the case of *b*, for example, it is the 8 minutes that the act lasts.

(2) If the quantity retained corresponds to the first operation (preparation), we *begin* with this operation; if it has to do with the second (presentation), we *end* with it. In the case of *b*, the quantity retained represents a presentation, and this act will therefore conclude the show.

(3) We cross out the line for which the allocation has been made in Table 17.1, and recommence these three procedures.

Example. If we cross out line *b*, the smallest remaining period is 10 minutes and represents the presentation of act *d*; hence *d* will end the acts still to be allocated and will immediately precede *b*, which is already allocated.

Position in the sequence

Iteration number								
1								*b*
2							*d*	
3						*c*		
4	(*e*)				*f*			
5	*e*				(*f*)			
6		*h*						
7			*a*	(*g*)				
8			(*a*)	*g*				

FIG. 17.3

After we have crossed out lines *b* and *d*, we allocate *c* (presentation), *f* (presentation), *e* (preparation), *h* (preparation), *a* (preparation), and finally, *g* (presentation).

Figure 17.3 shows the positions obtained in the sequence in the course of the successive iterations. The variants found (*e* can be allocated at the fourth iteration and *f* at the fifth, *a* at the last, and *g* at the last but one) in no way modify the final result: 13 minutes dead time.

TABLE 17.2

Act	Time (minutes)	
	Preparation	Presentation
a	15	25
b	10	12
c	12	11
d	8	10
e	9	15
f	15	12
g	18	20
h	12	16

A few days later the Alcazar troupe arrives at Veracruz, where the facilities of the local theatre enable the periods for preparing the acts to be reduced, but at the same time the artists in acts *b* and *h* have altered the duration of their numbers. The use of Johnson's algorithm results in the sequence *d*, *e*, *b*, *h*, *a*, *g*, *f*, *c*, giving a lost time of 8 minutes (Fig. 17.4).

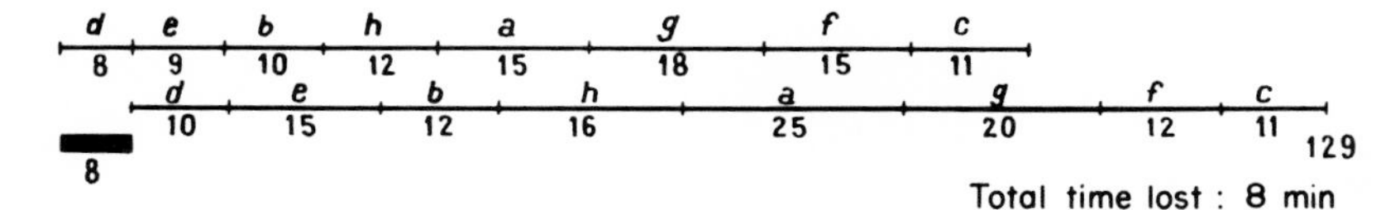

FIG. 17.4

Unfortunately, one evening a make-up woman is taken ill too late for her to be replaced or to alter the time of the performance, and the dead time is increased to 25 minutes (Table 17.3 and Fig. 17.5). After learning that the make-up assistant will be away for a week, the director, as usual, attempts to improve the sequence, eventually

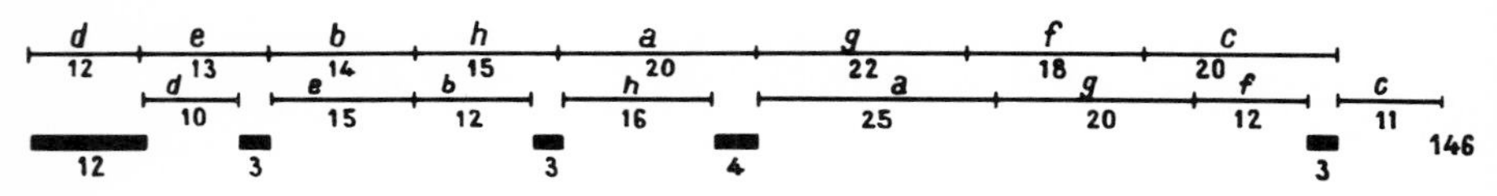

FIG. 17.5

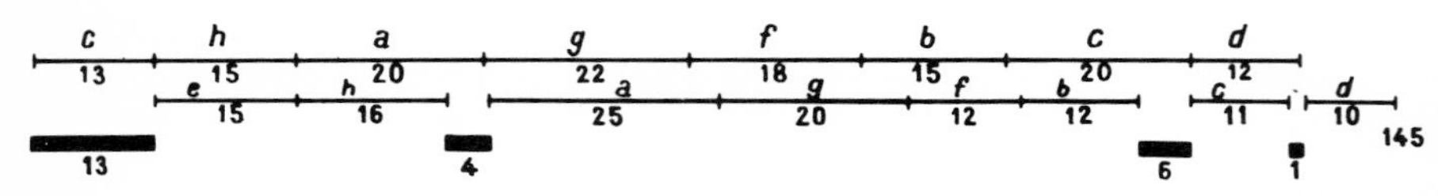

FIG. 17.6

producing that of Fig. 17.6 with a dead time of 24 minutes—not very brilliant, perhaps, but still an improvement.

TABLE 17.3

Act	Time (minutes)	
	Preparation	Presentation
a	20	25
b	15	12
c	20	11
d	12	10
e	13	15
f	18	12
g	22	20
h	15	26

Johnson's Algorithm

Our use of Johnson's algorithm shows that it can be employed for scheduling problems where n operations have to be carried out in two successive positions; indeed, it is, in certain cases, valid where three positions occur, but never for more. We shall now consider some cases of its industrial application.

Figure 17.7 contains a representation in diagrammatic form of a

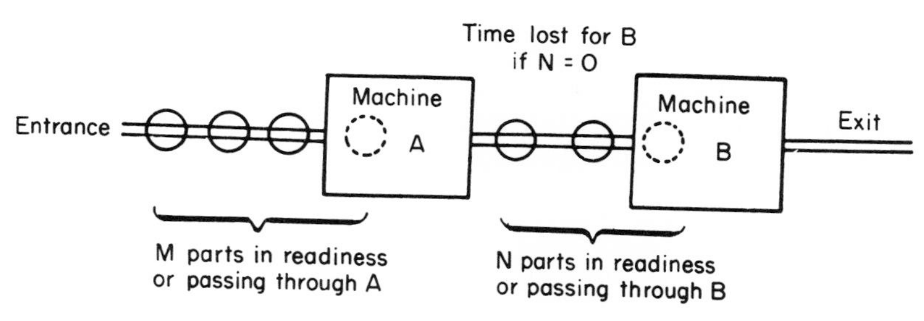

FIG. 17.7

repair shop comprising a reboring machine A and an internal rectifying machine B, which are used for diverse parts to the number of n. These parts are received in any order, and on account of their diversity, require very varying times for reconstruction. We shall take A_i and B_i for the respective times for repair of a part i on machines A and B.

The problem is to minimize the period of inactivity of machine B, that is, to find an order $p_1, p_2, ..., p_i, ..., p_n$ giving the least waiting time between the repair of part p_j and part p_{j+1}, the total being those of the successive j values.

Let us take T for the total period between the commencement of the reboring of the first part until the end of the repair of the last one, and X_i for the time wasted between the completion of operation p_{i-1} on machine B and the commencement of operation p_i on this machine. We have (Fig. 17.8),

$$T = \sum_{i=1}^{n} B_i + \sum_{i=1}^{n} X_i$$

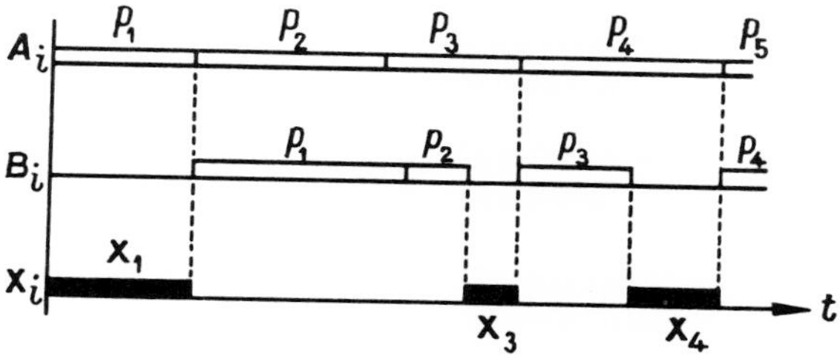

FIG. 17.8

and, as $\sum_i B_i$ is known, we must minimize

$$\sum_i X_i .$$

It will also be seen from Fig. 17.8 that $X_1 = A_1$, that $X_2 = A_1 + A_2 - B_1 - X_1$ if $A_1 + A_2 \geqslant B_1 + X_1$, and $X_2 = 0$ if $A_1 + A_2 < B_1 + X_1$.

Consequently we shall seek a value of X_2 such that

$$\begin{aligned} X_2 &= \max(A_1 + A_2 - B_1 - X_1; 0) \\ &= \max\Bigl(\sum_{i=1}^{2} A_i - \sum_{i=1}^{1} B_i - \sum_{i=1}^{1} X_i; 0\Bigr). \end{aligned}$$

Let us now examine the sum $X_1 + X_2$; we have

$$\begin{aligned} X_1 + X_2 &= X_1 + \max(A_1 + A_2 - B_1 - X_1; 0), \\ &= \max(A_1 + A_2 - B_1; X_1) \\ &= \max(A_1 + A_2 - B_1; A_1), \\ &= \max\Bigl(\sum_{i=1}^{2} A_i - \sum_{i=1}^{1} B_i; A_1\Bigr). \end{aligned}$$

In the same way

$$X_3 = \max\Bigl(\sum_{i=1}^{3} A_i - \sum_{i=1}^{2} B_i - \sum_{i=1}^{2} X_i; 0\Bigr)$$

and

$$\begin{aligned} \sum_{i=1}^{3} X_i &= \max\Bigl(\sum_{i=1}^{3} A_i - \sum_{i=1}^{2} B_i; \sum_{i=1}^{2} X_i\Bigr) \\ &= \max\Bigl(\sum_{i=1}^{3} A_i - \sum_{i=1}^{2} B_i; \sum_{i=1}^{2} A_i - B_1; A_1\Bigr). \end{aligned}$$

This formula can easily be extended to n times X_i for a certain order S of the p_i parts:

$$D_n(S) = \sum_{i=1}^{n} X_i = \max\Bigl(\sum_{i=1}^{n} A_i - \sum_{i=1}^{n-1} B_i; \sum_{i=1}^{n-1} A_i - \sum_{i=1}^{n-2} B_i ;...; A_1\Bigr),$$

which can still further be abbreviated to

$$D_n(S) = \max_{1 \leqslant r \leqslant n} \left(\sum_{i=1}^{r} A_i - \sum_{i=1}^{r-1} B_i \right),$$

which consists in taking the maximum of the differences obtained for each value of r, from 1 to n. Hence we can state

$$L_r = \sum_{i=1}^{r} A_i - \sum_{i=1}^{r-1} B_i ,$$

whence

$$D_n(S) = \max_{1 \leqslant r \leqslant n} L_r .$$

Let us now consider an order (S_1):

$$(S_1) = (p_1 , p_2 , p_3 ,..., p_{k-1} , p_k , p_{k+1} , p_{k+2} ,..., p_n)$$

and the order (S_2) obtained by inverting k and $k + 1$:

$$(S_2) = (p_1 , p_2 , p_3 ,..., p_{k-1} , p_{k+1} , p_k , p_{k+2} ,..., p_n).$$

The values of L_r^1 and L_r^2 obtained for the orders (S_1) and (S_2) are the same for each r, except possibly for $r = k$ and $r = k + 1$.

(1) Hence, we have

$$D_n(S_1) = D_n(S_2)$$

if

$$\max(L_k^1, L_{k+1}^1) = \max(L_k^2, L_{k+1}^2).$$

(2) If

$$\max(L_k^1, L_{k+1}^1) \neq \max(L_k^2, L_{k+1}^2),$$

one of the two orders (S_1) or (S_2) is preferable to the other.

The order (S_1), in which $k + 1$ follows k, will be better than (S_2), in which $k + 1$ precedes k, if

$$\max(L_k^1; L_{k+1}^1) < \max(L_k^2; L_{k+1}^2). \quad (1)$$

Hence,

$$\max(L_k^1; L_{k+1}^1) = \max\left(\sum_{i=1}^{k} A_i - \sum_{i=1}^{k-1} B_i;\ \sum_{i=1}^{k+1} A_i - \sum_{i=1}^{k} B_i \right)$$

and

$$\max(L_k^2; L_{k+1}^2) = \max\left(\sum_{i=1}^{k-1} A_i + A_{k+1} - \sum_{i=1}^{k-1} B_i; \sum_{i=1}^{k+1} A_i - \sum_{i=1}^{k-1} B_i - B_{k+1}\right).$$

Thus, we can write

$$\begin{aligned} \sum_{i=1}^{k-1} B_i - \sum_{i=1}^{k+1} A_i + \max(L_k^1; L_{k+1}^1) &= \max(-A_{k+1}; -B_k) \\ &= -\min(A_{k+1}; B_k) \end{aligned}$$

and

$$\begin{aligned} \sum_{i=1}^{k-1} B_i - \sum_{i=1}^{k+1} A_i + \max(L_k^2; L_{k+1}^2) &= \max(-A_k; -B_{k+1}) \\ &= -\min(A_k; B_{k+1}). \end{aligned}$$

Under these conditions, relation (1) becomes

$$-\min(A_{k+1}; B_k) < -\min(A_k; B_{k+1}),$$

or, again,

$$\min(A_k; B_{k+1}) < \min(A_{k+1}; B_k). \tag{2}$$

We conclude that $(..., p_k, p_{k+1}, ...)$ is preferable to $(..., p_{k+1}, p_k, ...)$, if

$$\min(A_k; B_{k+1}) < \min(A_{k+1}; B_k).$$

Let us therefore consider an order

$$(S') = (..., p_k, p_l, ...)$$

which can always be obtained by permutations. The order p_k, p_l will not have to be modified, if

$$\min(A_k; B_l) \leqslant \min(A_l; B_k); \tag{3}$$

this is satisfied if $A_k \leqslant B_l$, A_l, B_k, a relation which can be written

$$\min(A_k; B_k) \leqslant \min(A_l; B_l).$$

As a result, if we find a time A_k *less than all the other* A_l or B_l times in the table of times, we should *begin* with p_k ; if A_k is the equal smallest with certain A_l or B_l times, the order can still begin with p_k without any drawback.

Relation (3) is also satisfied if B_l is less than or equal to A_k, A_l, B_k, which can also be expressed as

$$\min(A_l; B_l) \leqslant \min(A_k; B_k).$$

Consequently, if the table of times contains a time B_l *less than all the other* A_k or B_k times, the order should *terminate* with p_l ; if the time B_l is the equal smallest with certain other A_k or B_k times, the order can still end with p_l without drawback.

It can now be seen that the order can be decided step by step according to Johnson's algorithm.

Extension to Three Positions

Johnson's algorithm is valid in the two particular cases:

$$\min A_i \geqslant \max B_i \qquad \text{and} \qquad \min C_i \geqslant \max B_i ,$$

for a series of n operations to be carried out in this order on three machines A, B, and C.

We then seek the times, using the sums of $A_i + B_i$ and $B_i + C_i$.

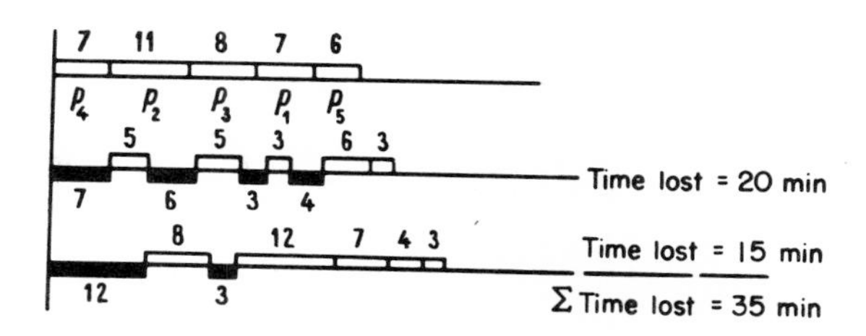

Fig. 17.9

Example. We are given operations defined by their durations A_i, B_i, and C_i on parts $p_1, \ldots, p_5$. Since the condition $\min A_i = 6 \geqslant \max B_i = 6$, for instance, is satisfied, we have the two tables:

	Reboring (A_i)	Milling (B_i)	Internal Repairs (C_i)
p_1	7	6	4
p_2	11	5	12
p_3	8	3	7
p_4	7	5	8
p_5	6	3	3

	$A_i + B_i$	$B_i + C_i$
p_1	13	10
p_2	16	17
p_3	11	10
p_4	12	13
p_5	9	6

and Johnson's algorithm enables us to choose

$$S = (p_4, p_2, p_3, p_1, p_5)$$

or

$$S = (p_4, p_2, p_1, p_3, p_5).$$

CHAPTER 18

DINNER À LA FRANÇAISE

(In Which We See That the Theory of Graphs and Boolean Algebra May Be Useful in the Kitchen)

At the present time, the French dinner, which is always a more complete meal than lunch, can consist, besides soup (and, perhaps, hors d'oeuvre or an entree), of three courses, one of which is invariably fish and another a roast. The third course can be either game or fowl or a ragout, and is always followed by salad and cheese. Although sweets are becoming popular again, a sweet is seldom served as well as pastry. To round off the meal, there is always fruit.

Because of this pattern, the sequence of the meal can be represented as a simple graph (Fig. 18.1), in which every route is practicable, since we have excluded the possibility of serving two entrees to the same person.

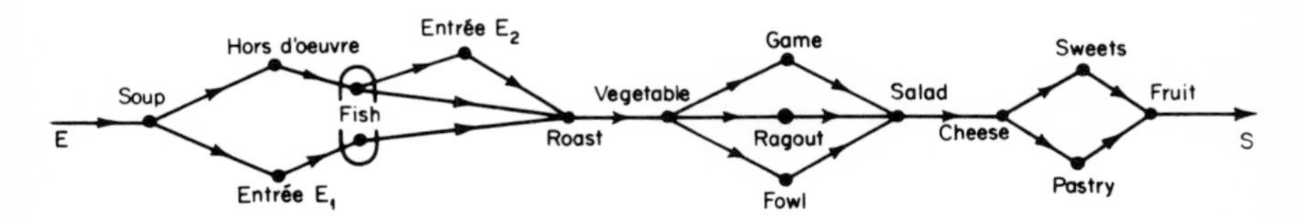

Fig. 18.1

At the same time, a taste derived from long years of civilization, and not yet vitiated by the abuse of the picnic or quick snacks for motorists (who seem the keener on high averages, the emptier their purses), dictates the choice of wines suited to a carefully chosen menu.

We have known for a long time that soup should be served without wine, and that artichokes, asparagus, and vinegar dressings require water as a beverage. For hors d'oeuvre, a light dry white wine or a very dry rosé are required, while melon needs a mellow white wine, and pâté de foie gras a sweet one. This last fact justified the former custom of serving white wines after the meat course, but it is now agreed that they may be served before the fish, and we then overlook the contradiction of the normal succession of wines. Oysters and shellfish require a dry white wine, but snails are better with a Bourgueil or a Burgundy.

Grilled fish must be accompanied by a dry white wine; for fish served with mayonnaise a semidry wine is more suitable. Finally, if the fish is served with a hot sauce, a mellow white wine is preferable. There are exceptions, of course, since fish stews and ragouts are served with the type of red wine used in their preparation.

It will be observed that two kinds of entree (each exclusive of the other) are shown in Fig. 18.1. With certain entrees such as fish rissoles, shrimps, whiting, lobster soufflé, pizza à la Nice,[1] and Croque-Monsieur du Pêcheur,[2] a white wine is clearly desirable, whereas other entrees such as truffle soufflé, kidneys, sausages, vol-au-vent, and Renaissance pies require a red wine. It is for this reason that we have shown the two entrees E_1 and E_2, the first of which may be chosen instead of the hors d'oeuvre, and the second of which comes between the fish and the roast.

The red wines, which make their appearance with the roast, vary in strength according to the course. A Beaujolais, for example, is quite strong enough for mutton or veal, whereas game requires full-bodied wines, and cheese should be accompanied by one of the best wines in the cellar served with all the care that such a wine deserves. Though red wine is normally served with cheese, a white wine can prove effective with a cheese made from goat's milk—an Alsace with a Munster, and a Meursault or a Cahors with Roquefort. Rich pastries require a sweet white wine, and ice cream or fruit need a semidry Champagne or a Vouvray.

This variety of appropriate wines, endorsed by a long tradition and rendered possible by the exceptional range of French wines, appears to increase almost to infinity the possible ways in which a complete meal can be represented graphically. In reality it subjects such a meal to the constraints of two well-established rules.

(a) Champagne excepted, it is customary to limit the wines served in the course of a meal to four.

[1] A pie made with onions and tomatoes.

[2] Pieces of fish or shellfish baked in the oven on pieces of buttered bread.

(b) The sequence of wines is subject to certain relations of order, recognized by all connoisseurs. These relations are:

$$\begin{aligned} \text{dry white} &< \text{mellow white} \\ \text{mellow white} &< \text{sweet white} \\ \text{light red} &< \text{full-bodied red} \\ \text{white (except sweet)} &< \text{red} \\ \text{red} &< \text{sweet white}, \end{aligned}$$

where the sign $<$ indicates that the wine shown on the left should be served before the one on the right.

These relations will be symbolized as

$$\begin{array}{l \vdots l} a < b & a \dotplus b < d \dotplus e, \\ b < c & d \dotplus e < c, \\ d < e & \end{array}$$

where a is the dry white, b the mellow white, c the sweet white, d the light red, e the full-bodied red, and introduce a *complete order* for the sequence of wines in the sense given to the term by mathematicians.

A short time ago our old friend Robert Felix Faber, a true gourmet, was to entertain to dinner the Grand Master of the Order of Hospitaliers, that enquiring and courteous devotee of Bacchus, M. de Saint-Pierre. After summoning his cook and lecturing her on the excellence required for the meal, he again sent for her several days before the dinner and obtained the menu she had drawn up:

MENU

Soup

Hors d'oeuvre

Fish with hot sauce

Entree

Roast with garnishings

Game (depending on available choice)

Salad

Cheese

Fruit

Our friend at once thought of the five classes of wines, and decided to produce a graph of the menu. After he had drawn the diagram of Fig. 18.2, he realized that the cook's menu would force him to serve

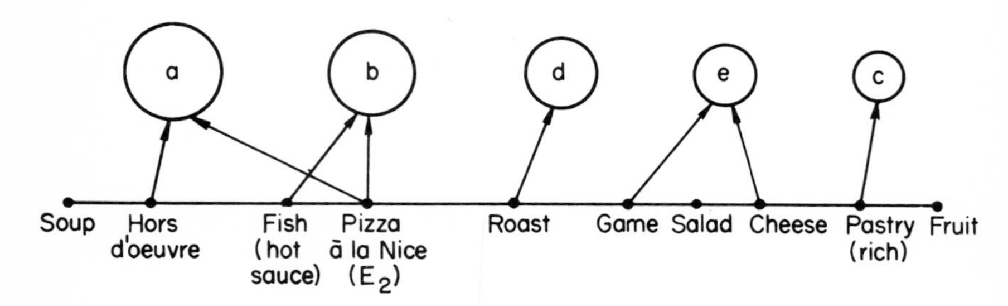

FIG. 18.2

five different wines and thus transgress rule (a). He therefore summoned her again, and it was agreed that the roast should be a leg of mutton *pré-salé*, and that the pastry requiring a sweet wine would be replaced by a mocha which could suitably be accompanied by the same dry Champagne served with the fruit.

Having thus preserved the sacrosanct rule (a), our friend took an inventory of his cellar and was astonished to find the great variety of solutions to his problem. The day before the dinner, he recalled our old friendship and, armed with the menu and the inventory of his cellar, appeared with a request that we should extricate him from his difficulty. Anxious to be of help to him, we first examined the inventory which is now shown in Table 18.1.

Enticed by so much promise, even if the dates of the wines were lacking, we started to sound him for his preferences.

"Are there not any prohibitions or obligatory connections you can suggest for the sequence of these nectars?"

"Indeed there are! I have given a lot of thought to the question, and if I serve No. 1, Nos. 10, 7, and 8 cannot follow it. Numbers 2, 7, and 8 would not be suitable after No. 3, nor should Nos. 5 and 9 precede No. 10. Numbers 4 and 10 would seem flat, which they are not, if they followed No. 6. Number 2 would not be suitable in a sequence with 10, 17, or 18, nor 8 with 10 and 11. Finally, Nos. 19 and 13 should not be served close together. As for the obligatory connections, you would not be a connoisseur without realizing that if I serve a No. 10 and need a more full-bodied wine to follow it, this must be No. 11.

TABLE 18.1

WINE INVENTORY OF R. F. FABER

Number	Class	Appellation	Quantity
1	*a*	Muscadet : Domaine de la Vente	32
2	*b*	Mâcon viré	14
3	*a*	Graves sec : Château Carbonnieux	27
4	*b*	Pouilly Fumé	39
5	*a*	Pouilly Fuissé	46
6	*a*	Sylvaner	57
7	*b*	Riesling	33
8	*b*	Gewürztraminer de Zellenberg	13
9	*a*	Crézancy (Cher)	51
10	*d*	Bordeaux : Cru de la Barre	98
11	*e*	Mouton-Rotschild	69
12	*d*	Chiroubles : Château de Javernand	181
13	*d*	Beaune : Clos des Mouches	33
14	*e*	Vosne-Romanée	52
15	*e*	Côtes du Rhône : Crozes Hermitage	37
16	*e*	Châteauneuf-du-Pape Beaucastel	42
17	*d*	St Nicolas de Bourgueil	63
18	*d*	Côtes de Chinon	7
19	*b*	Graves moelleux	53
20	*c*	Sauternes : Chateau-Caillou	31

There is a similar connection between 13 and 14, and Nos. 15 and 16 must follow each other in that order, although they belong to the same group."

After listening to these views we proceeded to draw the graph shown in the upper portion of Fig. 18.3, which embodies the above information.

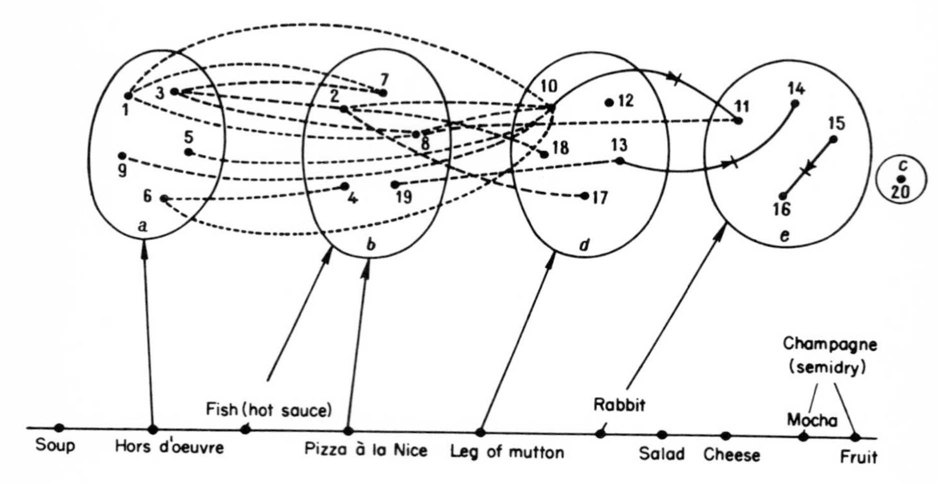

FIG. 18.3

The prohibitions were shown by dashed lines, the obligatory connections in the usual way, the arrows between the different classes implying all the permitted relations.

It now appeared to us that there were indeed a great variety of solutions and that the discussion of the problem might prove extremely protracted.

"But isn't there a particular wine you would like to offer your guest which could be served with one of the courses your cook has chosen?"

"To be sure! Monsieur de Saint-Pierre and I had a discussion about Cru de la Barre which I consider an excellent Bordeaux. It would go marvellously with Marie's way of serving roast mutton."

"Well, in that case, there are only two possible sequences for the wines to accompany your feast

$$3 - 4 - 10 - 11$$

or

$$3 - 19 - 10 - 11,$$

apart from the semidry Champagne you intend serving with the mocha and the fruit."

The reader could have discovered these solutions as follows: since wine No. 10 may not be preceded by 1, 5, 9, 6, 2, or 8, and a class *a* wine should be served with the hors d'oeuvre, the only possible wine with which to begin is No. 3. Only Nos. 4 and 19 may legitimately follow it and, finally, No. 10 should be succeeded by No. 11.

As soon as we informed our friend that he had only two choices, Château Carbonnieux, Pouilly Fumé, Cru de la Barre, and Mouton-Rotschild or Château Carbonnieux, Graves moelleux, Cru de la Barre, and Mouton-Rotschild, he replied that he had, in point of fact, only one choice, the second one, and would serve Bordeaux throughout the meal. He was so grateful for this solution that he insisted on our presence at the dinner for the Grand Master, and then hurried home to start bringing his excellent red wines to room temperature.

At the dinner our conversation turned mainly to the wines we were drinking, and the Grand Master was astounded to learn that the sequencing problems of the cellar could be solved by the use of graphs or Boolean algebra. We even undertook to establish subtle equivalence classes for a well-stocked cellar by means of Foulkes' algorithm, but we are not sure that our premise was taken very seriously.[3]

Conclusion

The reader who has followed us to the end will realize that we have never attempted to mislead him. The intentionally flippant tone and the comical subjects used as examples were only the sugar which coats the pill. Let us hope that this method has made it easier to grasp the serious concepts on which the anecdotes were based, and that, like the great Rabelais, we have enabled men of good will to discover a measure of *substantific marrow* in these pages.

[3] J.-A. Ville, professor at the Faculty of Science in Paris, has used the mathematical treatment of cooking recipes for purposes of instruction. See *Moyens automatiques de gestion*, Dunod, Paris, 1961, p. 202.

BIBLIOGRAPHY

General Bibliography

[Numbers in brackets are chapter numbers.]

[5, 6, 7, 16] Berge, C., "Théorie des graphes et applications." Dunod, Paris, 1958.

[1, 4, 5, 6, 7, 10, 13, 15] Churchmann, C. W., Ackoff, R. L., and Arnoff, E. L., "Éléments de recherche opérationnelle." Dunod, Paris, 1961.

[1, 4, 8, 9, 12, 13] Faure, R., Boss, J. P., and Le Garff, A., "La recherche opérationnelle." Presses Univ. de France, Paris, 1961.

[1, 4, 6, 7, 8, 9, 12, 13] Kaufmann, A., "Méthodes et modèles de la recherche opérationnelle," Vol. I. Dunod, Paris, 1959.

[10, 12, 14] Kaufmann, A., Faure, R., and Le Garff, A., "Les jeux d'entreprises." Presses Univ. de France, Paris, 1960.

[1, 2, 3, 10] Lesourne, J., "Technique économique et gestion industrielle." Dunod, Paris, 1958.

[10, 14, 15] Luce, R. D., and Raiffa, H., "Games and Decisions." Wiley, New York, 1957.

[1, 2, 8, 14] Massé, P., "Le choix des investissements." Dunod, Paris, 1959.

[4, 10, 13] McCloskey, J. F., and Trefethen, F. N., "Introduction à la recherche opérationnelle." Dunod, Paris, 1958.

[4, 9, 12] McCloskey, J. F., and Coppinger, J. M., "Recherche opérationnelle. Cas pratiques et méthodes." Dunod, Paris, 1959.

[1, 4, 8, 9] Morse, P. M., "Queues, Inventories and Maintenance." Wiley, New York, 1958.

[10, 13, 14] Von Neumann, J., and Morgenstern, O., "Theory of Games and Economic Behavior," 3rd ed. Princeton Univ. Press, Princeton, New Jersey, 1953.

[3, 10, 12] Rosentiehl, P., and Gouila-Houri, A., " Les choix économiques. Décisions séquentielles et simulations." Dunod, Paris, 1960.

[Diverse] Saaty, T. L., "Mathematical Methods of Operations Research." McGraw-Hill, New York, 1959.

[Diverse] Sasieni, Vaspan, and Friedmann, "Operations Research, Methods and Problems." Wiley, New York, 1959.

[10, 12, 14] Shubik, M., "Strategy and Market Structure." Wiley, New York, 1959.

[Diverse] "Notes on Operations Research." M.I.T. Press, Cambridge, Massachusetts, 1959.

[Diverse] Thrall, R. M., Coombs, C. H., and Davis, R. L., "Decision Process." Wiley, New York, 1954.

[10, 13] Vajda, S., "The Theory of Games and Linear Programming." Wiley, New York, 1957.

[1, 2, 3, 13] Vaszonyi, A., "Scientific Programming in Business and Industry." Wiley, New York, 1958.

Bibliography According to Chapter

Chapter 1

Bowman, E. H., and Felter, R. B., "Analysis for Production Management." Richard D. Irwin, 1957.

Brown, R. G., "Statistical Forecasting Inventory Control." McGraw-Hill, New York, 1959.

Faiveley, G., Sur un problème de stockage avec capacité limitée. *Proc. 6th Congr. TIMS, Paris, 1961.* Pergamon Press, Oxford.

Fort, R., Étude de l'optimum d'équipement et d'exploitation d'un réservoir souterrain de gaz, à capacité limitée. *Proc. 2nd Congr. Intern. Rech. Opérationnelle, Aix-en-Provence, 1960.* Dunod, Paris.

Fry, T. C., "Probability and Its Engineering Uses." Van Nostrand, New York, 1928.

Lesourne, J., La régulation simultanée de la production et des stocks. *Rev. Soc. Franc. Rech. Opérationnelle* **1** (No. 2), 1957. Dunod, Paris.

Littlefield, P., The determination of the economic size of production orders. Thesis, Massachusetts Inst. of Technol., Cambridge, 1924.

Loeb, P., Le contrôle économique des stocks. *Proc. 6th Congr. TIMS, Paris, 1961.* Pergamon Press, Oxford.

Magee, J. F., "Production Planning and Inventory control." McGraw-Hill, New York, 1958.

Manson, N., Le contrôle de la production en usine. *Proc. 6th Congr. TIMS, Paris, 1961.* Pergamon Press, Oxford.

Melese *et al.*, La gestion des pièces de rechange dans la sidérurgie. *Proc. 2nd Congr. Intern. Rech. Opérationnelle, Aix-en-Provence, 1960.* Dunod, Paris.

Michel, F. J., Méthode universelle de gestion rationnelle des stocks des ateliers de réparation, etc. *Proc. 8th Congr. TIMS, Bruxelles, 1961.* Pergamon Press, Oxford.

Raymond, F. E., "Quantity and Economy in Manufacture." McGraw-Hill, New York, 1931.

Roy, B., Recherche d'un programme d'approvisionnement ou de production. *Rev. Soc. Franc. Rech. Opérationnelle* **1** (No. 4), 1957. Dunod, Paris.

Seigneurin, M. A., Régulation de production dans une usine à vente saisonnière. *Rev. Soc. Franc. Rech. Opérationnelle* **1** (No. 2), 1957. Dunod, Paris.

Ventura, E., Application de la programmation dynamique à la gestion d'un stock. *Proc. 2nd Congr. Intern. Rech. Opérationnelle, Aix-en-Provence, 1960.* Dunod, Paris.

Whitin, T. M., "The Theory of Inventory Management." Princeton Univ. Press, Princeton, New Jersey, 1953.

Chapter 2

Bellman, R., "Dynamic Programming." Princeton Univ. Press, Princeton, New Jersey, 1957.

Bellman, R., Combinatorial processes and dynamic programming. *Proc. 10th Symp. Appl. Math.* Am. Math. Soc., 1960.

DREYFUS, S. E., "Dynamic Programming and the Calculus of Variations." Academic Press, New York, 1965.

HOWARD, R. A., "Dynamic Programming and Markov Processes." Wiley, New York, 1960.

KALABA, R., On some communications network problems. *Proc. 10th Symp. Appl. Math.* Am. Math. Soc., 1960.

KAUFMANN, A., and CRUON, R., "La programmation dynamique et ses applications." Dunod, Paris. In press.

CHAPTER 3

BARTLETT, M. S., "Stochastic Processes." Cambridge Univ. Press, London and New York, 1956.

BHARUCHA-REID, A. T., "Elements of the Theory of Markov Processes and Their Applications." McGraw-Hill, 1960.

FELLER, W., "An Introduction to Probability Theory and Its Applications," Vol. I, 2nd ed. Wiley, 1957.

FRECHET, M., "Recherches théoriques sur le calcul des probabilités, Traité du calcul des probabilités, publié par E. Borel," 1937–1938.

HOWARD, R. A., "Dynamic Programming and Markov Processes." Wiley, New York, 1960.

KAI LAI CHUNG, "Markov Chains with Stationary Transition Probability." Springer, Berlin, 1960.

KAUFMANN, A., and CRUON, R., "Les phénomènes d'attente." Dunod, Paris, 1961.

PILÉ, G., Étude fonctionnelle de certains processus de Markov homogènes. *Rev. Soc. Franc. Rech. Opérationnelle* No. 14, 1st trim. Dunod, Paris, 1960.

CHAPTER 4

CHANTAL, R., Sur des probabilités relatives au trafic aérien des aéroports. *Travaux* **37** (1953).

DELCOURT, J., Problèmes de la congestion d'un port pétrolier. *Proc. 2nd Congr. Intern. Rech. Opérationnelle, Aix-en-Provence, 1960.* Dunod, Paris.

DESCAMPS, R., Calcul direct des probabilités d'attente dans une file. *Rev. Soc. Franc. Rech. Opérationnelle*, No. 11, 2nd trim. Dunod, Paris, 1959.

DHONDT, A., Le processus d'attente à plusieurs stations avec entrées poissoniennes et durées de service exponentielles. *Proc. 8th Congr. TIMS, Bruxelles, 1961.* Pergamon Press, Oxford.

FELLER, W., see list for Chapter 3.

FRY, T. C., see list for Chapter 1.

GIRAULT, M., Quelques exemples d'analyse opérationnelle des files d'attente et de stockage. *Coll. Rech. Opérationnelle, Aix-Marseille, Nov. 1956.*

GIRAULT, M., "Initiation aux processus aléatoires." Dunod, Paris, 1959.

KAUFMANN, A., and CRUON, R., see list for Chapter 3.

KAUFMANN, A., and CRUON, R., Le processus de Galliber. *Rev. Soc. Franc. Rech. Opérationnelle*, No. 12, 3rd trim. Dunod, Paris, 1959.

LEVY, P., Convergence des séries aléatoires et loi normale. *Compt. Rend.* **234** (1952).

MIASKIEVICZ, L., Étude des files d'attente dans un magasin d'outillage. *Rev. Soc. Franc. Rech. Opérationnelle* **1** (No. 4). Dunod, Paris, 1957.

Morse, P. M., Application de la théorie des files d'attente à la gestion de stocks et à l'entretien des machines. *J. Rech. Opérationnelle*, Paris, Sept. (1957)

Palm, C., Étude des délais d'attente. *Erricson Technics* **5** (1947).

Pollaczek, F. S., Sur l'application de la théorie des fonctions au calcul des certaines probabilités continues utilisées dans la théorie des réseaux téléphoniques. *Ann. Inst. Poincaré* **10** (1946).

Pollaczek, F. S., Délais d'attente des avions... . *Compt. Rend.* **234** (1952).

Pollaczek, F. S., Généralisation de la théorie des probabilités au système téléphonique sans dispositif d'attente. *Compt. Rend.* **236** (1952).

Pollaczek, F. S., Sur la répartition des périodes d'occupation ininterrompue d'un guichet. *Compt. Rend.* **234** (1952).

Pollaczek, F. S., Sur une généralisation de la théorie des attentes. *Compt. Rend.* **236** (1953).

Vaulot, A. E., Délais d'attente des appels téléphoniques au hasard. *Compt. Rend.* **222** (1946).

Ventura, E., Application de la théorie des files d'attentes... . *Rev. Soc. Franc. Rech. Opérationnelle* **2** (No. 6). Dunod, Paris, 1958.

Volberg, D., Problème de la queue stationnaire et non-stationnaire. *Compt. Rend. USSR* **24** (1939).

Chapter 5

Dwyer, P. S., The solution of the Hitchcock transportation problem with a method of reduced matrices. Statistical Lab., Univ. of. Michigan, Ann Arbor, Michigan, 1955.

Flood, M. M., On the Hitchcock distribution problem. *Pacific J. Math.* **3** (1953).

*Ford, L. R., Network flow theory. Rand Corp. Paper P-923, Santa Monica, California, 1956.

Ford, L. R., and Fulkerson, D. R., A simplex algorithm for finding maximal networks flows and an application to the Hitchcock problem. Rand Rept. RM.-1-604, Rand Corp. Santa Monica, California, 1955.

Ford, L. R., and Fulkerson, D. R., Maximal flow through network. *Can. J. Math.* **8** (1956).

Ford, L. R., and Fulkerson, D. R., Dynamic network flow. Rand Corp. Paper P-967, Santa Monica, California, 1956.

Fulkerson, D. R., and Dantzig, G. B., Computation of maximal flows in networks. Rand Mem. RM-1489, Santa Monica, California, 1955.

Gale, D., A theorem on flows in networks. *Pacific J. Math.* **7** (1957).

Ghouila-Houri, A., Recherche du flot maximum dans certains réseaux lorsqu'on impose une condition de bouclage. *Proc. 2nd Congr. Intern. Rech. Opérationnelle, Aix-en-Provence, 1960.* Dunod, Paris.

Hitchcock, F. L., The distribution of a product from several sources to numerous localities. *J. Math. Phys.* **20** (1941).

Matthys, G., Flot optimum dans un réseau à capacités de faisceaux. *Proc. 2nd Congr. Intern. Rech. Opérationnelle, Aix-en-Provence, 1960.* Dunod, Paris.

Orden, A., The transhipment problem. *Management Sci.* **2** (1956).

*Roy, B., Contribution de la théorie des graphes à l'étude des problèmes d'ordonnancement. *Proc. 2nd Congr. Intern. Rech. Opérationnelle, Aix-en-Provence, 1960.* Dunod, Paris.

VIDALE, M. L., A graphical solution of the transportation problem. *J. Operations Res. Soc. Am.* **4**, April (1956).

CHAPTER 6

BERGE, C., Sur la déficience d'un réseau infini. *Compt. Rend.* **245** (1957).

DANTZIG, G., FULKERSON, R., and JOHNSON, S., Solution of a large scale traveling, salesman problem. *J. Operations Res. Soc. Am.* **4** (1954).

*EGERVARY, J., Matrixok kombinatorius Tulajdonsàgairòl. *Math. Fiz. Lapok* **38** (1931).

*FLOOD, M. M., The traveling salesman problem. *J. Operations Res. Soc. Am.* **4**, Feb. (1956).

FLOOD, M. M., The traveling salesman problem. *In* "Operations Research for Management" (McCloskey and Coppinger, eds.), Vol. II. John Hopkins Press, Baltimore, 1956.

FROBENIUS, G., Über matrizen mit nichtnegativen Elementen. *Sitzungsber. Berliner Akad.* **23** (1912).

KÖNIG, D., "Théorie der endlichen und unendlichen Graphen," 1912. Engl. ed. by Chelsea, New York, 1950.

KÖNIG, D., and VALKO, J., Über mehrdeutige Abbildungen von Mengen. *Math. Ann.* **95** (1926).

KUHN, H. W., The traveling salesman problem. *Proc. 6th Symp. Appl. Math.* McGraw-Hill, New York.

KUHN, H. W., A combinatorial algorithm for the assignment problem. Bryn Mawr College, Pennsylvania.

KUHN, H. W., The hungarian method for the assignment problem. *Nav. Res. Log. Quart.* **2**, Mar./June (1955).

CHAPTER 7

APPELL, P., Le problème géométrique des déblais et remblais. *Mem. Sci. Math.* **27** (1928).

DANTZIG, G. B., in Koopmans, T. C., see below.

DWYER, P. S., see list for Chapter 5.

FLOOD, M. M., see list for Chapter 6.

GLEYZAL, A., An algorithm for solving the transportation problem. *J. Res. Natl. Bur. Std.* **54** (No. 4), April (1955).

HOUTHAKKER, H. S., On the numerical solution of the transportation problem. *J. Operations Research Soc. Am.* **3** (No. 2), May (1955).

KANTOROVITCH, L., On the translocation of masses. *Dokl. Akad. Nauk USSR* **37** (1942).

KOOPMANS, T. C., "Activity Analysis of Production and Allocation," Cowles Comm. monograph. Wiley, New York, 1951.

KOOPMANS, T. C., and REITER, S., "A Model of Transportation."

MONGE, Déblai et remblai. *Mem. Acad. Sci.* (1781).

CHAPTERS 8 AND 9

BELLMAN, R., "Notes on the Theory of Dynamic Programming, III"; "Equipment Replacement Policy." Rand Rept. P-632, Jan., Santa Monica, California, 1955.

BOITEUX, M., Comment calculer l'amortissement. *Rev. Econ. Polit.*, Jan. (1956).

Chung Kai Lai, and Polland, H., An extension of renewal theory. *Proc. Am. Math. Soc.* **3** (1952).

Descamps, R., Prévision statistique des avaries et calcul des volants et rechanges. *DOCAERO.*, No. 41–43, Nov. (1956) and Mar. (1957). Min. Air, Paris.

Dreyfus, S. E., A generalized equipment replacement study. Rand Rept., March, 1957. Santa Monica, California.

Janin, R., Le choix des équipements. *Cahiers Semin. Econ., CNRS* **3** (1956).

Kelly, L'entretien préventif est-il justifié? *Rev. Soc. Franc. Res. Opérationnelle*, No. 10. Dunod, Paris.

Mercier, R., Politique de remplacement et amortissements. *Proc. 8th Congr. TIMS, Bruxelles, 1961.* Pergamon Press, Oxford.

Sasieni, N. W., A Markov chain process in industrial replacement. *Operations Res. Quart.* **7** (No. 1), Dec. (1956).

Terborgh, B., "Dynamic Equipment Policy." McGraw-Hill, New York, 1949.

Vaur, P., Éléments de sélection des investissements obtenus à l'aide d'un modèle linéaire. *Proc. 2nd Congr. Intern. Rech. Opérationnelle, Aix-en-Provence, 1960.* Dunod, Paris.

Chapter 10

Berge, C., Théorie générale des jeux à *n* personnes. "Mémorial des sciences mathématiques." Gauthier-Villars, Paris, 1957.

Chanier, P., La théorie des jeux conduit-elle à un renouvellement des notions fondamentales dans les sciences humaines? *ISEA*, No. 99 (1960).

Chantal, R., Stratégie et tactique dans un problème de concurrence. *Trav. Meth.*, Sept. (1956).

Chorafas, D. N., "Operations Research for Industrial Management." Reynold, 1958.

Cushen, W. E., Operational gaming. *In* "Operations Research for Management" (McCloskey and Coppinger, eds.), Vol. II. John Hopkins Press, Baltimore, 1956.

Dantzig, G. B., *In* "Iterative Solution of Games by Fictitious Play" (G. W., Brown, ed.). Wiley, New York, 1951.

Feeney, G., Market simulation and marketing games. *Proc. 8th Congr. TIMS, Bruxelles, 1961.* Pergamon Press, Oxford.

Guilbaud, G. T., "Leçons sur les éléments principaux de la théorie mathématique des jeux." CNRS, 1954.

Jacot, S., Stratégie et concurrence, Ph. D. Thesis, Univ. de Lyon, April, 1961.

Karlin, S., "Mathematical Methods and Theory in Games, Programming and Economics," Vol. 2. Addison-Wesley, Reading, Mass., 1959.

Kuhn, H. W., and Tucker, A. W., "Contributions to the Theory of Games," Vols. I and II. Princeton Univ. Press, Princeton, New Jersey, 1950, 1957.

McKinsey, J. C. C., "Introduction to the Theory of Games." McGraw-Hill, New York, 1952.

Nash, J. F., Equilibrium points in *n* person games. *Proc. Natl. Acad. Sci.* **36** (1950).

Neumann, J. von, Zur theorie der Gesellschaftspiele. *Math. Ann.* **100** (1928).

Neumann, J. von, A certain zero-sum two-persons game equivalent to the optimal assignment problem. *Ann. Math. Stud.* **28** (1953).

Shubik, M., Games, decisions and industrial organization. *Management Sci.* **6** (1960).

THIONET, M., Recherche d'une stratégie efficace contre la fraude. *Proc. 2nd Congr. Intern. Rech. Opérationnelle, Aix-en-Provence, 1960.* Dunod, Paris.

VASZONYI, A., Gaming techniques for management planning and control. *Proc. 8th Congr. TIMS, Bruxelles, 1961.* Pergamon Press, Oxford.

WALD, A., "Statistical Decisions Functions." Wiley, New York, 1950.

WILLIAMS, J. D., "The Compleat Strategyst." McGraw-Hill, New York, 1954.

CHAPTER 11

BERKELEY, E. C., "Giant Brains or Machines That Think." Wiley, New York, 1949.

BERKELEY, E. C., "Symbolic Logic and Intelligent Machines." Reinhold, New York, 1959.

BOLL, M., and REINHART, J., "Les étapes de la logique." Presses Univ. de France, Paris, 1946.

BOLL, M., "Manuel de la logique scientifique." Dunod, Paris, 1948.

BOOLE, G., "The Mathematical Analysis of Logic," 1847. See 1951 edition by Blackwell, Oxford.

BOOLE, G., "Investigation of the Laws of Thought," 1854. New ed. by Dover, New York.

BOURBAKI, N., "Éléments de math," Book I, Part I, Chap. I. Hermann, Paris, 1954.

CALDWELL, S. H., "Switching Circuits and Logical Design." Wiley, New York, 1958.

CARNAP, R., "L'ancienne et la nouvelle logique." Hermann, Paris, 1933.

CHAUVINEAU, "La logique moderne." Presses Univ. de France, Paris, 1959.

CHURCH, A., "Introduction to Mathematical Logic." Princeton Univ. Press, Princeton, New Jersey, 1956.

CURRY, H. B., "Leçons de logique algébrique." Gauthier-Villars, Paris, 1952.

DENIS-PAPIN, FAURE, KAUFMANN, "Cours de calcul booléien appliqué." Albin Michel, Paris.

DOGSON, C. L., "Symbolic Logic," 1897.

FORTET, R., L'algèbre de Boole et ses applications en recherche opérationnelle. *Cahiers Centr. Belge Rech. Opérationnelle,* No. 4 (1959).

GONSETH, F., "Qu'est-ce la logique?" Hermann, Paris, 1937.

KUNTZMANN, J., "Algèbre de Boole." Dunod, Paris.

LANGER, S. K., "An Introduction to Symbolic Logic." Houghton, Boston, Massachusetts, 1951.

NAMIAN, *Cours de l'Univ. de Grenoble.*

PFEIFFER, J. E., Symbolic logic. *Sci. Am.* **6**, Dec. (1950).

QUINE, V. W., "A Way to Simplify Truth Functions," 1955.

RAYMOND, F. H., "L'automatique des informations." Masson, Paris, 1958.

REICHENBACH, H., "Introduction à la logistique." Hermann, Paris, 1939.

RUSSEL, B., and WHITEHEAD, A. N., "Principia mathematica," 2nd ed. Cambridge Univ. Press, London and New York, 1925–1927.

SHANNON, C. E., A symbolic analysis of relay and switching circuits. *Trans. Am. Inst. Electr. Eng.* **57** (1938).

SIKORSKI, H., "Boolean Algebra." Ergebnisse Springer.

TARSKI, A., "Introduction to Logic and to Methodology of the Deductive Sciences." Oxford Univ. Press, London and New York, 1941.

TOUCHAIS, M., "Les applications techniques de la logique." Dunod, Paris, 1956.

VENN, J., "Symbolic Logic." Macmillan, New York, 1894.

Chapter 12

ALBERTS, W. E., System simulation. *Proc. 7th Ann. Natl. Conf. AIIE, Washington, May 1956.*

BAUER, W. F., The Monte-Carlo method. *J. Soc. Ind. Appl. Math.* **6** (1958).

BROWN, A. A., An operational experiment illustrating use of the Monte-Carlo method. M.I.T. Press, Cambridge, Massachusetts, 1953.

BROWN, R. G., A general purpose inventory-control simulation. *Rept. System Simulation Symp. AIIE, May 1957.*

BROWN, R. G., "An Inventory Control Simulation." Little, Brown, Boston, Massachusetts, 1958.

FAIR, W. R., Analogue computations of business decisions. *J. Operations Res. Soc. Am.* **1** (No. 4) (1953).

GAUSSENS, P., Le développement optimal d'un réseau de distribution d'énergie électrique. *Proc. 2nd Congr. Intern. Rech. Opérationnelle, Aix-en-Provence, 1960.* Dunod, Paris.

GALLIHER, H. P., Monte-Carlo simulation studies. *Proc. System Simulation Symp. AIIE, May 1957.*

GEISLER, M. A., Integration of modelling and simulating in organizational studies. *Proc. 6th Congr. TIMS, Paris, 1961.* Pergamon Press, Oxford.

HOUSEHOLDER, A. S., FORSYTHE, G. E., and GERMAND, H. H., The Monte-Carlo method. *Proc. of Symp. Washington.* U. S. Govt. Printing Office, 1951.

KINSLEY, E. R., The managerial use of industrial dynamics as illustrated by a company growth model. M.S. Thesis, Massachusetts Inst. of Technol., Cambridge, Massachusetts, 1959.

MALCOLM, D. G., System simulation. A fundamental tool for industrial engineering. *J. Ind. Eng.* **9** (No. 3) (1958).

MARKOWITZ, H. M., and COOK, S. E., "A Flow Shop Simulation Model," 1958.

MEYER, H. A., *Symp. Monte-Carlo Methods.* Wiley, New York, 1954.

ROSENSTIEHL, P., and SIMOND, M., Tour d'horizon sur la simulation. *Proc. 6th Congr. TIMS, Paris, 1961.* Pergamon Press, Oxford.

SHUBIK, M., Simulation, its uses and potential. Anticip. Proj. Expository and Devt. papers Nos. 1, 2, 3, 4, G.E.C., 1958, 1959.

STENGEL, J., Recherches dans le domaine des processus heuristiques de décision. *Proc. 2nd Congr. Intern. Rech. Opérationnelle, Aix-en-Provence, 1960.* Dunod, Paris.

VENTURA, E., Étude du roulage dans une mine par les méthodes de simulation. *Proc. 2nd Congr. Intern. Rech. Opérationnelle, Aix-en-Provence, 1960.* Dunod, Paris.

Proc. Natl. Simulation Conf. IRE, Dallas, 1956.

Symp. Prediction of Performance of Large-Scale Systems. The Univ. of Michigan, Rept. 2354-11-5, 1959, Ann Arbor, Michigan.

Symp. III on Simulation and Computing Techniques. N.A.D.C., U.S.N., Port Washington, New York, 1953.

Chapter 13

BELLMAN, R., On a new iterative algorithm for finding the solution of games and linear programming. Rand Rept. P-473, 1953, Santa Monica, California.

BELLMAN, R., On the computational solution of linear programming problems involving almost block diagonal matrices. *Management Sci.* **3** (July) (1958).

BERLINE, C., and WELS, J., Étude des problèmes économiques du raffinage à l'aide de la théorie des programmes linéaires. *5th Congr. Petrol., New York, 1959.*

CARTERON, J., Du bon usage des programmes linéaires. *Rev. Soc. Franc. Rech. Opérationnelle* **2** (No. 6) (1958).

CHARNES, A., AND COOPER, W. W., Chance-constrained programming and linear decision rules. *Proc. 8th Congr. TIMS, Bruxelles, 1961.* Pergamon Press, Oxford.

CHARNES, A., COOPER, W. W., and HENDERSON, A., "An Introduction to Linear Programming." Wiley, New York, 1953.

COURTILLOT, M., Étude de la variation de tous les paramètres d'une programmation linéaire. *Proc. 2nd Congr. Intern. Rech. Opérationnelle, Aix-en-Provence, 1960.* Dunod, Paris.

DANTZIG, G. B., Computational algorithm of the revised simplex method. Rand Mem., RM-1266, 1953, Santa Monica, California.

DANTZIG, G. B., Linear programming under uncertainty. Rand Rept., RM-1374, 1954, Santa Monica, California.

DANTZIG, G. B., Developments in linear programming. Rand Rept., RM-1281, 1954, Santa Monica, California.

DANTZIG, G. B., Recent advances in linear programming. Rand Rept., 1955, Santa Monica, California.

DANTZIG, G. B., New methods in math. programming. *Proc. 2nd Congr. Intern. Rech. Opérationnelle, Aix-en-Provence, 1960.* Dunod, Paris.

DANTZIG, G. B., FORD, L. R., and FULKERSON, D. R., A primal dual algorithm. Rand Rept., 1954, Santa Monica, California.

DANTZIG, G. B., and ORCHARD-HAYS, W., The product form for the inverse in the simplex method. *Math. Tables Aids Comput.*, No. 46 (1954).

DANTZIG, G. B., and ORCHARD-HAYS, W., Alternate algorithm for the revised simplex method. Rand Mem., RM-1268, 1954, Santa Monica, California.

DESPORT, L., Programmation linéaire. Thesis, Fac. Sci. Marseille, 1961.

DORFMAN, SAMUELSON, and SOLOW, "Linear Programming and Economic Analysis." McGraw-Hill, New York.

GALE, D., KUHN, H. W., and TUCKER, A. W., "Linear Programming and the Theory of Games."

GASS, S. I., "Linear Programming. Methods and Applications." McGraw-Hill, New York, 1958.

GOMORY, R., Essentials of an algorithm for quadratic programming. *Bull. Am. Math. Soc.*, April (1958).

KANTOROVITCH, L. V., Mathematical methods of organization and planning of production. *Management Sci*: **6** (No. 4) (1960).

KOOPMANS, T. C., "Activity Analysis of Production and Allocation." Wiley, New York, 1951.

KUHN, H. W., and TUCKER, A. W., Linear inequalities and related systems. *Ann. Math. Stud.* (1956).

LAMBERT, F., Programmes linéaires mixtes. *Proc. 8th Congr. TIMS, Bruxelles, 1961.* Pergamon Press, Oxford.

LESCAULT, J., Programmes linéaires et calculateurs électroniques. *Rev. Soc. Franc. Rech. Opérationnelle* **1** (No. 4) (1957).

MASSÉ, P., and GIBRAT, R., Applications of linear programming computing techniques. *Management Sci*: **4** (Jan.) (1958).

PIGOT, D., L'application de la méthode simplexe aux grands programmes linéaires. *Proc. 2nd Congr. Intern. Rech. Opérationnelle, Aix-en-Provence, 1960.* Dunod, Paris.

SYMONDS, G. H., Linear programming: The solution of rafinery problems. Esso Standard Oil Rept., New York, 1955.

THERME, M., Résolution et discussion graphique d'une programmation non-linéaire.

VENTURA, E., La détermination du plan optimum de production d'énergie électrique. *Pub. SOFRO*, Paris, 1955.

CHAPTER 14

ALLAIS, M., Le comportement de l'homme rationnel devant le risque. *Econometrica* **21** (1953).

ALLAIS, M., "Fondements d'une théorie positive des choix comportant un risque et critique des postulats et axiomes de l'école américaine." Imp. Nationale, Paris, 1955.

FOURGEAUD, C., and NATAF, A., Consommation en prix et revenus réels et théorie des choix. *Econometrica* **17** (No. 3) (1959).

HURWICZ, L., "Optimality Criteria for Decision Making Under Ignorance." 1951.

LUCE, R. D., "Individual Choice Behavior." Wiley, New York, 1959.

MASSÉ, P., Propos incertains. *Rev. Soc. Franc. Rech. Opérationnelle*, No. 11 (1959).

CHAPTER 15

ACKOFF, R. L., On a science of ethics. *Phil. Phenom. Res.* **9** (No. 4) (1949).

AILLERET, M. P., L'introduction de la mesure dans la notion de qualité du service d'une distribution d'électricité. *Bull. Soc. Franc. Elec.* (Jan.) (1956).

ARROW, K. J., "Social Choice and Individual Values." Wiley, New York, 1951.

BARBUT, M., Quelques aspects de la décision rationnelle. *Les temps modernes*, No. 164, Oct. (1959).

CHURCHMAN, C. W., Values and measurement costs. *Proc. 8th Congr. TIMS, Bruxelles, 1961.* Pergamon Press, Oxford.

CHURCHMAN, C. W., "Why Measure?" Wiley, New York, 1959.

DAVIDSON, D., MCKINSEY, J. C. C., and SUPPES, P., Outlines of a formal theory of value. Rept. 1, Stanford value th. proj., Feb., 1954.

DEHEM, "Traité d'analyse économique." Dunod, Paris, 1958.

FLAMENT, C., Analyse des structures préférentielles intransitives. *Proc. 2nd Congr. Intern. Rech. Opérationnelle, Aix-en-Provence, 1960.* Dunod, Paris.

FLAMENT, C., Comportement de choix et échelle de mesure, I et II. *Bull. Cent. Etudes Rech. Psychotech.* (1960).

HERTZ, D. B., Measurement in research and development. *Proc. 8th Congr. TIMS, Bruxelles, 1961.* Pergamon Press, Oxford.

KAUFMANN, A., and BARD, A., Établissement d'un indice de richesse des communes. *In* "Moyens automatiques de gestion." Dunod, Paris, 1961.

KREWERAS, G., Sur une possibilité de rationaliser les intransitivités. *Colloque du C.N.R.S. sur la décision, May 1959.*

MALINVAUD, E., L'agrégation dans les modèles économiques. *Cahiers du Seminaire d'Économétrie,* (No. 4). C.N.R.S., Paris, 1956.

PARETO, V., "Manuel d'économie politique," 2nd ed. Girard, Paris, 1927.

VAN DER BOGAARD, P. J. M., and VERSLUIS, J., The design of socially optimal decisions. *Proc. 2nd Congr. Intern. Rech. Opérationnelle, Aix-en-Provence, 1960.* Dunod, Paris.

POLYA, G., Kombinatorische Anzahlbestimmungen für Gruppen, Graphen und chemische Verbindungen. *Acta Math.* **68** (1937).

RICARD, M. J., and QUENNET, J., Deux exemples d'application de la théorie des graphes à l'exploitation ferroviaire. *Proc. 2nd Congr. Intern. Rech. Opérationnelle, Aix-en-Provence, 1960.* Dunod, Paris.

VEBLEN, O., "Analysis Situs." Am. Math. Soc., New York, 1931.

CHAPTER 16[1]

FLAMENT, C., Analyse pluridimensionnelle des structures hiérarchiques intransitives. *Bull. Cent. Etudes Rech. Psychotech.* **7** (1958).

FLAMENT, C., Fonction caractéristique d'un graphe et ligne de Hamilton. *Bull. Cent. Etudes Rech. Psychotech.* **8** (1959).

FLAMENT, C., Nombre de cycles complets dans un réseau de communications. *Bull. Cent. Etudes Rech. Psychotech.* **8** (Nos. 1, 2) (1959).

FLOOD, M. M., An alternative proof a theorem of Konig as an algorithm for the Hitchcock distribution problem. *10th Symp. Appl. Math.* Am. Math. Soc., New York, 1960.

FORD, L. R., and FULKERSON, D. R., A primal-dual algorithm for the capacited Hitchcock problem. Rand Corp., RM-P8-27, 1956, Santa Monica, California.

FOULKES, J. D., Directed graphes and assembly schedules. *10th Symp. Appl. Math.* Am. Math. Soc., New York, 1960.

HARARY, F., and NORMAN, R. Z., Graph theory as a mathematical model in social science. Univ. of Michigan, Ann Arbor, Michigan, 1953.

HEISE, G. A., and MILLER, G. A., Problem solving by small groups using various communications nets. *J. Abnormal and Social Psychol.* **46** (1951).

KALABA, R., On some communication network problems. *10th Symp. Appl. Math.* Am. Math. Soc., New York, 1960.

KAUFMANN, A., GRABOWSKI, B., and THOUZERY, J., "L'analyse des réseaux électriques à tubes et à transistors." Ed. Eyrolles, Paris.

KAUFMANN, A., Mise en équation et résolution des réseaux électriques par la méthode tensorielle. Min. de l'Air, S.I.D.T., Paris, 1954.

KIRCHHOFF, G., Über die Auflösung der Gleichungen, auf welche man bei der Untersuchung der linearen Vertheilung galvanischer Ströme geführt wird. *Ann. Phys. Chem.* **72** (1847).

KIRCHHOFF, G., Uber den Durchgang eines elektrischen Strömes durch eine Ebene, insbesondere durch eine Kreisformige. *Ann. Phys. Chem.* **64** (1845).

KÖNIG, G., "Theorie der endlichen und unendlichen Graphen." Leipzig, 1936; Engl. ed. by Chelsea, New York, 1950.

KRUSKAL, J. B., On the shortest spanning subtree of a graph and the traveling salesman problem. *Proc. Am. Math. Soc.* **7** (1956).

KUHN, H. W., The hungarian method for the assignment problem. *Nav. Res. Quart.* **2** (1955).

[1] See also references for Chapters 5 and 6, particularly those preceded by an asterisk.

MASON, S. J., Some properties of signal flow graphe. *Proc. IRE* **41** (Sept.) (1953), **44** (July) (1956).

MATTHYS, G., and RICARD, M., Étude du débit maximum entre deux triages. *Rev. Soc. Franc. Rech. Opérationnelle* **15**, 2nd trim. (1960).

MILNOR, J. W., "Games Against Nature." 1951.

SAVAGE, L. J., The theory of statistical decision. *J. Am. Math. Soc.* **46** (Mar.) (1951).

SAVAGE, L. J., "The fundations of statistics." Wiley, New York, 1954.

WALD, A., Contribution to the theory of statis. estimation and testing hypothesis. *Ann. Math. Stat.* **10** (1939).

WALD, A., Fundations of a general theory of sequential decisions functions. *Econometrica* **15** (1947).

WALD, A., "Sequential Analysis." Wiley, New York, 1947.

CHAPTER 17

AKERS, S. B., and FRIEDMANN, J., A non-numerical approach to production scheduling problems. *J. Operations Res. Soc. Am.* **3** (No. 4) (1955).

BARANKIN, E. W., The scheduling problem as an algebraic generalization of ordinary, linear programming. Log. Res. Proj. Univ. of California, Los Angeles, 1952.

BELLMAN, R., Math. aspects of scheduling theory. Rand. Rept., P-651, 1955, Santa Monica, California.

BEN ISRAËL, A., CHARNES, A., and GRAVER, L. L., Some integer-programming theorems and scheduling with start-up costs. *Proc. 8th Congr. TIMS, Bruxelles, 1961.* Pergamon Press, Oxford.

BOWMAN, E. H., The schedule sequencing problem. *J. Operations Res. Soc. Am.* **7** (No. 5) (1959).

DE CARLO, C. R., The use of automatic and semi-automatic processing equipment and production and inventory control. Case Inst. of Technol., Cleveland, Ohio, 1954.

FLOOD, M. M., Operations research and logistics. Office of Ordnance Res., Durham, North Carolina, 1955.

HARE, V. C., and HUGLI, W. C., Applications of O. R. to production scheduling and inventory control. Case Inst. of technol., Cleveland, Ohio, 1955.

JOHNSON, S. M., Optimal two and three-stage production schedules with set up times included. *Nav. Res. Quart.* **1** (No. 1) (1954).

KARUSH, W., and MOODY, L. A., Determination of feasible shipping schedules for a job shop. *J. Operations Res. Soc. Am.* **6** (No. 1) (1958).

KILBRIDGE, M., and WESTER, L., The assembly line problem. *Proc. 2nd Congr. Intern. Rech. Opérationnelle, Aix-en-Provence, 1960.* Dunod, Paris.

MELESE, J., and BARACHE, J., Comment poser efficacement un problème de contrôle de production. *Proc. 2nd Congr. Intern. Rech. Opérationnelle, Aix-en-Provence, 1960.* Dunod, Paris.

MOORE, F. G., "Production Control." McGraw-Hill, New York, 1951.

ROWE, A. J., and JACKSON, J. R., Research problems in production routing and scheduling. Res. Rept., No. 46, Univ. of California, Los Angeles, 1955.

ROWE, A. J., Dynamic evaluation of scheduling decision rules using computer simulation, 1958.

ROWE, A. J., Sequential decision rules in production scheduling, U.C.L.A., 1958.

ROY, B., Contribution de la théorie des graphes à l'étude des problèmes d'ordonnancement. *Proc. 2nd Congr. Intern. Rech. Opérationnelle, Aix-en-Provence, 1960*. Dunod, Paris.

SISSON, R. L., Methodes of sequencing in job shops. *J. Operations Res. Soc. Am.*, Jan. (1959).

INDEX

Mathematics in Science and Engineering

A Series of Monographs and Textbooks

Edited by RICHARD BELLMAN, *University of Southern California*

23. A. Halanay. Differential Equations: Stability, Oscillations, Time Lags. 1966

24. M. N. Oguztoreli. Time-Lag Control Systems. 1966

25. D. Sworder. Optimal Adaptive Control Systems. 1966

26. M. Ash. Optimal Shutdown Control of Nuclear Reactors. 1966

27. D. N. Chorafas. Control System Functions and Programming Approaches (In Two Volumes). 1966

28. N. P. Erugin. Linear Systems of Ordinary Differential Equations. 1966

29. S. Marcus. Algebraic Linguistics; Analytical Models. 1967

30. A. M. Liapunov. Stability of Motion. 1966

31. G. Leitmann (ed.). Topics in Optimization. 1967

32. M. Aoki. Optimization of Stochastic Systems. 1967

33. H. J. Kushner. Stochastic Stability and control. 1967

34. M. Urabe. Nonlinear Autonomous Oscillations. 1967

35. F. Calogero. Variable Phase Approach to Potential Scattering. 1967

36. A. Kaufmann. Graphs, Dynamic Programming, and Finite Games. 1967

37. A. Kaufmann and R. Cruon. Dynamic Programming: Sequential Scientific Management. 1967

38. J. H. Ahlberg, E. N. Nilson, and J. L. Walsh. The Theory of Splines and Their Applications. 1967

39. Y. Sawaragi, Y. Sunahara, and T. Nakamizo. Statistical Decision Theory in Adaptive Control Systems. 1967

40. R. Bellman. Introduction to the Mathematical Theory of Control Processes, Volume I. 1967; Volume II. 1971 (Volume III in preparation)

41. E. S. Lee. Quasilinearization and Invariant Imbedding. 1968

42. W. Ames. Nonlinear Ordinary Differential Equations in Transport Processes. 1968

43. W. Miller, Jr. Lie Theory and Special Functions. 1968

44. P. B. Bailey, L. F. Shampine, and P. E. Waltman. Nonlinear Two Point Boundary Value Problems. 1968

45. Iu. P. Petrov. Variational Methods in Optimum Control Theory. 1968

46. O. A. Ladyzhenskaya and N. N. Ural'tseva. Linear and Quasilinear Elliptic Equations. 1968

47. A. Kaufmann and R. Faure. Introduction to Operations Research. 1968

48. C. A. Swanson. Comparison and Oscillation Theory of Linear Differential Equations. 1968

49. R. Hermann. Differential Geometry and the Calculus of Variations. 1968

50. N. K. Jaiswal. Priority Queues. 1968

51. H. Nikaido. Convex Structures and Economic Theory. 1968

52. K. S. Fu. Sequential Methods in Pattern Recognition and Machine Learning. 1968

53. Y. L. Luke. The Special Functions and Their Approximations (In Two Volumes). 1969

54. R. P. Gilbert. Function Theoretic Methods in Partial Differential Equations. 1969

55. V. Lakshmikantham and S. Leela. Differential and Integral Inequalities (In Two Volumes). 1969

56. S. H. Hermes and J. P. LaSalle. Functional Analysis and Time Optimal Control. 1969

57. M. Iri. Network Flow, Transportation, and Scheduling: Theory and Algorithms. 1969

58. A. Blaquiere, F. Gerard, and G. Leitmann. Quantitative and Qualitative Games. 1969

59. P. L. Falb and J. L. de Jong. Successive Approximation Methods in Control and Oscillation Theory. 1969

60. G. Rosen. Formulations of Classical and Quantum Dynamical Theory. 1969

61. R. Bellman. Methods of Nonlinear Analysis, Volume I. 1970

62. R. Bellman, K. L. Cooke, and J. A. Lockett. Algorithms, Graphs, and Computers. 1970

63. E. J. Beltrami. An Algorithmic Approach to Nonlinear Analysis and Optimization. 1970

64. A. H. Jazwinski. Stochastic Processes and Filtering Theory. 1970

65. P. Dyer and S. R. McReynolds. The Computation and Theory of Optimal Control. 1970

66. J. M. Mendel and K. S. Fu (eds.). Adaptive, Learning, and Pattern Recognition Systems: Theory and Applications. 1970

67. C. Derman. Finite State Markovian Decision Processes. 1970

68. M. Mesarovic, D. Macko, and Y. Takahara. Theory of Hierarchial Multilevel Systems. 1970

69. H. H. Happ. Diakoptics and Networks. 1971

70. Karl Astrom. Introduction to Stochastic Control Theory. 1970

71. G. A. Baker, Jr. and J. L. Gammel (eds.). The Padé Approximant in Theoretical Physics. 1970

72. C. Berge. Principles of Combinatorics. 1971

73. Ya. Z. Tsypkin. Adaptation and Learning in Automatic Systems. 1971

74. Leon Lapidus and John H. Seinfeld. Numerical Solution of Ordinary Differential Equations. 1971

75. L. Mirsky. Transversal Theory, 1971

76. Harold Greenberg. Integer Programming, 1971

77. E. Polak. Computational Methods in Optimization: A Unified Approach, 1971

78. Thomas G. Windeknecht. General Dynamical Processes: A Mathematical Introduction, 1971

79. M. A. Aiserman, L. A. Gusev, L. I. Rozonoer, I. M. Smirnova, and A. A. Tal'. Logic, Automata, and Algorithms, 1971

80. Andrew P. Sage and James L. Melsa. System Identification, 1971

81. R. Boudarel, J. Delmas, and P. Guichet. Dynamic Programming and Its Application to Optimal Control, 1971

In preparation

Alexander Weinstein and William Stenger. Methods of Intermediate Problems for Eigenvalues Theory and Ramifications

G. Arthur Mihram. Simulation: Statistical Foundations and Methodology

William S. Meisel. Computer-Oriented Approaches to Pattern Recognition

Edward Angel and Richard Bellman. Dynamic Programming and Partial Differential Equations

F. V. Atkinson. Multiparameter Eigenvalue Problems, Volume I

Bruce A. Finlayson. The Method of Weighted Residuals and Variational Principles: With Application to Fluid Mechanics, Heat and Mass Transfer

D